Beyond the First
Degree

SRHE and Open University Press Imprint
General Editor: Heather Eggins

Current titles include:

Mike Abramson *et al.* (eds): *Further and Higher Education Partnerships*
Catherine Bargh, Peter Scott and David Smith: *Governing Universities*
Ronald Barnett: *Improving Higher Education: Total Quality Care*
Ronald Barnett: *The Idea of Higher Education*
Ronald Barnett: *The Limits of Competence*
Ronald Barnett: *Higher Education: A Critical Business*
Tony Becher (ed.): *Governments and Professional Education*
Hazel Bines and David Watson: *Developing Professional Education*
John Bird: *Black Students and Higher Education*
Jean Bocock and David Watson (eds): *Managing the Curriculum*
David Boud *et al.* (eds): *Using Experience for Learning*
Angela Brew (ed.): *Directions in Staff Development*
Ann Brooks: *Academic Women*
Robert G. Burgess (ed.): *Beyond the First Degree*
Frank Coffield and Bill Williamson (eds): *Repositioning Higher Education*
Rob Cuthbert: *Working in Higher Education*
Heather Eggins (ed.): *Women as Leaders and Managers in Higher Education*
Roger Ellis (ed.): *Quality Assurance for University Teaching*
Maureen Farish *et al.*: *Equal Opportunities in Colleges and Universities*
Shirley Fisher: *Stress in Academic Life*
Sinclair Goodlad: *The Quest for Quality*
Diana Green (ed.): *What is Quality in Higher Education?*
Susanne Haselgrove (ed.): *The Student Experience*
Robin Middlehurst: *Leading Academics*
Henry Miller: *The Management of Change in Universities*
Jennifer Nias (ed.): *The Human Nature of Learning: Selections from the Work of M.L.J. Abercrombie*
Keith Noble: *Changing Doctoral Degrees*
Gillian Pascall and Roger Cox: *Women Returning to Higher Education*
Graham Peeke: *Mission and Change*
Moira Peelo: *Helping Students with Study Problems*
John Pratt: *The Polytechnic Experiment*
Tom Schuller (ed.): *The Changing University?*
Peter Scott: *The Meanings of Mass Higher Education*
Michael Shattock: *The UGC and the Management of British Universities*
Harold Silver and Pamela Silver: *Students*
Anthony Smith and Frank Webster: *The Postmodern University?*
John Smyth (ed.): *Academic Work*
Geoffrey Squires: *First Degree*
Imogen Taylor: *Developing Learning in Professional Education*
Kim Thomas: *Gender and Subject in Higher Education*
David Warner and Elaine Crosthwaite (eds): *Human Resource Management in Higher and Further Education*
David Warner and Charles Leonard: *The Income Generation Handbook* (Second Edition)
David Warner and David Palfreyman (eds): *Higher Education Management*
Graham Webb: *Understanding Staff Development*
Sue Wheeler and Jan Birtle: *A Handbook for Personal Tutors*
Thomas G. Whiston and Roger L. Geiger (eds): *Research and Higher Education*
Jenny Williams: *Negotiating Access to Higher Education*
John Wyatt: *Commitment to Higher Education*

Beyond the First Degree

Graduate Education, Lifelong
Learning and Careers

Edited by
Robert G. Burgess

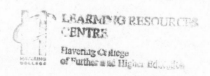

The Society for Research into Higher Education
& Open University Press

Published by SRHE and
Open University Press
Celtic Court
22 Ballmoor
Buckingham
MK18 1XW

and 1900 Frost Road, Suite 101
Bristol, PA 19007, USA

First published 1997

A catalogue record of this book is available from the British Library

ISBN   0 335 19977 1 (hb)   0 335 19976 3 (pb)

Library of Congress Cataloging-in-Publication Data
Beyond the first degree: graduate education, lifelong learning, and
  careers / edited by Robert G. Burgess.
      p.   cm.
    Precedings of the 1997 annual conference of the Society for
  Research into Higher Education.
    Includes bibliographical references and index.
    ISBN 0–335–19977–1 (hardcover). – ISBN 0–335–19976–3 (pbk.)
    1. Universities and colleges – Great Britain – Graduate work –
  Congresses. 2. Universities and colleges – Graduate work –
  Congresses. 3. Continuing education – Great Britain – Congresses.
  4. Continuing education – Congresses. I. Burgess, Robert G.
  II. Society for Research into Higher Education. Conference (1997)
  LB2371.6.G7B49   1997
  378.1'55'0941 – dc21   97–20166
                                                                    CIP

Typeset by Graphicraft Typesetters Ltd., Hong Kong
Printed in Great Britain by St Edmundsbury Press Ltd., Bury St Edmunds, Suffolk.

Contents

Notes on Contributors

Robert G. Burgess is Pro-Vice-Chancellor, Director of CEDAR (Centre for Educational Development, Appraisal and Research) and Professor of Sociology at the University of Warwick. His main teaching and research interests are in social research methodology, especially qualitative methods and the sociology of education, and in particular the study of schools, classrooms and curricula. He has written ethnographic studies of secondary schools and is currently working on case studies of schools and higher education. His main publications include: *Experiencing Comprehensive Education* (1983), *In the Field: An Introduction to Field Research* (1984), *Education, Schools and Schooling* (1985), *Sociology, Education and Schools* (1986), *Schools at Work* (1988 with Rosemary Deem), *Implementing In-Service Education and Training* (1993 with John Connor, Sheila Galloway, Marlene Morrison and Malcolm Newton), and *Research Methods* (1993), together with 20 edited volumes on qualitative methods and education. He was recently President of the British Sociological Association and is currently President of the Association for the Teaching of the Social Sciences and founding Chair of the UK Council for Graduate Education. He is a member of the Council of the Economic and Social Research Council and Chair of the ESRC's Postgraduate Training Board.

Helen Connor is a freelance researcher specializing on graduate labour market studies. Over the last ten years, she has undertaken numerous studies on postgraduate employment in the UK, including various student follow-up surveys and employer-based research on postgraduate skill requirements, mainly on behalf of the Research Councils. These have covered a number of science and social science disciplines, and were done at the Institute for Employment Studies (IES), based at the University of Sussex, where she is now an Associate Fellow.

Keith Dugdale is currently the Director of the joint Careers Service of the Universities of Manchester and UMIST and was formerly the Careers Service Director at the University of Strathclyde. From 1989 to 1991 he held office as President of the Association of Graduate Careers Advisory Services

(AGCAS) which represents over 120 Higher Education Careers Services in the UK. While working in Scotland he directed the Scottish Graduate Careers Programme, a collaborative initiative involving all HE Careers Services in Scotland in the delivery of graduate advice and career planning.

Chris Duke was educated at Cambridge and London and taught at Woolwich Polytechnic (now Greenwich University) and Leeds before becoming in turn foundation Director of Continuing Education at the Australian National University and founding Professor of Continuing Education at the University of Warwick. He is now Deputy Vice-Chancellor of the University of Western Sydney and UWS Nepean Member President. He has occupied Australian, British, European, Asian and other international positions of leadership in non-governmental and professional organizations for non-formal and continuing education for development. He remains incorrigibly committed to widely accessible, recurrent education and to the highest quality of lifelong learning.

Edward Holdaway was born in Australia and received his undergraduate education there. Since obtaining his PhD, he has been associate Professor (1968–74) and Professor (1974–97) of educational administration at the University of Alberta, Canada. He was also Director of Institutional Research and Planning from 1978 to 1987. Professor Holdaway has been Editor of *The Canadian Administrator*, has had editorial responsibilities with several other journals, and has served as President of the Canadian Educational Researchers' Association and Chair of the Research Policy Committee of the Social Science Federation of Canada. His teaching and research interests include graduate programmes, job satisfaction, administrative behaviour, and organizational effectiveness.

Jules B. LaPidus received his bachelor's degree from the University of Illinois and MS and PhD degrees from the University of Wisconsin. His field of specialization is medicinal chemistry. In 1958 he joined the faculty of Ohio State University as Assistant Professor of Medicinal Chemistry, and was Professor of Medicinal Chemistry from 1967 to September 1984. In 1972 he was appointed Associate Dean for Research in the graduate school at Ohio State University and became Dean of the Graduate School and Vice-Provost for Research in 1974. In 1984 he became President of the Council of Graduate Schools in Washington DC.

Barbara Merrill is a Senior Researcher in the Department of Continuing Education, University of Warwick. Previously, she worked in the field of secondary and community education. Her research interests include access issues, especially the access of non-traditional adult students to higher education from a comparative European perspective, gender and adult education. Her recently completed PhD looked at mature women students in universities, using biographical, feminist and sociological approaches. Her current research includes comparative European projects on access and APEL. Recent publications consist of journal articles on access and mature women students. She is also coordinator of the ESREA Access Network.

Mary J. Osborn received her PhD in Biochemistry from the University of Washington (Seattle, Washington) in 1958. She joined the Department of Microbiology, University of Connecticut Health Center as Professor in 1968 and has chaired that department since 1980. Her interests in graduate education arose from her experiences, and those of her colleagues, in educating and mentoring PhD students in a medical school setting. A member of the National Academy of Sciences, she was a member of the Academies' Committee on Science, Engineering and Public Policy during the study on graduate education in science and engineering, and was part of the guidance group responsible for production of the report 'Reshaping the Graduate Education of Scientists and Engineers'.

Millicent E. Poole is Vice-Chancellor at the Edith Cowan University. She has had a distinguished career in education and the social sciences. Her major research contributions are in four fields: life span development, language and cognition, policy research, and general education. She has served as Chair of the Australian Research Council Social Sciences Sub-discipline Panel, was a member of the ARC Strategic Review of Research in Education, and is on the Board of the Australian Council for Educational Research. Her current responsibilities include staffing, resourcing, strategic planning in the Faculties and Institute of the Arts, the Graduate School, external relations coordination, the Library, educational technology, building and capital planning, and equal opportunity.

Raymond H. Spear has been Dean of the Graduate School at the Australian National University since its establishment in 1990. He is a Nuclear Physicist, with PhD and DSc degrees from the University of Melbourne. His research interests are in nuclear spectroscopy and the study of nuclear processes relevant to astrophysics. He was born at Bendigo, Victoria in 1933 and was educated at Williamstown and University High Schools and the University of Melbourne where he was a Senior Lecturer in Physics until he moved to the ANU in 1964. He has held sabbatical appointments at the California Institute of Technology and McMaster University.

Susan Weil is Professor of Social and Organizational Learning and Founder/ head of the new SOLAR centre at Nene College of Higher Education, Northampton. Previous posts include Head of Higher Education and Fellow in Organisational Learning at the Office for Public Management, Associate Director of the Royal Society of Arts Higher Education for Capability Initiative, and Senior Lecturer/Consultant at the Centres for Higher Education Studies and Staff Development, University of London. She was elected Chair of the Society for Research into Higher Education from 1990 to 1992, was awarded a Fellowship in 1994 from the University of Wolverhampton for her innovative work in student-centred learning and institutional development, and is the author/editor of many books, chapters, development materials and journal articles.

Preface

The chapters in this volume constitute the precedings of the 1997 Annual Conference of the Society for Research into Higher Education. This edited collection has the same title as the Conference and takes up three themes: graduate education, lifelong learning and careers. However, the chapters published in this volume can only reflect some of the issues to be covered at the conference and are therefore focused on a series of interconnected themes that were discussed with contributors.

In all sections of the volume attention is given to postgraduate education. In Part 1 readers can locate discussions of graduate education in the United Kingdom in an international context to allow areas of convergence and divergence to be examined and explored. In Part 2, the concept of lifelong learning is examined, again using national and international examples but in relation to postgraduate education and training. In Part 3, student careers are examined in relation to first degree courses and higher degree courses in the UK before turning, in chapter 10, to links that can be made between postgraduate education and careers drawing on a policy discussion in the United States. Taken together the chapters in this volume are designed to stimulate discussion and dialogue about issues beyond the first degree that focus on postgraduate education.

In common with studies in other areas of higher education, the topics covered are of central concern to researchers, policy makers and practitioners. Accordingly, the contributors have been drawn from these three constituencies so that they can identify topics for the research agenda, for policy discussions and for practice. The result is a collection of essays that demonstrate how researchers, policy makers and practitioners analyse major issues and problems concerning graduate education, lifelong learning and careers. It is hoped that the material presented here will provide insights for students engaged in the academic study of education, as well as for researchers and practitioners who deal with these issues through their work in higher education.

The shape of this volume is a result of discussions with members of the conference committee: Paul Anderson, Heather Eggins, Lee Harvey, Phil

Harvey, Ian McNay, Mike Shattock, Geoffrey Squires and Margaret Wallis who invited me to edit the precedings. Finally, I am indebted once again to Su Powell for her excellent secretarial services in preparing the manuscript for publication. As always, any errors or omissions are my own.

Robert G. Burgess

Introduction

1

The Changing Context of Postgraduate Education in the United Kingdom

Robert G. Burgess

Studies in higher education have devoted relatively little attention to post-graduate education and training. Instead, researchers have tended to follow the interests of policy makers and practitioners by focusing on undergraduate programmes. As Burton Clark has commented:

> the first degree level has historical primacy, predominates numerically and possesses a deep hold on traditional thought and practice. It comes first in budget determination, public attention and the concerns of governments. Graduate or advanced education is then prone to develop at the margin as an add on of a few more years of unstructured work for a few students.
>
> (Clark, 1993: 356)

Yet this portrait of higher education based on research conducted in England, France, Germany, Japan and the USA in the late 1980s is gradually changing as a major shift occurs from an élite to a mass system of higher education. In this context, there has been some rethinking of the goals and purposes of postgraduate education and its role in meeting the need for a highly trained and skilled workforce in many countries worldwide, where postgraduate education is seen to have a role in underpinning a modern competitive economy (Gellert, 1993; Pratt, 1995; Harris, 1996). Such developments have resulted in a range of debates about doctoral training and research, the purpose of vocational taught master's degrees, the link between employment, training and postgraduate education, and the impact of postgraduate work on future careers. Many of these issues have been taken up by researchers, policy makers and practitioners in the United Kingdom and elsewhere and it is therefore the purpose of these chapters to sketch out some key areas of debate through an analysis of postgraduate education, lifelong learning and student careers. In each part of this volume evidence is drawn from different higher education systems so that reflections on the UK can be placed in a broader context. In this respect,

Table 1.1 Higher education students in United Kingdom higher education institutions (1994–5)

	Full-time	Sandwich	Full-time and sandwich	Part-time	Other	Part-time and other	Total
Postgraduate							
Research for a higher degree	44,738	1	44,739	26,821	15,401	42,222	86,961
Taught course for a higher degree	45,920	67	45,987	81,221	14,957	96,178	142,165
Other taught postgraduate	38,236	749	38,985	65,168	2046	67,214	106,199
Total	128,894	817	129,711	173,210	32,404	205,614	335,325
Undergraduate							
First degree	714,570	118,229	832,799	162,768	197	162,965	995,764
Other undergraduate	103,218	10,902	114,120	121,761	343	122,104	236,224
Total	817,788	129,131	946,919	284,529	540	285,069	1,231,988
Total	946,682	129,948	1,076,630	457,739	32,944	490,683	1,567,313

Source: HESA, 1996: 5.

Table 1.2 All students by domicile and level of course (1994–5)

	Postgraduate students	% of UK/Overseas
UK domiciled		
England	212,540	80.1
Wales	11,289	4.3
Scotland	24,026	9.0
Northern Ireland	9257	3.5
Channel Islands and Isle of Man	504	0.2
United Kingdom (country unknown)	7865	3.0
Total	265,481	100.0
Overseas domiciled		
European Union	20,238	29.0
Other Europe	5721	8.2
Africa	6215	8.2
Asia	22,992	32.9
Australasia	1124	1.6
Middle East	4228	6.1
North America	6454	9.2
South America	1863	2.7
Other Overseas (region unknown)	1009	1.4
Total	69,844	100.0

Source: HESA, 1996: 7.

the chapters are designed to examine major developments and achievements in postgraduate education and training, and to assess these developments in graduate education in relation to lifelong learning and future careers. Many readers of this volume will want to examine issues in postgraduate education in the UK, and it is for this reason that this chapter begins with a survey of some of the main trends and developments in the UK before relating them to issues discussed by other contributors to this volume.

The scope of graduate education in the UK

Since 1979, the number of postgraduate students in the UK has risen from around 100,000 to 335,325. The current scale and scope of postgraduate education in the UK is reflected in the figures provided in Table 1.1, which facilitates comparisons with undergraduate student numbers.

Postgraduate students constituted 21 per cent of those in higher education in the academic year 1994–5. However, the numbers in the system prompt questions about trends, about the balance of postgraduate research students and postgraduate taught students, the proportions of students studying full-time and part-time, and the kinds of courses and training programmes that are followed (cf. Burgess, 1994, 1996).

These developments in student numbers rely on postgraduates being recruited worldwide. Indeed, the main trends in the student market are revealed in Table 1.2.

Table 1.3 All UK postgraduate students by subject area, level of course and mode of study (1994–5)

	Postgraduate		
	Full-time	*Part-time*	*Total*
Medicine and dentistry	3.1	3.1	3.1
Subjects allied to medicine	2.8	4.5	3.9
Biological sciences	6.0	3.2	4.3
Veterinary science	0.3	0.1	0.2
Agriculture and related subjects	1.5	0.5	0.9
Physical sciences	8.2	3.1	5.1
Mathematical sciences	1.7	0.7	1.1
Computer science	4.6	2.7	3.4
Engineering and technology	11.1	6.0	7.9
Architecture, building and planning	3.4	2.6	2.9
Social, economic and political studies	9.9	8.5	9.0
Law	6.0	2.5	3.9
Business and administrative studies	9.2	22.8	17.5
Librarianship and information science	1.6	1.0	1.3
Languages	4.3	2.9	3.5
Humanities	3.5	3.3	3.4
Creative arts and design	3.2	1.6	2.2
Education	17.9	19.1	18.6
Combined	1.7	11.7	7.8
Total	100.0	100.0	100.0

Source: HESA, 1996: 7.

Table 1.4 Nature of study of postgraduate new entrants in the UK 1989–90 to 1993–4 (000s)

	1989–90	*1990–1*	*1991–2*	*1992–3*	*1993–4*	*% change since 1992–3*
Research for a postgraduate qualification	10.4	11.3	11.9	12.7	13.9	9.1
Taught higher degrees	18.0	20.5	24.5	26.5	29.2	10.2
Other taught courses	12.2	12.1	13.9	14.3	15.0	5.0
Charged home fees	26.9	29.4	35.2	38.2	41.8	10.1
Charged other fees	13.7	14.4	15.0	15.6	16.3	4.8
Total	40.6	43.9	50.2	53.5	58.1	8.6

Source: Table L, Universities Statistical Record, 1994: 10.

These data suggest that postgraduate work like research is international. Indeed, the data automatically prompt questions about the importance of international markets, especially in Asia, for the future of postgraduate recruitment. Does the UK have to maintain its position in the postgraduate marketplace worldwide if the rapid developments of postgraduate education and training are to be sustained? But how are some of these trends reflected in subject areas? Table 1.3 focuses on patterns of student enrolment in different subject areas and especially on the proportion of full-time and part-time students. However, it also reveals several trends: the relative proportions of full-time and part-time students; the concentration of part-time students in business studies and education; the concentration of postgraduate students in the social sciences.

Such data carry implications for the training of highly qualified people in different subject fields and raises issues concerning patterns of funding and future careers. But what have been the main trends in the UK in recent years? Table 1.4 shows the increase in graduate student numbers in the early 1990s.

While there were 58,119 full-time postgraduate students in the UK in 1993–4, the largest group of students have been concentrated on taught courses. Indeed, between 1989–90 and 1993–4 full-time postgraduates on taught courses increased by 62 per cent, while part-time postgraduates increased by 85 per cent. As these students were on one-year taught courses, it is important to consider the relationship between master's courses and undergraduate courses and the link between master's programmes and vocational training including continuing professional development (Burgess, 1997). Indeed, do master's courses act as a 'top-up' to an undergraduate programme – a continuation and development of advanced work? To what extent are such courses part of continuing professional development? Such a range of questions give rise to a number of concerns that have been identified in postgraduate systems worldwide. These include:

- the organizational structures required to implement postgraduate education;
- quality issues in postgraduate education and training;
- the role of education versus training at postgraduate level;
- academic versus vocational purposes of postgraduate education;
- labour market considerations within and beyond higher education

(Burgess and Schratz, 1994; Blume, 1995a, 1995b; Holdaway, Deblois and Winchester, 1995).

It is to some of these issues that we now turn.

Organizational structures

The scale and scope of postgraduate education has resulted in members of universities having to consider the kinds of organizational structure that might be most appropriate for the delivery of graduate programmes. In these circumstances, many higher education institutions in Britain have turned to the United States with its graduate school model for the delivery of all aspects of postgraduate work from recruitment and admission through to the delivery of programmes and the award of degrees and diplomas (for a similar trend in Australia see Chapter 3 in this volume). However, in the UK and elsewhere such models have had to be adapted to the current organizational arrangements of higher education institutions in order to allow postgraduate education to become an integral part of the organization rather than being 'superimposed' or 'bolted on'.

In the early 1990s only two institutions in the UK had adopted the graduate school model (Burgess, Hogan, Pole and Sanders, 1995). However, by the mid-1990s the UK Council for Graduate Education was able to report on a survey they conducted in which 33 higher education institutions had a graduate school and 23 others were considering putting such a structure in place (UKCGE, 1995).

But what form does a graduate school take? Within the UK a number of models have been developed at different levels in the system:

- *Programmes*, where a graduate school structure is associated with a particular degree scheme – often a taught course at master's level.
- *Departments*, where increases in student numbers at departmental level have resulted in a graduate school organization being put in place to handle all graduate matters for taught course and research students.
- *Faculty* models, that link together postgraduate work across a range of disciplines and offer the potential for some economies of scale in terms of course provision, training and supervision. In some instances, this model has been linked with the research activities of the faculty concerned and the development of a research and graduate school.
- *Institution-wide* models, whereby the graduate school covers all areas of academic work within an institution. All members of staff are automatically members of the graduate school that is responsible for every aspect of the life and work of postgraduate students.
- *Regional* models, which link together students and staff in particular disciplines within a geographical area covering several institutions.

In general, there is considerable potential for UK institutions to develop graduate school models to fit their social and academic circumstances. However, in research terms we need to ask: how do graduate schools operate? What is their role? And, ultimately, how effective are graduate schools in the provision of education and training and enhancing the student experience? On these areas there is much work to be done.

Education versus training: an 'old' debate revisited

Central to all the discussions and commentaries on postgraduate education and training is a debate concerned with the predominant characteristics of postgraduate work. In the UK it can be seen in the report of the Robbins Committee, which states:

> the preparation of a master's dissertation or a doctoral thesis on a comparatively narrow subject is too often regarded as the sole or the most important form that work towards a higher degree should take. In many subjects the preparation of a thesis is not enough ... we recommend that the kind of training by formal instruction and seminars provided in the best graduate schools should be provided for research students in this country.
>
> (Robbins, 1963, para. 257)

It is this concern with postgraduate training and the process of 'doing research' that is often juxtaposed with postgraduate education and the product of research as represented by the PhD thesis. The result is a debate that has continued for some 30 years about the purpose of postgraduate work – is it education or is it training? Indeed, echoes of this could be heard in various pronouncements during the 1980s. First, in the Swinnerton-Dyer Report (1982), which emphasized the importance of including some taught courses within doctoral training. Second, in the inquiry chaired by Graham Winfield for the Economic and Social Research Council, which recommended two different types of doctoral study: a knowledge-based PhD and a training-based PhD (Winfield, 1987). Indeed, the training-based model has been widely adopted through the production of ESRC's training guidelines for each social science discipline, which have been linked to a recognition exercise whereby only those departments adhering to the guidelines for general and subject specific training would be recognized to hold research council studentships (ESRC, 1991, 1996).

While the ESRC has made much of the running concerned with postgraduate training, it is not confined to this Council alone. In the 1990s, the British Academy introduced training in the Humanities linked with a 1 + 3 model (one year of training through a master's degree followed by three years of doctoral study). Similarly, in the natural sciences a report from the Royal Society of Chemistry took up similar themes when it stated:

> It is essential that supervisors should do everything possible to convince their students of the need to obtain a detailed knowledge of a range of topics related to their research as well as a general knowledge of their subject.
>
> (Royal Society of Chemistry, 1995, section 4.1)

Here, it was argued that the PhD in Chemistry needed to incorporate training in professional, communication, personal and technical skills. This was a major theme in the 1993 White Paper on Research Policy which stated:

> The arrangements for the training of postgraduate scientists and engineers will be developed so that the MSc can become the normal initial postgraduate degree in science, engineering and technologies and that

the PhD training for those who progress beyond the Master's degree is properly underpinned. Greater attention will be given to the relevance of postgraduate training for all careers.

(OST, 1993)

This theme continues to the present day, but we need to conduct further research on the process of postgraduate education and training (cf. Burgess, 1994). Among the questions that need to be addressed by researchers, policy makers and practitioners are: What constitutes training at postgraduate level? What effect does training have upon the postgraduate experience? How far is the training that is delivered relevant for careers within and beyond higher education (an issue that is examined by Osborn in Chapter 10). However, alongside a discussion of training and the provision of courses has been a debate about quality in higher education in general and postgraduate programmes in particular.

Quality issues in postgraduate education and training

As Harvey (1995) has indicated, 'quality is an important feature of every facet of higher education' and cannot be taken for granted. Indeed, five broad approaches to quality in higher education have been identified by Harvey and Green (1993):

- The *exceptional*, where quality is seen as special, distinctive and élitist. It is linked to excellence.
- *Perfection*, whereby quality is seen as flawless. The notion of quality is 'democratized' and has the potential to be achieved by all.
- *Fitness for purpose*, when quality is seen as fulfilling a customer's requirements (i.e. fulfilling the educational needs of students).
- *Value for money*, involving a return on investment by government or by individuals (in the case of postgraduate students those who are Research Council or British Academy sponsored as opposed to those who are self-financing).
- *Transformation*, whereby quality involves a change – the empowerment of students through the acquisition and development of new knowledge and skills.

But how might these criteria be applied to postgraduate taught courses and research? How can quality be achieved and evaluated in postgraduate education and training? At the micro-level, studies have been concerned with quality management and quality control through admission, monitoring and upgrading of doctoral work (Burgess, Pole and Hockey, 1994) and through the examination process (Phillips, 1994). However, these issues can also be explored across a range of higher education systems as in Holdaway's contribution to this volume (Chapter 4).

Postgraduate work, vocationalism and lifelong learning

Much of the work conducted at postgraduate level has a vocational orientation while fulfilling personal as well as public purposes. This was summed up by the Harris Committee when their report stated:

> Postgraduate education in all its forms serves the needs of individuals, it stimulates their minds and enables them to learn new skills and acquire new knowledge, and to develop intellectual and cultural appreciation – and by all these means to enhance their chances of a rewarding and personally satisfying life.

However, the report continued:

> In the public realm, postgraduate education contributes directly to wealth creation. Postgraduate study remains a principal vehicle for the development of the next generation of some of the best minds of the nation working at the forefront of their subjects and carrying the research of the country forward.
>
> (Harris, 1996: 15)

The committee identified a number of areas where it believed postgraduate education made a significant contribution. This included the proportion of qualified people required by industry and commerce who could contribute to innovation and technological development through the acquisition of skills and knowledge. In these terms, the economic significance of postgraduate education was very similar to the situation portrayed some 30 years earlier in the Robbins Report (1963). However, an essential difference was the importance of postgraduate education for lifelong learning whereby individuals require professional updating and reskilling for the purposes of employment.

Some indication of the contribution postgraduate education makes to lifelong learning can be deduced through the growing importance of part-time study at graduate level. Indeed, the age of students participating in part-time postgraduate study provides a further indication of lifelong learning at graduate level. In 1994–5, 37 per cent of part-time postgraduates were in the age range 30–9 and 23 per cent in the age range 40–9 (similar trends are also noted in Chapter 2 by LaPidus on the United States). However, the Harris Committee went further in concluding:

> that well into the next century there will be increased demand for postgraduate education, in part as a vehicle for lifelong learning.
>
> (Harris, 1996: 28)

But what constitutes lifelong learning? What form might this take at postgraduate level? Several of these conceptual issues are explored in Part 2 of this volume where Duke and Merrill (Chapters 5 and 6) provide examples drawn from higher education systems worldwide, while Weil (Chapter 7) examines a local example in micro-detail that links lifelong learning with postgraduate training.

The concept of lifelong learning has been defined by Longworth and Davies in the following way:

> Lifelong learning is the development of human potential through a continuously supportive process which stimulates and empowers *individuals* to acquire all the knowledge, values, skills and understanding they will require throughout their lifetimes and to apply them with confidence, creativity and enjoyment in all roles, circumstances and environments.
>
> (Longworth and Davies, 1996: 22)

They indicate how increases in the number of mature students engaged in postgraduate courses demonstrates the way in which lifelong learning can fulfil the needs of individuals and companies. Taking an example from the Rover Group in the UK, they demonstrate how the demands of the skilled workforce require learning that will satisfy the needs of the company and the individual. In this respect, lifelong learning and postgraduate study can be explored in relation to future careers (a topic that is examined in Part 3).

The labour market and careers

Postgraduate study has always been associated with labour market considerations. Levels of graduate unemployment may, in recent years, have assisted UK higher education institutions to recruit graduates from first degree programmes to engage in postgraduate study. A proportion of students have decided to enter programmes of further study rather than employment at the time of graduating from a first degree course (for details of the context see Chapter 8 by Dugdale).

However, in 1993 the Advisory Board for Research Councils argued that:

> There should be a wide range of graduate training opportunities to meet the strategic needs of the economy and society. The qualifications gained should place their emphasis on: the application of existing knowledge; project management skills; communication skills; and team work. The objectives of these schemes should be to service more effectively the demand from individuals for a diversity of career paths and from labour markets for very highly qualified manpower.
>
> (Advisory Board for the Research Councils, 1993)

Certainly, these themes recurred in the White Paper of 1993 (OST, 1993), and in turn led to the establishment of master's degrees providing training. These degree programmes, it was argued, would benefit the requirements of industry and commerce as well as academia, thus providing high-level skills that would be of relevance to employers beyond the academic world. This is a crucial issue, as some studies conducted by members of the Institute of Manpower Studies (now Institute of Employment Studies) revealed that many employers could see no advantage to employing students who had undergone doctoral training rather than first degree students (Bulmer, McKennell and Schonhardt-Bailey, 1994; Connor, 1994). Certainly, this theme recurred in the Harris Report's Task Force devoted to employment outside the academic world. Although the Task Force argued that post-graduates were critical to investment and international competitiveness given their improved skills and knowledge, they were forced to conclude that:

> Postgraduate qualifications, although relevant to many generalist and specialist jobs, are rarely prerequisites. Most employers tend to use level of first degree attainment as the primary recruitment factor.
>
> (Harris, 1996: 87)

However, evidence on the levels of employment and unemployment among those who have taken a postgraduate qualification suggest that a higher degree does help students in the labour market (for a detailed consideration of this issue see Chapter 9 by Connor).

One area that has always required individuals who have undergone postgraduate training is higher education. Yet training, especially at doctoral level, is not the only requirement currently being asked of those who want to join the academic profession. Indeed, the Harris Committee's Academic and Research Base Employers' Task Force gave a timely warning when it stated:

> While doctoral training is essential for entry to the academic and research base labour markets (except in certain specialised subjects where vocational qualifications and relevant professional experience may be of equal importance), it is rarely sufficient.
>
> (Harris, 1996: 89)

Such remarks suggest that a re-evaluation of the skills required by those going into the academic and non-academic labour markets would be timely. In the United States, this has been done by the Committee on Science, Engineering and Public Policy in its report 'Reshaping the Graduate Education of Scientists and Engineers' (COSEPUP, 1995). The issues that confront us are discussed in Chapter 10 by Osborn and also by LaPidus (Chapter 2), thus demonstrating the link between postgraduate education and training and labour market considerations.

However, the chapters in this volume may also lead to debates about more radical issues such as the shape and substance of the PhD, the training provided, the provision of postgraduate study to fulfil the demands of lifelong learning and future careers. Yet it is important for agendas to be set by policy makers and practitioners as well as researchers in higher education.

Developing the policy agenda

With the expansion of postgraduate education it is essential for policy makers and practitioners to examine critically aspects of policy and practice. Among the key issues that require consideration are:

1. *The role of training.* Much has been written about the role of training for master's students and those engaged in doctoral training as well as the links between them. However, it is essential for the academic community not merely to relate to the latest shift in government policy, but rather to consider what fundamental components of research training are essential and appropriate for students engaged in an academic or vocational course at postgraduate level.

2. *Specialization.* Trends in first degree courses and in postgraduate education have resulted in increased specialization especially at master's level. Yet, this has implications for student recruitment and the use of resources – might institutions consider the extent to which collaboration might occur in order to conserve academic resources?

3. *Lifelong learning.* Many of the courses provided at postgraduate level meet vocational demands. The academic community needs to consider how this could be extended and developed. How might graduate education be developed to meet the lifelong learning and national training targets? Could graduate education become centrally involved in the delivery of continuing vocational education and professional updating?

4. *Employment.* Students who engage in postgraduate courses often give vocational reasons for engaging in further study. Yet evidence from the academic labour market makes it difficult to see larger numbers of new posts being available in higher education, while evidence from employers suggest that postgraduate qualifications are rarely prerequisites for employment (Harris, 1996). In these circumstances, consideration needs to be given to promoting postgraduate education among potential employers and entering into discussions about the appropriate skills and knowledge that are required. This may require higher education institutions to rethink the kinds of training they provide, especially at doctoral level (Burgess, 1997) – a theme that is discussed in the Australian context in Chapter 3 by Poole and Spear.

Developing the research agenda

We have already noted that higher education is a small and specialized field of academic study as relatively few researchers choose to study the world with which they are very familiar. The result is that Becher, Henkel and Kogan (1994) have been able to specify a number of gaps and a series of research questions that need to be addressed if researchers are to develop their understanding of postgraduate education. But how is this to be done in a familiar setting? The sociologist Pierre Bourdieu offers researchers who move into this field the following advice:

> The sociologist who chooses to study in his own world in its nearest and most familiar aspects should not, as the ethnologist would, domesticate the exotic, but if I may venture the expression exoticize the domestic.
>
> (Bourdieu, 1988: xi)

But how might this be achieved? We do not only need macro-policy studies but also micro-studies of postgraduate education. There are a number of ways in which we might move forward to realize this objective:

1. Research on postgraduate education needs to cross all subject areas – disciplinary and interdisciplinary.
2. The orientation of the research on postgraduate education might take up the concerns not only of academics but also of administrators and policy makers. In these circumstances, some practitioner-based research inquiries could be developed.
3. Research on postgraduate education needs to be cumulative so as to develop specific theoretical, and substantive themes.
4. International and comparative studies need to be developed so as to facilitate:

   (a) comparisons of policy at a macro-level;
   (b) studies of policy implementation at a micro-level.

5. Studies of the structure, content and delivery of postgraduate research could be conducted by examining:

   (a) graduate school models and their effectiveness;
   (b) the academic and vocational content of postgraduate courses;
   (c) the extent to which postgraduate education provides professional development.

6. Researchers working in this area could develop the ways in which their work might link with enquiries in such fields as:

   (a) politics and policy making in higher education;
   (b) higher education management;
   (c) curriculum and pedagogy in higher education;
   (d) teaching and learning in higher education.

7. Research on the labour market effects of postgraduate study demand a qualitative as well as a quantitative approach with students and their employers.
8. Dissemination by researchers concerned with higher education needs to engage with policy makers and practitioners.

In these ways, it is hoped that more systematic work will be conducted in the areas covered by this volume.

Conclusion

Postgraduate education and training has shifted from being a fringe activity in higher education institutions to commanding a role that takes centre stage. In recent years, there have been numerous reports from government and the research councils about postgraduate study in the UK. For many coming to this volume (and to the SRHE Conference), their knowledge and experience of postgraduate education will be limited to the United Kingdom in the recent past. Accordingly, this chapter and in turn this volume attempts to provide evidence that will allow that experience to be located in a broader context and related to national and international concerns. The issues that are discussed in the following chapters need to continue to be examined at local, national and international levels as researchers, policy makers and practitioners explore whether there are links to be made between postgraduate education, lifelong learning and future careers beyond the first degree.

References

Advisory Board for the Research Councils (1993) *Nature of the PhD: A Discussion Document.* London: HMSO.

Becher, T., Henkel, M. and Kogan, M. (1994) *Graduate Education in Britain.* London: Jessica Kingsley Publishers.

Blume, S. (ed.) (1995a) *Research Training: Present and Future.* Paris: OECD.

Blume, S. (1995b) 'Extended Review of the Internationalisation of Research Training in the EU'. Unpublished paper.

Bourdieu, P. (1988) *Homo Academicus.* Oxford: Polity.

Bulmer, M., McKennell, A. and Schonhardt-Bailey, C. (1994) Training in quantitative methods for postgraduate social scientists: the other side of the fence, in R. G. Burgess (ed.) *Postgraduate Education and Training in the Social Sciences: Processes and Products* (pp. 182–203). London: Jessica Kingsley Publishers.

Burgess, R. G. (ed.) (1994) *Postgraduate Education and Training in the Social Sciences: Processes and Products.* London: Jessica Kingsley Publishers.

Burgess, R. G. (1996) Trends and developments in postgraduate education and training in the UK, *Journal of Education Policy,* 11(1): 125–32.

Burgess, R. G. (1997) Revolution required to keep boom on track, *The Times Higher Education Supplement,* 7 March.

Burgess, R. G., Hogan, J. V., Pole, C. J. and Sanders, L. (1995) Postgraduate research training in the United Kingdom, in S. Blume (ed.) *Research Training: Present and Future* (pp. 135–57). Paris: OECD.

Burgess, R. G., Pole, C. J. and Hockey, J. (1994) Strategies for managing and supervising the social science PhD, in R. G. Burgess (ed.) *Postgraduate Education and Training in the Social Sciences: Processes and Products* (pp. 13–33). London: Jessica Kingsley Publishers.

Burgess, R. G. and Schratz, M. (1994) Editorial introduction, *Zeitschrift fur Hochshuldidaktik,* 18(2), 148.

Clark, B. R. (ed.) (1993) *The Research Foundations of Graduate Education.* Berkeley: University of California Press.

Connor, H. (1994) Doctoral social scientists and the labour market, in R. G. Burgess (ed.) *Postgraduate Education and Training in the Social Sciences: Processes and Products* (pp. 167–81). London: Jessica Kingsley Publishers.

COSEPUP (1995) *Reshaping the Graduate Education of Scientists and Engineers.* Washington: National Academy Press.

ESRC (1991) *Postgraduate Training Guidelines.* Swindon: ESRC.

ESRC (1996) *Postgraduate Training Guidelines,* 2nd edn. Swindon: ESRC.

Gellert, C. (1993) The conditions of research training in contemporary German universities, in B. R. Clark (ed.) *The Research Foundations of Graduate Education.* Berkeley: University of California Press.

Harris, M. (1996) *Review of Postgraduate Education.* London: HEFCE.

Harvey, L. (1995) Editorial, *Quality in Higher Education,* 1(1), 5–14.

Harvey, L. and Green, D. (1993) Defining quality, *Assessment and Evaluation in Higher Education,* 18, 9–34.

HESA (1996) *Students in Higher Education Institutions 1994/95. Reference Volume.* Cheltenham: HESA.

Holdaway, E., Deblois, C. and Winchester, I. (1995) *Organisation and Administration of Graduate Programs.* Canada: University of Alberta.

Longworth, N. and Davies, W. K. (1996) *Lifelong Learning.* London: Kogan Page.

OST (1993) *Realising Our Potential.* White Paper. London: HMSO.

Phillips, E. M. (1994) Quality in the PhD: points at which quality may be assessed, in R. G. Burgess (ed.) *Postgraduate Education and Training in the Social Sciences: Processes and Products* (pp. 124–46). London: Jessica Kingsley Publishers.

Pratt, J. (1995) The future of higher education: the editorial, *Higher Education Review,* 27(3), 3–7.

Robbins, L. (1963) *Higher Education.* London: HMSO.

Royal Society of Chemistry (1995) *The Chemistry PhD – the Enhancement of Quality.* London: Royal Society of Chemistry.

Swinnerton-Dyer, P. (1982) *Report of the Working Party on Postgraduate Education.* London: HMSO.

UKCGE (1995) *Graduate Schools.* Coventry: UKCGE.

Universities Statistical Record (1994) *University Statistics 1993–94 Students and Staff,* Vol. I. Cheltenham: Universities Statistical Record.

Winfield, G. (1987) *The Social Science PhD: the ESRC Inquiry on Submission Rates.* London: ESRC.

Part 1

Graduate Education

2

Issues and Themes in Postgraduate Education in the United States

Jules B. LaPidus

Introduction

Three factors currently provide a framework for virtually all discussions of education in the United States: money, politics and technology. Of course, these factors affect education in all countries, but the specific nature of the educational system, the level of education being discussed, and the conditions defining the dimensions of any factor at a particular time and place, provide a context in which to examine what is happening in any single country, and to compare that with what is happening elsewhere.

With respect to the educational system in the United States, the most important point is that there is no Ministry of Education; that is, there is no branch of the federal government that has responsibility or authority for all educational institutions. Thus, while problems or concerns may be national or global in scope, solutions are local, sometimes at the state level (for public universities), or, more often, at the individual institution level. A good example is the recent review of doctoral programmes carried out in the State of Ohio.

The Ohio State Board of Regents, which has budgetary authority for allocation of state funds, as well as authority to decide which institutions may grant specific degrees, reviewed all doctoral programmes, discipline by discipline, in the 12 public universities in the state. The impetus was a concern that the state was investing too much money in doctoral education, coupled with a perception that doctoral students were having difficulty in finding jobs and, therefore, that too many PhDs were being produced. In the field of history, for example, there were eight doctoral programmes in the state. Following review, the Board of Regents announced that henceforth only two would be eligible to receive state support. The other six could choose to continue offering the degree, but would receive no funding from the state for that purpose. What is far more common is for individual institutions to cut back on their graduate programmes, or to reduce the enrolments in those programmes based on an institutional assessment of priorities, mission, student demand and funds available.

Another point worth noting is the idea of a graduate school, that is, a central university office devoted entirely to issues involving graduate education. This is a characteristic of universities in the United States, and provides a focal point for considering the structure, nature, and quality of graduate programmes across disciplines. Graduate deans, in contact with graduate students and faculty in all departments, bring issues of broad concern, such as the ones discussed in this chapter, to the attention of the graduate community. In this way, the graduate school acts as an advocate for research and graduate education and coordinates the development of policies that affect graduate education in the institution.

The level of education discussed here is what is usually referred to in the United States as graduate education (postgraduate education in many other countries). For purposes of this chapter, here are definitions of three categories of graduate education:

1. Graduate certificate programmes
2. Master's programmes

   • Practice-oriented master's programmes
   • Traditional master's programmes

3. Doctoral programmes

Each of these will be discussed in terms of their current state and how they are being affected by the factors to be described next.

Money

Since the late 1980s, money has been harder to get. The current mode is one of constriction rather than expansion or even stability. A word much in use is 'downsizing', describing a need to redefine what an organization can accomplish with fewer resources, and to develop smaller and more focused operations, both in universities and in industry. There is some difference of opinion about whether this actually is happening, or whether the need for efficiency – for doing more with less – is having specific effects on the size and nature of the workforce. An example would be the recent increase in the number and percentage of part-time or adjunct faculty being hired, in many cases to replace retiring full-time tenured faculty. Another is the increasing difficulty being experienced by new PhDs in finding research jobs. In either case, the driving force is not the improvement of education or research, or even the desire to decrease size and scope, but rather the need to reduce costs while dealing with an increasing workload and a more competitive environment.

Politics

Three issues currently dominate political discussions relative to higher education. The first is race, an issue that affects every aspect of American life. For the past 30 years, universities have been increasing the access of minorities and women to higher education. This usually has taken the form of programmes and financial assistance 'targeted' on certain groups of American citizens who had historically been excluded from universities and particularly from advanced study. Included were African-Americans, Latinos, American Indians, people with disabilities and, in some cases, women (in fields such as engineering and the physical sciences). At the graduate level, literally hundreds of university, state, and federal programmes were initiated to provide fellowships and recruitment and retention activities for these groups. Much of this has taken place using the general strategy of affirmative action, which involves not simply opening the doors to let people in, but taking specific steps to seek out, encourage and promote success among students from the aforementioned groups.

Recent actions, particularly in the University of California system, in the courts in some states and by the voters in the State of California in passing the California Civil Rights Initiative, prohibit consideration of race, gender, national origin or ethnicity, as factors in decisions relating to hiring, admission or the award of financial aid. The effect this will have on participation in graduate education by the groups mentioned above is uncertain, but many other universities, states and the federal government will be considering the future of affirmative action over the next few years. The debate about affirmative action will certainly be acrimonious and emotional, and almost any action will likely be challenged in the courts (as it currently is in California). While this all plays out, graduate students and potential graduate students, along with the institutions that provide graduate programmes, will face a very uncertain future.

The second political issue has to do with immigration policy. Over the past 25 years, the United States, like many other countries, has experienced a large increase in immigration, particularly from Latin America and Asia. Until recently, most attention by both local and federal government agencies was devoted to taking action against illegal immigrants. The focus now has shifted to legal immigrants, and is related, in part, to the success that many recent immigrants have had in the higher education system and the workforce. This has led to some resentment, particularly in states such as California, where the majority of students on some campuses are Asian-Americans, and has been compounded by the large influx of foreign students over the past 20 years, mostly from China, Taiwan, Korea, India and Japan.

Added to this is a new flow of immigrants from Russia and the Newly Independent States (formerly parts of the Soviet Union). Many of these immigrants are scientists, engineers or mathematicians and are seen by some as an asset in terms of adding highly skilled people to the workforce.

For US citizens in these fields who are having difficulty finding jobs, the reaction is quite different, since they are likely to view immigrants as extra competition in the job market. For example, a number of young American mathematicians has recently formed a group with the express purpose of trying to change immigration law to restrict entry of foreign mathematicians into the United States. This is directly related to a particularly bad job market for new PhDs in this field. In addition, foreign graduate students tend to be concentrated in precisely those fields where the greatest difficulty has been encountered in attracting American minorities and women. Thus xenophobia grows, and more resentment builds about foreign students and scientists 'displacing' Americans.

The third political factor has to do with human resources, particularly the relationship of doctoral production to the current or projected job market. Most studies of this issue define the primary job market as being tenure track positions in universities. While that is the historical view, it does not represent reality in some fields (engineering, some of the sciences) where industry has been the major employer for some time. In either case, starting in 1992–4, new PhDs in the sciences began to encounter difficulties in finding jobs directly related to their training. This last point is important; chemists have expected to get jobs doing research in chemistry, mathematicians doing research in mathematics. While the unemployment rates have remained low, the so-called underemployment rate has increased. This is not a new phenomenon in the humanities and arts, but it is unusual in the sciences and engineering, and has resulted in great public interest.

Exacerbating the problem is the fact that in the late 1980s and early 1990s a number of books, reports and articles appeared projecting a large shortage of faculty in particular, and of scientists and engineers in general, beginning in the mid-1990s (Bowen and Schuster, 1986; Bowen and Sosa, 1989; Atkinson, 1990). Projections of this kind are extremely unreliable since the only thing one can predict with certainty is that unanticipated events will take place that will invalidate projections. This is what has happened now, and many new PhDs feel that they were misled and exploited. There is a good deal of bitterness and resentment which is leading to recommendations to reshape graduate education to prepare better students for a wide variety of jobs and careers.

The four items just discussed:

● cutbacks in funds, particularly in support for academic and industrial research positions;
● changes in the options available to universities for the recruitment and retention of students and faculty historically under-represented in graduate study and in the academic and industrial workforce;
● changes in immigration policy that would affect the ability of people in other countries to come to the United States for advanced study and for jobs in the academic and industrial workforce;

- the production of more PhDs than can currently be accommodated into the academic and industrial workforce;

intersect at a number of points and create a complex economic and political milieu in which graduate education is buffeted by prevailing and countervailing winds of change.

Technology

This term is being used as a catch-all to refer to various technological developments that can be used in education. For the most part, it means interactive audio/video (A/V) and, increasingly, computers and the Internet. It is usually associated with the idea of distance education, but does not have to be. Technology, as used here, relates to how a thing is done; distance education refers to where it is done. The use of A/V usually means that students go somewhere and participate in a class being offered somewhere else. This occurs in real time, and students can interact with faculty and other students. This has great advantages for students who cannot come to the university for classes. It also allows universities to extend their service areas and thus acquire more students.

The major interest in technology, however, is in the use of the Internet to provide education directly through a computer in the student's room or home. Interactions can take place through e-mail and/or 'chat rooms'. Students have access to an incredible amount of information on their own time and in their own place. This has given rise to the idea of the 'virtual classroom' and, by extension, the 'virtual university', which has no physical dimensions and exists only in cyberspace. Currently, the Governors of 15 western states are cooperating to create 'The Western Governors University' which will be a virtual university comprising courses and programmes from all the universities in the states involved. This in effect creates a virtual consortium which, to be effective, must develop ways to create programmes, transfer credit and grant degrees. Meanwhile, some institutions are offering undergraduate and graduate courses and certificates, as well as some graduate programmes entirely on-line.

Several driving forces are operating here. One is the availability of intriguing technology which is getting better and faster by the moment. Another is the possibility of making information available to people anywhere, anytime. Yet another is the idea that these techniques will be very efficient in delivering education since one faculty member, theoretically, could interact with a huge number of students. In addition, much less classroom space would be needed, which would give rise to additional cost savings. Actually the same issues arose as a consequence of another technology – the printing press – and probably stimulated much the same kind of debate that is taking place today. No one is quite sure whether the quality of education will improve or deteriorate, and doctoral theses are being written about the role of human contact in the learning process, but the use of computers in the educational process is compelling and unavoidable.

This is not the place to argue the pros and cons of 'virtual' education. What is important is to recognize that the use of technology, as described here, intersects with the other factors discussed previously, particularly as it relates to money and to the nature of the academic job market. In more subtle ways, it also relates to racial and gender issues in so far as these are invisible on the Internet.

Graduate education in the United States

The preceding discussion of some of the factors and structural components that affect higher education in the United States will serve as background for consideration of the various components of graduate education. Before doing so, however, it will be useful to provide a brief overview of the enterprise.

As of 1995, approximately 1.7 million postgraduate students were enrolled in US colleges and universities. There are approximately 2700 institutions of higher education in the US, and some 1600 of them have some kind of post-baccalaureate offerings. The majority of graduate students (about three-

Figure 2.1   Graduate enrolment, 1974 to 1994

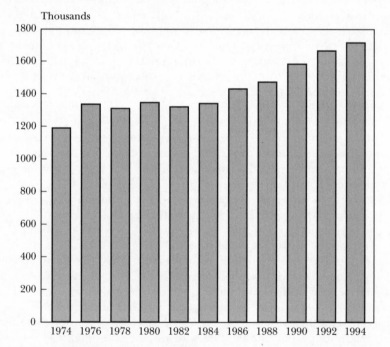

Source: Snyder, Hoffman and Geddes (1996).

Table 2.1 Trends in master's degree production, 1974 to 1994

	1974	1978	1982	1986	1990	1994
Business	32,644	48,326	60,763	66,689	76,676	92,759
Education	112,610	119,038	91,601	74,801	84,881	98,938
Engineering	15,379	16,398	17,939	21,657	24,775	29,756
Humanities	25,326	22,704	20,752	19,181	21,113	24,944
Life sciences	18,570	24,448	26,540	27,387	28,572	35,519
Physical sciences	13,172	11,972	13,712	17,579	19,272	20,186
Public administration/ services	12,077	18,341	17,416	15,692	17,399	21,833
Social sciences	24,997	23,719	22,758	21,354	23,576	28,375
Other*	22,258	26,674	24,065	24,227	28,037	34,760
Total	277,033	311,620	295,546	288,567	324,301	387,070

* Includes architecture, communications, home economics, law, library science, military technologies, parks/recreation, protective services, and transportation and material moving.
Source: Snyder, Hoffman and Geddes (1996).

Table 2.2 Trends in doctoral degree production, 1974 to 1994

	1974	1978	1982	1986	1990	1994
Education	7241	7194	7251	6649	6511	6695
Engineering	3147	2423	2646	3376	4894	5822
Humanities	5170	4231	3561	3461	2822	4745
Life sciences	4964	5041	5709	5734	6604	7736
Physical sciences	4976	4193	4291	4807	5859	6822
Social sciences	5882	6038	5837	5893	6093	6614
Professional/other*	1667	1755	1816	1982	2284	2583
Total	33,047	30,875	31,111	31,902	36,067	41,017

* Includes business and management, communications, architecture, home economics, law, library science, parks and recreation, public administration, social work, and theology.
Source: Simmons and Thurgood (1995).

quarters) are enrolled in 400 of the largest institutions. Overall enrolment over the past 20 years is shown in Figure 2.1. The apparent stability from the mid-1970s to the mid-1980s is somewhat misleading in that during the period in question there was a decrease in the number of US citizen males offset by an increase in women and international students. Doctoral degree production began to increase in 1986, and this trend has continued to the present time, with each successive year representing a new high. Much the same thing can be said for master's education. Trends in degree production for both degree levels are illustrated in Tables 2.1 and 2.2.

Table 2.3 The new American graduate student

	Master's	Doctoral
Enrolment		
Full-time	30%	58%
Part-time	70%	42%
Demographics		
Female	56%	38%
Minority (US and permanent residents)	14%	17%
African American	6%	7%
American Indian	1%	1%
Asian	4%	7%
Hispanic/Latino	4%	3%
Age		
Average age	33	33
Over 30	54%	59%
Over 40	23%	21%
Marital status and dependants		
Married	54%	52%
With dependants	27%	24%
Average number of dependants	2	1.7

Source: Council of Graduate Schools (1996).

A useful way to describe today's graduate student appears in Table 2.3. Things have changed from the time most current faculty were graduate students, a fact that many may not realize as they design programmes, establish standards and set expectations. The modern American graduate student probably has very different goals, in terms both of careers and lifestyle, and these can affect the time it takes to get degrees, the way one sees education as part of life, the research problems one chooses and the jobs one seeks.

Certificate programmes

These are the least well characterized of all post-baccalaureate programmes. The idea is an old one: to provide 'official' recognition of some activity in which the student has been engaged. In most cases, the certificate represents accomplishment, as measured in the usual academic ways (tests, papers). In some cases, it may represent attendance at a certain number of sessions. In either case, there is a tremendous variation in certificate programmes in terms of length, requirements, offering entity and purpose. Certificates may be awarded for work accomplished during a weekend or over several years. The ultimate value to the student has to do, of course, with what is learned but, in a very practical sense, it also relates to the value of the particular credential in the marketplace.

Certificate programmes can be offered by anyone, but the usual purveyors are colleges and universities (often through their continuing or further education operations). Many professional societies provide certificates for participation in seminars, symposia or workshops. Some require this certification as a condition of continuing professional accreditation. An increasing source of certificate programmes is private vendors, who develop specific programmes to meet market demand or student interest. A good example of the former would be any number of programmes dealing with information and technology. A good example of the latter would be programmes offered by museums or galleries in art or connoisseurship. The latter may be taken purely for interest and personal development. The former, however, usually relate to a changing workplace and the need to keep current in order to keep one's job. Two rather graphic terms have been used to describe this situation: 'defensive credentialling', and 'just in time learning'. Both are self-explanatory.

A more classic type of post-baccalaureate offering is the area studies certificate. This often represents two years of study beyond the master's degree. Programmes are focused on an area, usually geographic, and students finishing such a programme are awarded a certificate in areas such as East Asian Studies, or Latin American Studies. These programmes tend to attract people in fields such as economics or political science who have specific interests in certain parts of the world.

Another major category is the teaching certificate. A student in a specific field might want to acquire such a certificate as a 'safety net' in case it proved difficult to get a research position. This would provide an option for the individual to obtain a teaching position, usually at the secondary (high school) level.

Certificates are perhaps the most rapidly expanding area of post-baccalaureate education. This is a natural consequence of a tight and rapidly changing job market. Those who have jobs want to make sure they keep them; those who don't, want to improve their chances of getting one. Thus, there is a great deal of consumer demand, and many education suppliers eager to claim their share of this market. As far as universities are concerned, this is a source of much-needed revenue. In addition, most certificate programmes are short term, may require little in the way of facilities and faculty, and can be offered relatively easily using modern technology, particularly the Internet.

Certificate programmes are firmly embedded in a matrix of money, politics and technology. Since they are not degree programmes, they are often offered through units other than the regular colleges. Professional colleges and continuing education units, however, have been aggressive in seeking new ways to provide university services to the public. This is not just to find additional sources of revenue, but to demonstrate the responsiveness of the university to the needs of the public, and to cultivate a loyal alumni group that will be financially and politically supportive of the university. Making these programmes readily available at times and in locations convenient for students is increasingly being done through various combinations of computer-assisted and interactive audio/video techniques. These programmes undoubtedly will continue to flourish, and questions of quality, costs and university priorities will continue to be raised.

Master's programmes

In 1993, Conrad, Haworth and Millar published the results of their extensive study of master's education in the United States. They interviewed 781 people associated with 47 master's programmes in 31 colleges and universities. The programmes were in 11 different fields, ranging from business through environmental studies to English. The people interviewed were students, faculty, administrators, alumni and employers. The investigators were interested in finding out how people involved in master's education evaluated their own experiences, how to interpret differences in experiences and, most particularly, what characteristics of master's programmes were thought to enhance the quality of the participants' experiences.

One of the important outcomes of the study was the finding that all of these programmes, regardless of field, could be grouped into four broad categories:

1. *Ancillary* programmes – individuals involved perceived these programmes in relation to PhD programmes in the same department. There was very little commitment, either by faculty or administrators, to the programme, except as preparation for the PhD.
2. *Career advancement* programmes – client-centred, career-oriented, 'expert' training. This kind of programme is intended to provide students with the skills and training needed for careers in various professional fields. A practitioner degree.
3. *Apprenticeship* programmes – similar to guilds, where student apprentices worked with faculty masters in order to become members of the guild.
4. *Community-centred* programmes – students and faculty work as a collegial learning community.

Most master's programmes in the arts and sciences fall into the first category. These are often referred to as traditional master's programmes. For the most part, programmes in the other three categories are related to preparation for, or advancement in careers. These are usually referred to as practice-oriented programmes.

Practice-oriented master's programmes
In a recent study of educational aspirations of baccalaureates one year after they had graduated (National Center for Education Statistics, 1993), 62 per cent indicated that they eventually planned to go on for a master's degree. The degree referred to by the vast majority of these people has come to be known as the practice-oriented master's degree. Roughly 85 per cent of all

master's degrees are in this category. Their major distinguishing feature is that they focus on the state of practice in a profession, rather than on the state of knowledge in a discipline. In addition, their purpose is to prepare people to practise a certain profession, or to improve and extend the abilities of those already practising. The most common of these degrees, in terms both of public understanding and numbers of students enrolled, are in business, education and engineering, followed by literally hundreds of degrees in much more specific areas.

Practice-oriented master's programmes tend to relate very closely to the current needs of the practice. Many involve significant participation by working practitioners, often as adjunct or part-time faculty. The majority of students in these programmes are part-time, and many receive partial payment of their tuition from their employers. The length of time required to complete such programmes varies, but is usually equivalent to between one and two years of full-time study.

Given the nature of the graduate student population, there is a great demand for programmes of this type at times outside traditional office hours. Universities have accommodated to this demand, initially by providing courses at night and on weekends, and later by developing video cassettes (courseware) that students can view at their convenience. This is simply a modern version of a correspondence course, with television replacing written material. Some universities have developed off-campus centres, close to where people live and work, where students can take courses and meet with faculty. This has been relatively easy for institutions located in urban areas, but somewhat more difficult for those in rural or remote locations. In many cases, institutions in this latter category have developed audio and video presentations so that students at a remote site could have access to courses, and technical advances have led to interactive audiovisual presentations that permit students to participate in class discussions.

With the availability of the Internet, universities are rapidly developing the capability of delivering complete master's programmes on-line. The most common of these is the Master of Business Administration (MBA), but a host of others are in preparation. As the use of the Internet expands, a number of issues arise that require attention. For the most part, these do not relate to the technology, which is here and will only get better. Instead, they relate to the way people learn, and to the problems encountered by universities in certifying the quality of a student's performance. This latter point becomes more complicated if students take courses from several different institutions. In that case, the student is, in effect, creating a virtual consortium, with no prior agreement on what constitutes a programme, and which institution will grant the degree.

We are still at the beginning of the era of hi-tech education. Particularly in certificate programmes and practice-oriented master's programmes, which usually require completion of a series of courses rather than the completion of a thesis, this form of delivery of degree programmes is becoming very popular, and can be very powerful in making seemingly endless resources available to students. We still do not know much about the real costs of these programmes, or whether they improve the ability of students to learn.

Traditional master's programmes

As pointed out previously, only 15 per cent of master's programmes fall into this category. For the most part, these are programmes in the arts and sciences. More to the point, however, is that they exist primarily in departments also offering a PhD. In this situation, master's programmes are often viewed as screening mechanisms for the doctoral programme. The term 'consolation prize' has sometimes been used to describe the role of the degree, in that it may be awarded to students who are not considered to be good prospects for the PhD programme. Indeed, master's programmes of this type are often simply the first part of PhD programmes, and concern has been expressed that students leaving with this kind of background are not prepared for any particular career.

Master's programmes, particularly those in the sciences, are a current topic of renewed interest in the United States, primarily in connection with what is thought by many to be an overproduction of scientists at the PhD level. Tobias and Chubin (1996), as well as others, have urged that the master's degree be revitalized and, in a sense, professionalized, to provide students interested in research-related careers an option for acquiring the appropriate training and credentials. Part of their argument is based on the assumption that PhDs in many research laboratories may be performing essentially technical functions that could be carried out just as well by well-trained master's graduates. Another important consideration is that the investment of time and money required to get a master's degree is much less than that required for the PhD. The outcome could be that research-related industry would have access to technically competent people who had spent two years rather than six in graduate school.

This idea brings to mind the distinction made by John Ziman (1968: 69) to the effect that, 'Scientific education is for research; technological education is for practice.' This emphasizes the point that master's education is most responsive to the needs of employers, while doctoral education has been most responsive to the needs of the disciplines. An important question is, is industry not hiring PhDs because they are 'overqualified' or because there is not enough money to increase scientific staffs? Certainly there are opportunities for people with a solid background through the master's level, particularly in areas such as biotechnology. How more extensive use of people with master's degrees would affect industrial positions for PhDs would depend on the way particular industries defined their scientific workforce. In a paper on science in Japan (Normile, 1996), industrial leaders as well as graduate students appear to be favouring the master's degree over the PhD, particularly in areas of applied research.

The future of the traditional master's degree is uncertain. If, as has been suggested, there is a market for people with this degree, particularly in industry, the reconceptualized degree may prove to be useful, for students, industry and universities. The real question is whether the academy will devote the time, thought and finances required to develop the traditional master's degree as one with its own integrity and purpose, which must go beyond serving either as a prelude to, or a gatekeeper for, the PhD.

Doctoral programmes

In the early 1990s several books appeared that provided analysis and discussion of the doctoral degree. One (Bowen and Rudenstine, 1992) was concerned primarily with factors affecting time to degree and completion rates in several disciplines. Cohort data from a small group of American research universities were analysed and discussed. Another (Clark, 1993) provided comparative information about doctoral education in five countries and speculated about the nature of graduate education. These studies created a climate of interest in doctoral education. Currently, the overriding issue is the relationship between doctoral education and the job market. In terms of supply, many people believe that we are producing too many PhDs and, in terms of demand, that there is a rapidly changing situation relative to the way the largest employers of PhDs carry out their work. There is a strong movement in higher education for significant reforms in doctoral education. Many reports have been written, conferences held and speeches delivered, all attempting to sort out this complicated business. In the next few pages, I shall try to present the issues and a variety of points of view pertaining to doctoral education.

In the United States, doctoral education was a rather small enterprise prior to the end of World War II. Those individuals who did seek doctoral degrees were strongly motivated to do research in an academic setting, and to teach. After the war ended, at least two dramatic changes took place. One had to do with the growth of the academic enterprise, fuelled by increasing numbers of students and a rising birth rate. Existing universities expanded, and new ones were created. There was a strong demand for faculty, and students were urged to go to graduate school in order to become the next generation of professors. Academic jobs were abundant.

The other change had to do with research. During the war years it had become apparent that PhDs could make significant contributions to the military-industrial research and development effort, and new industrial firms, particularly in fields such as chemistry, became interested in hiring PhDs. In addition, the federal government, prompted by leading scientist-statesmen like Vannevar Bush (1945/1980), decided that supporting academic research and graduate education was a good national investment. The successful launching of sputnik in 1957 added a strong component of international scientific rivalry, and even more money became available. The period 1958–72 represented unprecedented growth for universities and for graduate education.

There have been ups and downs since that time, but the basic picture, particularly from the mid-1970s to the mid-1980s, was one of stability. That changed in the late 1980s when doctoral production began a slow but steady increase that continues today. Two major studies (Bowen and Schuster, 1986; Bowen and Sosa, 1989) written during that time period suggested a strong demand for faculty in most fields, starting in the mid-1990s and extending into the next century. In addition a number of analyses led some people (e.g. Atkinson, 1990) to conclude that there would be a huge shortage of PhD scientists and engineers for all sectors of employment. People who entered graduate school in the late 1980s expected to find an abundance of job opportunities in industrial and academic research when they obtained their PhDs in the mid-1990s. That proved not to be the case.

In times of rapid change, the relatively long period between a student's decision to go to graduate school and the acquisition of the PhD (between five and seven years in most science and engineering fields) usually confound attempts to make valid projections, and can lead to serious mismatches between expectation and reality with regard to research positions, either in universities or in industry. This occurred during the late 1980s to mid-1990s and was related to a number of factors (the recession, the collapse of the Soviet Union and its effect on the defence budget, the demise of the superconducting supercollider) that no one had predicted. By 1993–4 new PhDs in many if not most fields were encountering some difficulties in finding the jobs they wanted, and while the unemployment rate stayed quite low (1–2 per cent) the underemployment rate and the length of time it took to get the first job were increasing (National Science Foundation, 1995). What was new (and newsworthy) was that this was occurring in the sciences and engineering.

For some years there had been a concern, largely in the university community, about the lack of jobs for humanists. Obviously, there was turnover, and jobs were available each year, but the situation was not quite that simple. For one thing, the overwhelming majority of PhDs in the humanities were seeking academic jobs. But many, if not most, young humanists were likely to want tenure track jobs, not just in academe, but in universities resembling the ones in which they got their degrees, and there were relatively few of those available. Jobs in other sectors of education were often viewed with disdain, particularly by faculty advisers of graduate students, and students got a fairly clear message that these 'other' jobs were only for those who could not make it in the research university. Exacerbating this situation was the uncapping of retirement age, thus allowing faculty to remain after the age of 70, and the fact that when senior faculty did retire or die, they were often replaced by part-time faculty. This permitted universities not only to save money, but to avoid the long-term commitment that accompanies tenure track appointments.

Apart from a few articles, mainly in the academic press, deploring this state of affairs, there was little interest in the topic. What humanists actually did was something of a mystery to those outside of the academy, and when people did find out, they tended to be surprised that anyone really expected to make a living reading and writing scholarly books, and discussing them with generations of students.

The situation was entirely different in the sciences and engineering. With the exception of a brief period in the early 1970s, new PhDs could be reasonably sure that they would find jobs doing research in their fields, and would have some options including postdoctoral work, faculty positions, government or industrial jobs or consulting. The projections made in the late 1980s and early 1990s indicated that this would only get better, so initial reports that new PhDs were encountering difficulties in finding jobs caused much consternation. In addition to articles in the publications of many of the scientific associations, stories appeared in the public press citing widespread unemployment among young scientists. Actually, as pointed out above, the unemployment rate for new PhDs has remained quite low. What has changed is that a larger number of graduates are having more difficulty getting the jobs they want (or believe they should want). This has led to a good deal of bitterness among recent graduates, as well as widespread calls for reform.

For some years, certain scientists and observers of science had been saying that we were producing far too many PhDs. David Goodstein (1993: 216), a well-known physicist, has stated that 'What we face . . . is a chronic, systemic oversupply of Ph.D.s, a rising tide of Ph.D.s that we seem helpless to stem.' The key words are chronic and systemic. Tobias, Chubin and Aylesworth (1995) suggested that there were three ways to view the current bad job market for PhDs: that it was cyclic, and if we just waited it out, it would get better; that it was a coincidence, that is, that we happened to have very high production at a time when employment opportunities were limited; or that it was systemic, and would not get better unless we took steps to change the system.

The idea of a systemic problem is related to the way we produce PhDs. Faculty members at research universities carry out programmes of research for which they need funding, laboratories, equipment and assistants. Universities need people to teach undergraduates, and since faculty members may spend an increasing amount of time doing research and teaching graduate students, the graduate students provide a source of teaching assistants as well as research assistants. Indeed, these two kinds of assistantships are the primary forms of financial support for graduate students in the sciences.

In thinking about the factors that determine how many graduate students a department should have, the future job market plays a small role, primarily because of reasons mentioned earlier, that is, projections over the period of time involved have been notoriously bad. Instead, facilities, advising capacity, student demand and the research and teaching obligations of the department (faculty) are the dominant factors. Since more has often been considered to be better, and since faculty are strongly motivated to be ever more productive in research to enhance their own careers and the reputations of their universities, faculty may be seeking as many graduate students as they can handle. If one assumes that a large number of the PhDs produced in this process obtain jobs in research universities, and that all of them will have doctoral students, the system does indeed have all the attributes of the Sorcerer's Apprentice. But the system does not work quite that way.

For one thing, there has been a continuing decline over the last 20 years in the percentage of new PhDs in the sciences and engineering who seek academic jobs. In the physical sciences and engineering it is currently between 20 and 40 per cent, with the majority going primarily to industry. Furthermore, most academic jobs will not be in research universities. Thus, only a relatively small percentage of PhDs will become producers of more PhDs.

For another, the system is self-correcting in a way, since changes alluded to earlier are causing some universities to contract their graduate programmes, and, in addition, to replace regular faculty with part-time faculty. For the most part, only regular faculty members serve as advisers of doctoral students. In addition, the state of the job market is not a secret and, particularly with the advent of the Internet, graduate students, faculty members and people considering graduate school have up-to-date information from the field. For example, first year graduate enrolment in physics has declined by over 20 per cent during the last few years, at least in part because of the extensive discussion of the bad job market in that field.

All of that being said, a real problem exists when smart and motivated young people spend five to seven years as graduate students getting a first-rate education, and are then told that they are surplus goods in a glutted market. In order to address this problem in a systematic way, the Committee on Science, Engineering, and Public Policy (COSEPUP) of the National Academy of Sciences, the National Academy of Engineering, and the Institute of Medicine, initiated a study in 1993. Their report, *Reshaping the Graduate Education of Scientists and Engineers* (1995), has received widespread discussion among graduate deans, and others interested in research policy and graduate education. Like many reports of this kind, however, it probably has not been discussed as widely as it should be among faculty members and graduate students.

The COSEPUP report made several general and a number of fairly specific recommendations. It took a strong stand against any broad-based attempts to reduce doctoral production, advised against any systemic attempt to reduce foreign student enrolment, and encouraged continuing vigorous activities to increase the number of women and minority students studying science at the graduate level. The report went on to suggest a number of changes in the way that universities interact with students. Among these are:

1. provide better information on employment options;
2. broaden graduate programmes to include courses and experiences that go beyond the student's dissertation research;

3. strengthen the master's degree to make it a viable option for students who decide not to pursue the PhD;
4. decrease time to degree;
5. provide more federal support for graduate students in the form of training grants, whose purpose is education, rather than on research grants, the purpose of which is to produce research;
6. try to develop better national data on employment options and trends;
7. facilitate a national discussion on issues in graduate education.

Many universities are currently examining their graduate programmes in the light of these and other recommendations. In addition, a number of important topics, such as the rapid development of interdisciplinary programmes, the effects of technology on the way scholarly activities are carried out, and the role and nature of postdoctoral students in the workforce, are also being considered. A basic issue, however, and one that will continue to be at the heart of any discussion of doctoral education, is how to balance the encouragement of young people to pursue advanced study with the public policy concerns about support, and the changes in the way employers view the workforce.

Conclusion

Graduate education is in a state of flux, reflecting changes taking place in society. As those involved with graduate education attempt to understand its purpose and value in contemporary terms, questions are being posed that are as old as education itself:

Who are we? (Who are the faculty and students in terms of race, ethnicity, gender, nationality and other factors?)
What do we do? (What is the nature of graduate education?)
How do we do it? (What are our processes and procedures?)
How well do we do it? (How do we define quality?)
Finally, what difference does it make whether we do it or not?

Although these questions are timeless, the answers are not. They are affected by the factors and forces described in this chapter. Today's universities, far from being 'ivory towers', are vital parts of the society in which they exist. Much of their claim on public support, particularly at the graduate level, depends on how they respond to the educational needs of their constituents. The development of new kinds of graduate programme and of new ways of delivering them, coupled with the task of providing high quality education at reasonable cost to large numbers of people, are responsibilities that universities must assume. To do all of this while retaining the essential nature of the university as a place where scholarship and learning flourish is the challenge before us.

References

Atkinson, R. (1990) Supply and demand for scientists and engineers: a national crisis in the making, *Science*, 27 April.

Bowen, H. and Schuster, J. (1986) *American Professors: A National Resource Imperiled.* New York: Oxford University Press.

Bowen, W. G. and Rudenstine, N. L. (1992) *In Pursuit of the Ph.D.* Princeton, NJ: Princeton University Press.

Bowen, W. and Sosa, J. (1989) *Prospects for Faculty in the Arts and Sciences.* Princeton, NJ: Princeton University Press.

Bush, V. (1980) *Science – The Endless Frontier.* Washington, DC: The National Science Foundation. New York: Arno Press (original publication date 1945).

Clark, B. R. (ed.) (1993) *The Research Foundations of Graduate Education: Germany, Britain, France, United States, Japan.* Berkeley, Los Angeles and Oxford: University of California Press.

Committee on Science, Engineering, and Public Policy (COSEPUP) of the National Academy of Sciences, the National Academy of Engineering, and the Institute of Medicine (1995) *Reshaping the Graduate Education of Scientists and Engineers.* Washington, DC: National Academy Press.

Conrad, C. F., Haworth, J. G. and Millar, S. B. (1993) *A Silent Success: Master's Education in the United States.* Baltimore, MD: The Johns Hopkins Press.

Council of Graduate Schools (1996) The new American graduate student, *CGS Communicator*, 29(8), October.

Goodstein, D. (1993) Scientific Ph.D. problems, *The American Scholar*, 62(2).

National Center for Education Statistics (1993) *Occupational and Educational Outcomes of Recent College Graduates One Year After Graduation: 1991, Statistical Analysis Report* (No. 93–162, p. 10). Washington, DC: National Center for Education Statistics.

National Science Foundation (1995) For 1993, doctoral scientists and engineers report 1.5 per cent unemployment rate but 4.3 per cent underemployment, *Data Brief*, 15 March.

Normile, D. (1996) Corporate concerns and costs clamp down on PhD output, *Science*, 4 October.

Simmons, R. O. and Thurgood, D. H. (1995) *Summary Report 1994: Doctorate Recipients from United States Universities.* Washington, DC: National Academy Press.

Snyder, T. D., Hoffman, C. and Geddes, C. M. (1996) *Digest of Education Statistics 1996.* Washington, DC: US Department of Education, National Center for Education Statistics.

Tobias, S. and Chubin, D. (1996) New degrees for today's scientists, *Chronicle of Higher Education*, 12 July.

Tobias, S., Chubin, D. and Aylesworth, K. (1995) *Rethinking Science as a Career: Perceptions and Realities in the Physical Sciences.* Tucson, AZ: Research Corporation.

Ziman, J. (1968) *Public Knowledge: An Essay Concerning the Social Dimension of Science.* Cambridge: Cambridge University Press.

Further reading

Boyer, E. (1990) *Scholarship Reconsidered: Priorities of the Professorate.* Princeton, NJ: The Carnegie Foundation for the Advancement of Teaching.

Council of Graduate Schools (1990) *The Doctor of Philosophy Degree.* Washington, DC: Council of Graduate Schools.

Council of Graduate Schools (1991) *International Graduate Students: A Guide for Graduate Deans, Faculty, and Administrators.* Washington, DC: Council of Graduate Schools.

Council of Graduate Schools (1993) *Enhancing the Minority Presence in Graduate Education, V: Summer Research Opportunity Programs – Voices and Visions of Success in Pursuit of the Ph.D.* Washington, DC: Council of Graduate Schools.

Council of Graduate Schools (1994) *Master's Education: A Guide for Faculty and Administrators.* Washington, DC: Council of Graduate Schools.

The Government-University-Industry Research Roundtable (1989) *Science and Technology in the Academic Enterprise: Status, Trends, and Issues.* A discussion paper. Washington, DC: National Academy Press.

The Government-University-Industry Research Roundtable (1992) *Fateful Choices: The Future of the US Academic Research Enterprise.* A discussion paper. Washington, DC: National Academy Press.

Patel, C. (1995) *Reinventing the Research University.* Proceedings of a symposium held at UCLA on 22–23 June 1994. Los Angeles, CA: Regents of the University of California.

President's Council of Advisors on Science and Technology (1992) *Renewing the Promise: Research Intensive Universities and the Nation.* Washington, DC: US Government Printing Office.

3

Policy Issues in Postgraduate Education: An Australian Perspective

Millicent E. Poole and Raymond H. Spear

The changing context

Australian higher education is undergoing a period of rapid transformation under a new (1996) conservative coalition government. During the previous 13 years of the Labour incumbency, policy in relation to postgraduate studies was based on the principles of increasing access and greater participation, the positioning of Australia in terms of economic growth globally, and building strategic alliances with the Asia-Pacific economies. During this period major developments relating to higher education as they affected postgraduate students were: more attention to issues of equity and access; greater emphasis on continuing education and skills upgrading; the introduction of the Higher Education Contribution Scheme; the introduction of postgraduate course fees and full-fee paying arrangements for overseas students; development of closer links with industry; enhanced concern with quality issues; and, in the aftermath of the abolition of the binary system and resulting institutional amalgamations, increased focus on research in many of the new institutions.

With the change of government, there has been a shift from growth to contraction of the higher education sector with an emphasis on quality, diversity and choice. This is part of a philosophical belief that a major shift of funding from the public sector needs to occur, that smaller government is desirable, and that users should pay a higher contribution to their education since higher education brings major private benefits.

Phillips (1996), a senior bureaucrat, argued recently that the present government's overall public policy orientation starts from a presumption that the private sector will always be more efficient than the public sector. This policy shift entails two marked tests for the justification of public policy interaction in any area, that is whether there has been (or would otherwise be) a market failure and/or whether there are overriding social policy criteria (such as in social welfare) so that government intervention is warranted. For education, which satisfies both tests, the question is not whether public funds will be made available, but how, and at what level. The new approach, as Phillips calls it, is based on 'best practice', meaning best practice especially in terms of a cost model, a client-focused model and contestability.

Phillips considered that how the whole system is funded will be a key policy issue during the current term of office of the new government. The government is currently looking at competition policy and the possibility of a common national approach to its implementation in higher education so that, for example, commercial arms which often involve close university–industry links, with associated postgraduate training especially in Cooperative Research Centres, will have to be separately accountable and competitive in terms of neutral pricing so that there is not unfair competition with the private sector.

During this period of transformation, it is anticipated that the government will continue to fund postgraduate research and to provide postgraduate scholarships to assist in the process of training graduates for academe, business and industry. Phillips summed up the current policy focus under the coalition government as: (a) governments should be small, (b) organizations should be competitive, (c) contestability should be the overriding philosophy for the distribution of public funding and (d) the private sector is assumed to be more efficient than the public. It is within this framework that the radical change occurring in Australian higher education will unfold.

The major shift in policy direction has been a reduction in university operating grants from 1997 to 1999. The undergraduate load has been protected but public funding for postgraduate coursework (with the exception of education and nursing) has been reduced dramatically: up to 50 per cent over three years at some universities. This will impact on institutional funded postgraduate load.

In contrast to the reduction in operating grant funding for postgraduate coursework over the 1997–9 triennium, the new government will over the same period increase total funding for research in the higher education budget by $91.5 million for research infrastructure and $39.1 million for Australian Postgraduate Awards and Collaborative research grants. Targeted funding for university research will be directed at programmes to remedy deficiencies in infrastructure, encourage closer links between industry and universities and train high quality researchers. In the latter case, funds for postgraduate student awards have been increased by $9.3 million from a current level of about $80 million. Funding of the Cooperative Research Centres Programme aimed at promoting more effective cooperation between researchers in universities, government agencies and industry will rise by 6 per cent in real terms.

Under the present government a more user-pays philosophy is developing. This new orientation brings into play a new political correctness which leads to economic correctness, where the major social gains that were made in access and participation in postgraduate education in Australia under the previous government may well be lost. There will be greater public scrutiny of whether teaching and research can continue to be funded in the way that they have been previously. For example, there are discussions as to whether all universities should be funded for both research and teaching or whether some should be funded predominantly for teaching. Institutions are starting to examine rationalization with a focus on collaboration rather than competition in delivering a scarce resource (postgraduate training) in the geographically large and dispersed area of Australia.

In releasing its first Higher Education Budget Statement in August 1996, the new government announced that it had identified a range of issues which had the potential to re-shape the higher education system and that it would institute a review of higher education policy to examine the challenges for the next two decades. The terms of reference refer to broad social, economic, scientific and cultural needs, responding creatively and effectively to change, and to funding operations. Issues such as: the impact of advanced information and communications technology; the globalization and internationalization of higher education; and the role of higher education research in the broader national research and innovation system are identified. The level and nature of industry demand for higher education graduates and the contribution that graduates and research make to Australia's industrial competitiveness form part of the focus. In an address to the Business/Higher Education Round Table Annual General Meeting (Vanstone, 1996), the Federal Minister for Employment, Education, Training and Youth Affairs commented that policy settings should 'maximise the contribution of research to industry needs'. The Minister also reaffirmed the contribution of research to innovation: 'University based research makes a direct contribution to national innovation through the development of new knowledge, ideas and techniques.'

In discussing 'postgraduate' issues, there is a tendency to focus on *research* postgraduate issues which is partly a reflection of a wider tendency evident (rightly or wrongly) in the literature. There are a great many issues relating particularly to the provision of postgraduate coursework degrees, especially in view of the policy initiative to push the postgraduate coursework load into the full-fee paying area.

The policy debates concerning funding following a move to a more deregulated market approach have raised concerns about equity of access; availability of courses; the need to design income-contingent loan schemes; the effect of inertia-factors (e.g. tenure) on universities; response to market forces; commonalities/differences between Australian and international full-fee paying students; and premiums on fees to increase the basis of competition between universities. Another major set of issues relates to professional upgrading and the interaction between universities and industries. The notion of lifelong learning and professional development has encouraged a shift towards a user-pays model. The deregulation of the market has to date had little effect on postgraduate research degrees, but a greater impact on coursework enrolments. There has been a steady increase in Australian postgraduate fee-paying enrolments as a proportion of total Australian postgraduate load (from 15 per cent in 1994 to 18 per cent in 1995 and 23 per cent in 1996).

The Australian Vice-Chancellors' Committee (AVCC) issued in 1997 guidelines for the provision of postgraduate fee courses to Australian students by Australian universities. The principles being examined are: comparability; quality; access and equity; transparency; diversity; and accountability. The factors driving this include: the changing student population; growth in demand; modes of delivery; credit transfer and orientation; pressure on public funding; the emergence of the user pays principle.

The changing policy context in Australia has not been occurring in a vacuum. Poole (1995), in a paper entitled 'The framing of post graduate policy', drew parallels with the UK in terms of two major frames: the macro/ micro frame in which policy and practice are shaped (i.e. at the national and institutional levels) and the stratification/differentiation frame which operate in the traditional system (across institutions and disciplines). Poole argues that these frames and their inter-relationships are being challenged by governmental ('externalist') and pedagogical pressures ('internalist'). Stratification develops from policies and processes related to prestige (e.g. in Australia, some institutions resist pressure for growth in postgraduate coursework to protect an image of research degree training). Differentiation occurs through factors related to the spectrum of disciplines. For example, in Australia there are different infrastructure and fieldwork provisions for arts and science postgraduate students. As Poole (1995) argued, 'differentiation' and 'stratification' can occur even when a central policy relating to postgraduate education has been formulated and such frames come to define power, status, and a hierarchy related to universities, organizational units and disciplines.

In this changing framework universities are becoming more outward looking, and concentrating on better promotion of their particular strengths and areas of excellence in postgraduate teaching and research, as a more differentiated and competitive policy framework emerges.

Pressures for greater concentration of research degree studies

An area of increasing policy concern relates to increased diversity or differentiation within the system. Prior to 1988 there were only 19 universities in Australia, all of them engaged in research and postgraduate education. In 1988 the Australian government reorganized the system through a programme of mergers and upgrading of colleges of advanced education, which had conducted no research, and of institutes of technology, which had conducted very little. The net result is that today there are 39 universities, all of them involved in research and postgraduate education to some extent, and most of them aspiring to a higher research profile. This situation has substantially increased the tensions associated with the distribution of research funding by the federal government.

An international perspective on policy in relation to postgraduate studies is provided by Holdaway (1993), using data from Australia, the UK and Canada. He makes some very interesting comparisons. For example, on the general question of postgraduate education policy, he notes that, whereas in Australia an external pressure under the Labour government had been for the 'expansion of postgraduate research enrolments to meet demand for academic staff and needs of economy generally', in the UK postgraduate education was until very recently largely neglected as a policy question, while in Canada, it is a province or territory responsibility, so that federal government policy statements are rarely made.

Any analysis of the policy and practice of system-wide frames influencing postgraduate education must take account of the macro, national/international context of science and technology, of shifting educational traditions and values in higher education. Becher, Henkel and Kogan (1994) noted a transition from the classic 'academic actor' frame (a process of sponsored individuality) to a 'rational system-led' frame of policy making (i.e. more imposed). This is exemplified by the way in which the UK research training system is being brought into line with national economic and social policies, through the machinery of government concerned with research and graduate education becoming a part of the Office of Science and Technology within the Department of Trade and Industry. In other words, the link with science is seen as more important than the link with the rest of higher education – a major signal of a shifting frame, of the increasing emphasis on economic instrumentalism in graduate education policies.

These macro policy shifts are also evident in Australia, where there has been a searching reappraisal of research and postgraduate training, and various challenges to the traditional intellectual cultures through the emergence of institutional strategic policies for research concentration, selectivity and commercialization (Poole, 1994). New collaborative research cultures have been funded through federal funding schemes which concentrate research infrastructure and new modes of postgraduate training with an emphasis on commercialization and technology transfer. Such changes have not been unique to Australia: the process of strategic repositioning and cultural transformation in Australian universities has been part of a global phenomenon allying research and postgraduate training to global economic competitiveness, scarce resource utilization, and accountability for the outcomes (social, cultural, but mainly economic benefits). These trends are not temporary nor local, they are part of a worldwide process in which science is being transformed internally as it moves into new relationships with national economies, and where the higher education sector is expected to train graduate students who will contribute to and enhance economic competitiveness.

These same themes have been part of federal government policies in Australia under both the Labour and coalition governments. The new government has affirmed its commitment to these policy directions in the Science and Technology Budget Statement (McGauran, 1996).

The government has adjusted its priorities within science and technology to get a greater return for its investment. 'Targeted funding for University research under the Australian Research Council will grow significantly in real terms and will be directed at remedying deficiencies in infrastructure, encouraging greater industry funding of University research, and expanding post-graduate research' (ibid.).

The new policy imperatives in science and technology, outlined in the science and technology budget statement (ibid.), are aimed at:

positioning the Australian innovation system to service the national interests in the coming century. Australia's long-standing investment in basic and strategic research will underscore the nation's capacity to increase economic growth in the context of responsible management of the environment and to improve the standards of health, equity and social development. The imperative of sustaining rapid real growth in business and development is the sine qua non of bringing the skills and knowledge furnished through public sector research to real effect in the national interest.

With this changing framework, the research-council type of body has become an important allocative mechanism, driving and framing central policy values, in the competitive allocation of research funds and post-graduate scholarships and awards.

The range in magnitudes of the research efforts across the Australian university sector can be gauged to some extent from the allocation of federally funded Australian Postgraduate Awards (APA). *The Higher Education Funding Report for 1997–99 Triennium* (1996) indicated that for 1997 awards without stipend, which basically cover tuition fees, ranged across the 39 universities from 0 to 2360, the total number being 21,500. Awards with stipend, which provide tuition and a living allowance for up to three and a half years, ranged from 0 to 175, the total number being 1605. According to the Department of Employment, Education, Training and Youth Affairs (1996) *Selected Higher Education Student Statistics*, in 1996 the total number of PhD students at Australian universities was 22,696, and there were 10,855 students doing master's degrees by research. Thus it is evident that a large proportion of postgraduate research is dependent on federal funds. In addition, many students without APAs are supported by faculty research grants provided for staff by the Australian government. It is clear that the government is in a position to mould the character of the postgraduate research enterprise.

In 1993 the Government established a new formula for the allocation of APAs, designed to target assistance for postgraduate study more effectively. The formula is intended to gauge the quality of each institution's postgraduate education environment; it includes performance indicators such as number of higher degree completions and success in attracting research grants.

There are those who argue that it is in the nation's interest to enhance this trend to concentrate research and postgraduate training in institutions which have larger supervisory capacity, superior facilities and research infrastructure, and demonstrated research performance. Not surprisingly, there are others who contend that big is not necessarily beautiful, and that a greater concentration of postgraduate training in a smaller number of larger institutions would be inimical to the nation's interest, since high quality research, measured for example by citation indices, is often performed by individuals working in relatively small institutions.

Organization and structures

The number of graduate students at Australian universities has more than doubled over the past decade. From 1986 to 1996, the number of students enrolled for higher degrees by research increased from 13,896 to 33,560, and the total number of graduate students increased from 64,689 to 132,495 (Department of Employment, Education, Training and Youth Affairs, 1996).

This rapid expansion has stimulated re-evaluation of the ways in which graduate education is organized within the various universities. Each university now has a designated individual who has university-wide responsibility for the oversight of graduate education. In most cases the person concerned has the status of Dean, Deputy Vice-Chancellor, or Pro-Vice-Chancellor. About a dozen universities have established graduate schools, although the nature of these schools varies greatly.

The concept of the graduate school has developed over the past hundred years or so within the remarkably vigorous and successful US graduate education enterprise. The US graduate school is by no means a uniquely defined entity; the structure and responsibilities of graduate schools vary widely. Some US universities prefer to organize their graduate education in a largely devolved manner without a centralized graduate school, although virtually all of them have a Dean of Graduate Studies, or equivalent person. An excellent description of the North American situation is given in the policy statement *Organization and Administration of Graduate Education* (Council of Graduate Schools, 1990): 'The primary purpose of the graduate school in a university is to define and support excellence in graduate education, and the research and scholarship activities associated with it. No two universities are exactly alike, and the same is true for graduate schools.'

Until recently graduate education in the UK has been largely managed as an extension of undergraduate programmes, without a separate organization. However, in response to political and financial pressures, many UK universities in recent years have adopted more centralized graduate administration structures, including graduate schools in many cases. The publication *Graduate Schools: The Organisation of Graduate Education* by John Hogan (1994) presents an excellent and comprehensive review of the situation in the UK and elsewhere.

It is against this background that graduate schools have developed in some Australian universities. For example, the Australian National University graduate school, established in 1990, is designed to coordinate graduate education across the university and to enhance its quality; initiatives developed by a small centralized administration are combined with devolved activities by 39 university-wide graduate programmes. The University of Melbourne graduate school, established in 1994, is a rather more centralized operation, with the status of a faculty. Located in a substantial building, one of its main objectives is to maintain a collegial environment for staff and students, not only through a wide range of interdisciplinary academic interactions, but also through a variety of social experiences.

In most Australian universities, graduate education is patterned largely on the old UK model, with the emphasis being on discipline-based departments providing the human and physical research infrastructure, with a minimum of centralization.

In some of the newer universities, especially those in the Australian Technology Network (former Institutes of Technology), graduate students are concentrated in a few centres of national and/or international research excellence in each institution in order to optimize access to physical resources and, increasingly, to work on specific collaborative projects.

The nature of the PhD

The PhD in Australia is essentially a research-only degree, although some universities, in some disciplines, have introduced a limited amount of coursework, both formal and informal. In general, Australian PhD students must have completed a four-year first degree. The fourth ('honours') year consists of a mixture of coursework and research. Students entering an Australian PhD course will have already completed coursework that corresponds approximately to the mid-point of the coursework component of a US PhD.

The extent to which coursework or other innovations can be introduced into the Australian PhD course is limited by financial constraints. APA scholarships, which support a large proportion of students, are limited to a maximum of three and a half years, and similar limitations apply to most other awards. Each university determines its own course arrangements.

The traditional PhD, with its emphasis on production of a highly specialized thesis, is primarily geared to producing graduates capable of filling research positions in universities, industry and government. However, societal changes in recent years have meant that in Australia, as in many countries, PhD graduates increasingly find themselves ultimately working in non-research areas which do not require the particular disciplinary expertise acquired during their PhD programme. Even research-oriented industries increasingly contend that the traditional PhD training is inappropriate for the industrial situation. Universities are looking to broaden their PhD training so that graduates will be more widely employable and have a broadened vocational outlook. The Professional Doctorate discussed below is one response to this view, although many contend that to 'broaden' the PhD is to devalue its real purpose and appeal and its applicability.

The poles of the policy debate may be represented in the following quotations (Cioffi, 1995): 'Graduate education should be broadened so as to better prepare students for diverse – that is, non academic – careers . . . the vast majority of science doctorates find work outside academia'; and (Holden, 1995): 'any attempt to "hybridise" the PhD . . . is likely to be regarded by academics as a watered-down version of the real thing'.

Within the Australian context, a seminal paper entitled *Postgraduate Skills: A View from Industry* (Clark, 1996) under the general heading 'Preparing PhDs for the real world' contends that the quality of Australian PhD graduates could be significantly improved by supplementary training that 'need not require a lot of time'. Clark's comments have encouraged a process that has been under way in Australia for some time, as exemplified by the optional skills and methodology short courses and seminars provided by some graduate schools, as discussed earlier. According to Clark, skills needing development are teamwork, leadership, ability to view issues holistically. Greater breadth and experience would also enhance the employability of graduates.

Professional doctorates

In a report, *Higher Education Courses and Graduate Studies* (1990), the Higher Education Council of the National Board of Employment, Education and Training suggested that universities should consider the development of doctoral degrees:

> providing extended and advanced training in certain professional fields where projects and investigations are applied in nature, oriented to practice in the professions and where, in some cases, the setting might be industry-based rather than campus-based.

Although such degrees might be expected to contain 'significant elements of coursework', the Higher Education Council was firmly of the view that they should include 'substantial pieces of investigative work, projects and exercises', and suggested that: 'it would be misleading and unfortunate if such degrees came to be known as "coursework doctorates" rather than, say, "professional doctorates"'. The Higher Education Council (1990) specifically recommended that universities should:

> augment traditional doctoral programs, within the overall requirement that doctoral degrees include a substantial component of original research which significantly contributes to some area of knowledge, by

Table 3.1 Types of Australian professional doctorates (1996)

Field	Award	Number
Education	EdD	22
	DTeach	1
	DScEd	1
Business	DBA	9
	DOrgDyn	1
	DPA	1
Psychology	DPsych	4
	DClinPsych	1
	DHealthPsych	1
Health Sciences	DPH	2
	DHSM	1
	DNurs	1
Design	DEnvDesign	1
Architecture	DArch	1
Law	SJD	8
Humanities	DCA	2

broadening existing PhD guidelines or alternatively by introducing, on a pilot basis, professional doctoral degrees which require advanced application of existing knowledge and technology in professional fields such as engineering, accounting, law, education and nursing.

In response, by 1996, 29 Australian universities had introduced professional doctorates. The number and range of such doctorates is indicated in Table 3.1, taken from Shannon and Sekhon (1996).

Among the factors driving the introduction of these degrees, Jongeling (1996) identifies national and state government directions, employer dissatisfaction with current PhD programmes, and recommendations from professional organizations. Most of the candidates are part-time students working concurrently in their professional vocations.

The introduction of professional doctorates has not been without some controversy. Probably the chief cause of concern relates to the standard of the degrees offered. Comparison with the PhD is inevitable. What is meant by 'doctoral' level? Is it proper that universities should offer doctoral degrees at a level perceived to be below that of the PhD flagship? In response, it can be argued that the PhD itself is far from monolithic. Even PhDs of the English-speaking countries Canada, USA, UK and Australia are quite different. Indeed, significant variations occur across universities and disciplines within a given country. The structure and standard of Australian professional doctorates varies considerably, and, in fact, some of them appear to be more demanding than the traditional PhD (Maxwell and Shanahan, 1996).

Other concerns that have been raised include the following:

• Is there a need for national standardization?
• Some professional doctorates appear to have been introduced without significant consultation with the relevant professional bodies.
• Could not professional doctorates be embraced within the PhD framework?
• How to involve industry in supervision?
• Do universities have adequate/appropriate supervisory expertise?
• Entry standards – allowance for work experience?

It should be noted that master's degrees specifically designed to meet professional requirements are widely established and less controversial, and that innovation continues rapidly at that level.

Response to the information revolution

It is beyond the scope of this chapter to cover the huge impact that the 'information revolution' will have on higher education in general, or on postgraduate education in particular. It is possible to do little more than mention some of the factors to be considered in formulating policy.

The situation for Australian universities has been discussed recently in a paper issued by the Australian Vice-Chancellors' Committee entitled *Exploiting Information Technology in Higher Education: An Issues Paper* (1996). It is based largely on a paper produced in 1995 by the UK Joint Information Systems Committee. A report by James and Beattie (1995) concentrates on delivery technologies for postgraduate coursework. A key concern is the impact of information technology on graduate education and distance education, a concern also at the December 1996 meeting of the North American Council of Graduate Schools (CGS) held in San Francisco (e.g. papers entitled 'The Virtual University', 'Graduate Education in the Information Age' and 'Technology and the Graduate School').

At the research degree level the computer will continue its increasingly crucial role in all aspects of the research process itself, and in some disciplines will greatly increase the possibility of research students working off-campus, both through electronic transmission of information and through the increased possibility of supervision at a distance.

Probably the major impact of information technology on graduate education will occur through the application of distance learning to professional and technical master's degrees by coursework. Among the societal trends to be considered in policy formulation in this area are the following:

• Increased demand for lifelong learning:

> If the move towards a more flexible workforce . . . and decreasing job stability continues, there will be a need for graduates periodically to retrain and up-date their skills; the concept of life-long learning will become important. Forecasters in the USA say that the average work life in the future will consist of six or seven different careers, each requiring new skills, new attitudes, new values. One estimate is

that by the year 2000, 75 per cent of the workforce will need retraining. This will increase the demand for continuing post-experience adult education which may be largely, but not wholly, based on part-time study at home.

(Twigg, 1996)

- The information explosion. It has been estimated that knowledge doubles every seven years, and that the half-life of a technical degree is now about five years.
- The need to master rapidly developing new skills and technologies.
- Pressures to improve productivity, both within and outside the academy.
- The desire/need for students to work off-campus. This trend is strengthened by the increasing average age of graduate students whose adult attitudes and responsibilities often render existing classroom hours inconvenient, and whose approach to education is increasingly that of the consumer.

Naturally there are many who view changing trends with considerable scepticism, believing that there is no substitute for the education that occurs through the interaction of minds arising in person-to-person situations. There is also much concern about quality control in the face of increasing financial pressures and the temptation to offer 'soft' distance education via information technology.

Participation of women in postgraduate studies

Both the previous and the current federal governments affirmed their commitment to equity policy whereby institutions are required to report on the access, participation, success and retention rates of students in various designated equity groups (women in non-traditional areas of study and postgraduate courses, low socio-economic status, indigenous Australians, rural and remote and the disabled). Only patterns for women will be discussed in this chapter. However, as indicated earlier, the major social gains made in terms of access and participation in postgraduate education could be jeopardized by policy directions of the new government.

The participation of women in postgraduate studies has increased dramatically. Figure 3.1 shows postgraduate enrolments by gender 1991–6. Since 1995 the number of postgraduate female enrolments has exceeded male enrolments. Figure 3.2 shows a comparison of postgraduate enrolment by gender and level of course for 1991 and 1996. It indicates that women have a greater tendency than men to enrol in coursework degrees.

As noted by Barinaga (quoted in Caplan, 1993), there has been a 'funnelling effect' process operating whereby the retention and participation rates of women at the undergraduate level are not reflected fully in the research higher degrees area. Indeed, a recent Equity Project undertaken at a major Australian university entitled *Improving Women's Participation in Research Higher Degrees* (Monash Postgraduate Association, 1996), found that

Figure 3.1   Postgraduate enrolment by gender 1991–6

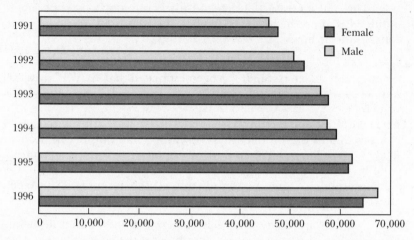

Source: Department of Employment, Education, Training and Youth Affairs (1996) and previous years.

Figure 3.2   Comparison of postgraduate enrolment by gender by level of course for 1991 and 1996

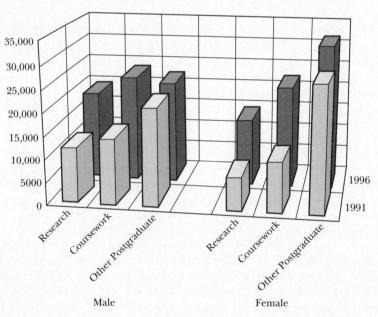

Source: Department of Employment, Education, Training and Youth Affairs (1996) and previous years.

'their participation rates in research higher degrees have improved. However, their participation rates in research higher degrees were significantly lower than at undergraduate level – even in those faculties in which women have high participation rates at the undergraduate level.'

The project found both structural and attitudinal barriers and constraints to account for this lower participation of women:

> Women at Monash University identified financial constraints, lack of role models and mentors, problems with supervision, the inflexibility of the institution and departments within it, the negative response of departments to women returning to study and to the experience and skills they bring, the unsupportive environment, the negative community attitudes to women doing postgraduate research all as barriers.

Various strategies were suggested to overcome these barriers and constraints and to try to reconfigure the funnelling or attrition process: 'that the University improve its links to the community; that it recognise part-time study as the best option for some women; more encouragement, mentors and networks for women and more resource higher degrees'. This suggests that macro policy frameworks of equity need to be underpinned by institutional policies which are outcomes oriented to change the 'tunnelling' effect process.

Concerns have also been expressed that women are disadvantaged by the government's deregulation of fees for postgraduate coursework study. The Stanley Report (1995) indicated that there was not sufficient evidence about differential participation in fee-paying postgraduate programmes by designated equity groups to cause concern, although it did find that the patterns of participation were significantly different between the sexes. The Higher Education Council has commissioned a study (Anderson *et al.*, 1997) on the impact of the introduction of postgraduate fees on designated equity groups of students which examines historical patterns of participation since the commencement of deregulation in 1989.

Strategies that have been widely used by universities to encourage greater participation of women in postgraduate studies (either research or coursework) include one-year full-time postgraduate re-entry scholarships which allow awardees to upgrade qualifications in order to become eligible for entry into postgraduate research degree courses. These scholarships are usually available to women resuming their academic studies following a period of family formation. Re-entry scholarships are usually based on the assumption that, on the successful completion of the re-entry phase, women will be integrated into mainstream research or coursework degree courses. In a discussion paper entitled *Women in Science, Engineering and Technology* (Women in Science, Engineering and Technology Advisory Group, 1995) such scholarships are seen to be particularly necessary for women wishing to re-enter training in science, engineering and technology, especially at the postgraduate level.

Internationalization

One of the major benefits of postgraduate training and research is the opportunity for international links. Australia has had a long association with overseas universities, initially with the Commonwealth, Europe, and the United States, and increasingly with the Asia-Pacific region.

Research students from overseas have made a major contribution to Australia's postgraduate training and research endeavours. Prior to 1986 almost all overseas students who came to Australia were either fully or partly subsidized by the government. From 1986, universities were permitted to offer places to overseas students at full cost, with the government setting minimum course fees for full-fee paying overseas students. Nationally, total student arrivals doubled between 1986 and 1989. The subsidized-student scheme was formally discontinued after the 1989 intake. All commencing overseas students are now full-fee paying; the fees being paid either privately, by Australian government scholarship, by some other sponsoring agency or by institutional scholarships.

In spite of the introduction of fees, there has been in recent years a major growth in internationalization of Australian postgraduate education – in student numbers, particularly for coursework degrees; in the provision of specialized services; in terms of curriculum content; and in the development of off-shore and twinning arrangements with overseas universities.

There is a maturing attitude and realization by government of the social and cultural, as well as the economic and intellectual benefits, of internationalizing Australian higher education. To assist this process there have been some policy initiatives such as the UMAP Scheme (University Mobility in Asia and the Pacific) to encourage student (including postgraduate) exchanges based on bilateral and consortium agreements. IDP Education Australia is Australia's international education organization, which: provides assistance to education systems overseas; promotes access to expertise; and facilitates the enrolment of international students in Australian education institutions, especially through a network of offices in 19 overseas countries.

The Australian Vice-Chancellors' Committee (AVCC) has developed a code of ethics to ensure consistent and caring procedures in the recruitment, reception, education and welfare of international students, and also to ensure that the students get 'value for money'. The AVCC also plays an important role in assisting universities to internationalize their functions and form cooperative links with higher education institutions in other countries.

The Overseas Postgraduate Research Scholarships Scheme (OPRS), which began in 1990, originally supported students from developing countries, but now the scholarships are available to students from most countries. The scholarships cover tuition fees and health benefits for 300 new students each year. The purpose of the scheme is to attract top quality overseas postgraduate students to areas of research strength in higher education institutions to support Australia's research effort. On the other hand the programme offers overseas students the opportunity to obtain a postgraduate qualification and to gain experience with leading Australian researchers. The expansion of the scheme to include most countries, together with the Scheme's objectives, mirrors other policy moves in the internationalization of Australian education, and places the scheme within a context of mutual benefit and reciprocity rather than within the previous policy phases of trade and aid (Grigg and McMahon, 1996).

Grigg and McMahon argue that the internationalization of Australian education is of great strategic importance and that the OPRS scheme has contributed greatly to this process. They comment:

> the Scheme is contributing in no small way to the international research and research training endeavours of the Australian Higher Education System. The international partnerships that exist because of the nature of the scheme, between international students and their academic supervisors, are contributing to the development of informal international networks with the potential to lead to invitations to collaborate, or to formal arrangements to participate in planned programs of research activity which transcend national boundaries. With the current pressure in the system to internationalise this is an important contribution. . . . As pointed out recently by Blume (1995), the internationalisation of research training has taken on a new significance, with governments in most OECD countries treating the international aspect of the activity as an important and complex policy issue. Where most networks, structures and resources for international mobility used to be at the postdoctoral level and driven largely by the scientific community, Blume points out that the impetus now is also coming from the centre, with governments becoming more directive with regard to international exchange mobility and research training programmes becoming the focus of serious interest in this regard.

The growth in numbers of international research students studying in Australia has been paralleled by an enhanced focus on international research collaboration. The 1997 ARC large research grants, announced in October 1996, contained a 44 per cent increase in grants awarded to projects involving an international partner. The government regarded the shift as underlining the 'need to encourage Australian researchers to establish links with high-quality researchers in other countries' (Illing and Windsor, 1996).

Quality issues

During the 1990s in Australia there has been a great emphasis on quality assurance in higher education (see, for example, Higher Education Council of the National Board of Employment, Education and Training, 1992; Cullen, 1992). A substantial contribution to the debate has come from the activities of the Committee for Quality Assurance in Higher Education, appointed by the federal government. This committee investigated and evaluated quality assurance procedures in each university in the years 1993, 1994 ('Teaching and Learning', Committee for Quality Assurance in Higher Education, 1993, 1994) and 1995 ('Research and Community Service', Committee for Quality Assurance in Higher Education, 1995). Funds were allocated to reward perceived good practice. Although this process was initially greeted with great scepticism, there can be little doubt that it did stimulate universities to look more closely at their process and performance with a view to continuing improvement.

Within the context of graduate education, one of the main issues is the supervision of research students. Supervision quality has long been one of the major concerns of postgraduate student associations, and it has featured prominently at meetings of Deans and Directors of Graduate Studies. It has been the subject of numerous research projects and conferences, and has spawned a substantial literature (see, for example, Moses, 1985, 1992; Cullen *et al.*, 1994). Individual universities have developed, and continue to develop, a variety of policies with respect to such matters as supervisory arrangements (panels or individual supervisors?); off-campus supervision; induction, training and accreditation of supervisors; monitoring of supervisory performance; development of initiatives to enhance the quality of supervision; formulation of codes of practice; and production of manuals on supervision for both students and staff.

A second major concern relates to the provision of resources and facilities for postgraduate research students. The Council of Australian Postgraduate Associations (CAPA) surveyed research facilities for postgraduate students in 1994, and found that in some cases the level of resources provided was substandard (Council of Australian Postgraduate Associations, 1994). The situation varies greatly from one university to another, and even within one university. CAPA argued that since research students are expected to produce work of an international standard they should be given facilities of equivalent standard. For many universities, provision of services suggested by CAPA for all research students would require difficult decisions concerning budgetary priorities.

Other quality issues include the availability of support services such as counselling, study skills advice, and statistical consulting, and the provision of induction programmes for newly enrolled research students, including instruction on thesis writing and relevant research methodologies.

Conclusion

At two National Seminars in 1996 (1996a, 1996b) the Deans and Directors of Graduate Studies in Australian Universities, have begun systematically to explore major policy issues which impact on their institutions at the micro level but which also have macro systems implications. System-wide issues which may become more issues for individual institutions or clusters of institutions, in an environment of diversity and differentiation, include: (a) infrastructure needs of research students; (b) the changing patterns of postgraduate education (e.g. professional doctorates, preparation of PhDs for the real world and the world of work, coursework master's degrees); (c) quality of postgraduate education (e.g. postgraduate induction, supervision, support); (d) innovations (e.g. flexible structures and mechanisms for the supervision of students on, off and across campuses and institutions); (e) skills development (e.g. teamwork, leadership, context awareness); (f) legal and quasilegal issues (e.g. intellectual property and ownership of data; mediation and grievance procedures for graduate students); (g) monitoring and evaluation (e.g. completion rates, the needs of international students); and (h) graduate schools – their role and function. Scholarly work (e.g. Zuber-Skerritt, 1996) on frameworks for postgraduate education include analyses of institutional frameworks, conceptual frameworks and practical frameworks. In this new period of review and transformation, it will become increasingly important for interaction to occur on major policy frames between the key stakeholders.

The policies relating to postgraduate education pose challenges and highlight possible tensions between macro and micro policy frames. Macro policies of access, participation, and contestability do not sit easily with increasing concentration, selectivity and differentiation among institutions and stratification between disciplines. As the Australian system becomes more market-oriented, and as new structures and modes for delivering postgraduate training occur, diversity will increase. Micro structures are also being transformed as the nature of postgraduate education responds to new possibilities (graduate schools, professional doctorates, interactive multimedia and distance learning). With a new government committed to user-pays principles, to downsizing the public sector, and reviewing higher education, the policy frameworks face transformation, in line with many of the pressures and patterns emerging in other OECD countries.

Acknowledgements

The authors are grateful to David Phillips, Linda Cooke and Rae Wells for their contributions.

References

Anderson, D., Johnson, R. and Milligan, B. (1997) *The Effects of the Introduction of Fee-Paying Postgraduate Courses on Access for Designated Groups.* Higher Education Council commissioned report no. 55. Canberra: Australian Government Publishing Service.
Australian Vice-Chancellors' Committee (1996) *Exploiting Information Technology in Higher Education: An Issues Paper.* Canberra.

Australian Vice-Chancellors' Committee (1997) *Guidelines for Postgraduate Fee Courses for Australian Students.* Canberra: AVCC.

Becher, A., Henkel, M. and Kogan, M. (1994) *Graduate Education in Britain* (p. 7). Jessica Kingsley Publishers.

Blume, S. (1995) Problems and prospects of research training in the 1990s, in *Research Training Present and Future.* Paris: Organisation for Economic Cooperation and Development.

Caplan, P. (1993) *Lifting a Ton of Feathers: A Woman's Guide to Surviving in the Academic World* (p. 173). Toronto: University of Toronto Press.

Cioffi, D. (1995) What lies in store for US graduate physics education? *Physics Today,* September, 79.

Clark, J. (1996) *Postgraduate Skills: A View from Industry. Meeting the Demands of R., D and E Leadership in a Rapidly Changing Social and Business Environment.* Paper presented to Australian Deans of Graduate Studies, 17 April, University of Technology, Sydney.

Committee for Quality Assurance in Higher Education (1993) *Report on 1993 Quality Review.* Canberra: Australian Government Publishing Service.

Committee for Quality Assurance in Higher Education (1994) *Report on 1994 Quality Review.* Canberra: Australian Government Publishing Service.

Committee for Quality Assurance in Higher Education (1995) *Report on 1995 Quality Review.* Canberra: Australian Government Publishing Service.

Council of Australian Postgraduate Associations (1994) *The Strategy Guide for Supervision.* Melbourne.

Council of Graduate Schools (1990) *Organization and Administration of Graduate Education.* Washington.

Cullen, D. J. (ed.) (1992) Proceedings of Quality in PhD Education Symposium held at the ANU, July 1992.

Cullen, D. J., Pearson, M., Saha, L. J. and Spear, R. H. (1994) *Establishing Effective Supervision.* Canberra: Australian Government Publishing Service.

Deans and Directors of Graduate Studies in Australian Universities (1996a) *Second Seminar.* Adelaide, 17 April.

Deans and Directors of Graduate Studies in Australian Universities (1996b) *Third Seminar.* Brisbane, 31 October–1 November.

Department of Employment, Education, Training and Youth Affairs (1996) *Selected Higher Education Student Statistics 1996.* Canberra: DEETYA.

Grigg, L. and McMahon, I. (1996) *The Internationalisation of Australian Higher Education: An Evaluation of the Contribution of the Overseas Postgraduate Research Scholarships Scheme.* Evaluations Program Report 2. Canberra: Australian Government Publishing Service.

Higher Education Council of the National Board of Employment, Education and Training (1990) *Higher Education Courses and Graduate Studies.* Canberra: Australian Government Publishing Service.

Higher Education Council of the National Board of Employment, Education and Training (1992) *Achieving Quality.* Canberra.

Higher Education Funding Report for 1997–99 Triennium (1996) Canberra: DEETYA.

Hogan, J. (1994) *Graduate Schools: The Organisation of Graduate Education.* CEDAR Papers 5. University of Warwick.

Holdaway, E. A. (1993) The organisation of graduate studies, in D. J. Cullen (ed.) *Quality in PhD Education.* Proceedings of the 1 July 1992 Symposium (pp. 23–32). Canberra: ANU.

Holden, C. (1995) The future of the PhD, *Science*, 270, 122.

Illing, D. and Windsor, G. (1996). Grants promote global research links, *The Australian*, 30 October, 35.

James, R. and Beattie, K. (1995) *Expanding Options: Delivery Technologies and Postgraduate Coursework*. Department of Employment, Education and Training, Evaluations and Investigations Program. Canberra: Australian Government Publishing Service.

Jongeling, S. (1996) *Professional Doctorates*. Paper presented at Seminar of Deans and Directors of Graduate Studies in Australian Universities, Adelaide, April. Sydney: UTS.

Maxwell, T. W. and Shanahan, P. J. (1996) Which Way for Professional Doctorates. Paper presented at Which Way for Professional Doctorates conference at Coffs Harbour, October.

McGauran, P. (1996) *Science and Technology Budget Statement 1996–97*. Canberra: Australian Government Publishing Service.

Monash Postgraduate Association Equity Project (1996) *Improving Women's Participation in Research Higher Degrees* (p. viii). Melbourne: Monash Printing Services.

Moses, I. (1985) *Supervising Postgraduates*. Sydney: HERDSA.

Moses, I. (ed.) (1992) *Research Training and Supervision*. Paper presented at ARC and AVCC conference, Canberra, May.

Phillips, D. (1996) First Assistant Secretary, Higher Education Division, Department of Employment, Education, Training and Youth Affairs. Presentation to meeting of Deputy Vice-Chancellors and Pro Chancellors (Academic), University of New South Wales, Sydney, November.

Poole, M. E. (1994) Melting 'Snow' and Shifting 'Cultures': the Strategic Repositioning of Australian Universities' Research and Development, *Higher Education Research and Development*, 13(2), 143–55.

Poole, M. E. (1995) The framing of post graduate policy, in *Higher Education and Technology: Blending Traditions*. HERDSA ACT 18 (pp. 15–29).

Shannon, A. and Sekhon, P. (1996) *Australian Professional Doctorates – 1*. Graduate School Discussion Paper 6. Sydney: UTS.

Stanley, G. (1995) *Report of the Committee to Review Fee-Paying Arrangements for Postgraduate Course*. Canberra: Australian Government Publishing Service.

Twigg, C. (1996) *Meeting Tomorrow's Learning Needs*. Paper presented at the annual meeting of the Council of Graduate Schools. San Francisco, December.

UK Joint Information Systems Committee (1995) *Exploiting Information Systems in Higher Education: an Issues Paper*.

Vanstone, A. (1996) *Address to Business/Higher Education Round Table Annual General Meeting*. 26 November.

Women in Science, Engineering and Technology Advisory Group (1995) *Women in Science, Engineering and Technology* (p. 7). Discussion paper. Canberra: Australian Government Publishing Service.

Zuber-Skerritt, O. (ed.) (1996) *Frameworks for Postgraduate Education*. Lismore: Southern Cross University Press.

4

Quality Issues in Postgraduate Education

Edward Holdaway

Widespread interest exists in ensuring that universities are operating effectively and efficiently. For example, in Australia the Department of Employment, Education and Training (1993: 295) observed that 'evaluation and performance reporting in higher education has been of increasing interest internationally over the last two decades'. Also, the Committee for Quality Assurance in Higher Education (1994) noted that many quality audit agencies have been established in different countries. This Committee provided three reasons for incorporating quality approaches in the university environment: (a) the intellectual heritage and ideals of universities require that criticisms be addressed; (b) the student mix at universities is changing, especially with respect to age and part-time status; and (c) the level of market competition is increasing. It also stated that quality has always been a concern, but that the present focus reflects general interest in society on 'more effective performance leading to greater customer satisfaction' (1994: 3).

Some governments (e.g. Australia and the UK) and the popular press (e.g. *Maclean's*, a Canadian weekly) seem to be obsessed with combining either weighted or unweighted measures of effectiveness on individual aspects into an overall measure or indicator of 'quality'. The size of operating grants provided by some governments is partly determined by performance of universities on these measures.

Postgraduate education is obviously an important element in these assessment activities. Although it varies across disciplines and programmes, postgraduate education is an integral component of the operations of most universities and is essential for a healthy national research culture. In this regard, Conrad, Haworth and Millar (1993) and Moses (1994) noted that the large growth in postgraduate enrolment in recent years, especially in course-based master's programmes, has generated increased interest in the quality of these programmes. This is coupled with perceptions that quality is dropping as reduced resources are insufficient to allow universities to cope appropriately with demands imposed by increased enrolment (Higher Education Council, 1992a: 3). Remote delivery ('distance education') is increasingly being used by many universities to accommodate more students. This trend has generated concerns about programme quality, but they are not discussed in this chapter.

Further evidence of widespread concern comes from New Zealand where all universities have implemented changes following expressions of discontent by postgraduate students about several matters, especially supervision, policies and procedures, funding, resources, and copyright and intellectual property (Rivers, 1996: 15).

This paper deals with (a) definitions of 'quality', (b) four classes of issues relevant to the quality of postgraduate education, and (c) some suggestions for addressing these issues. The content draws upon these sources: (a) literature and documents: (b) personal experiences as a supervisor, reviewer and researcher; and (c) an extensive international 1991–4 research project (Holdaway, Deblois and Winchester, 1995a, 1995b). This project used interviews to obtain detailed information from deans, postgraduate coordinators, experienced supervisors and postgraduate students, especially in Canada, Australia and the UK. Comprehensive questionnaires were also used but only in Canada.

The meaning of 'quality'

Many writers (e.g. Bulmer, 1992; Phillips, 1994) have stated that 'quality' (and its near synonyms of 'excellence' and 'effectiveness') is difficult to define. The *Times Higher Education Supplement* (1987) concluded that 'Quality, as in "top quality", is the central mystery of British higher education. It is a mystery in all the variants of meaning and nuance of which that word is capable.' Similarly, Bowen and Rudenstine, after conducting extensive research on US postgraduate programmes, observed that 'institutional quality is a notoriously elusive concept' (1992: 63) and 'no one knows how to measure this elusive attribute' (1992: 23). Further, the Higher Education Council (1992a: 5) proposed that for some people quality means 'comparative standards', while for others it means 'a level of superiority that is high, a degree of excellence'. The Higher Education Council (1992b: 6) also stated that 'no single workable "definition" of quality is possible', and that 'the literature generally argues that the best approach to quality is to look for characteristics of programs and of institutions which are valued by those whose needs the institution is seeking to meet'. This Council (1992a: 6) moved 'away from trying *to define* quality per se and towards *describing* the attributes [knowledge and skills] that graduates should acquire when exposed to quality higher education – in other words, to describe the qualities of an outcome'.

Another perspective was added by Cullen and Allen (1993) who stated that different consumers have different conceptions of quality. This leads to a distinction between internal perspectives (e.g. students, faculty, administration

Figure 4.1 Evaluations of selected inputs, processes and outputs as contributors to assessment of quality of postgraduate programmes

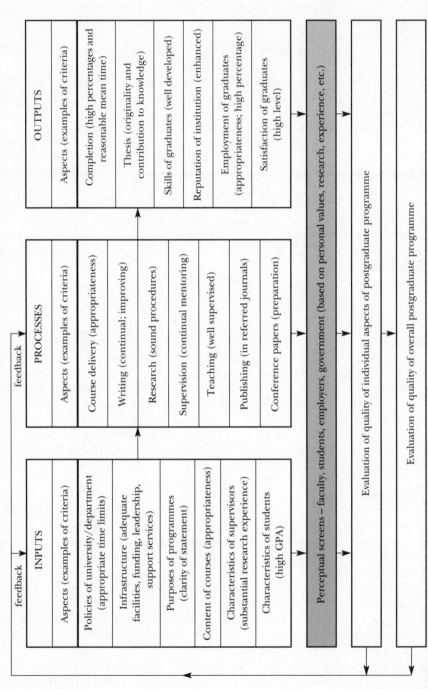

and boards of governors) and external perspectives (e.g. government agencies and employers). Cullen and Allen also suggested 'that the possible confusion over process and product should be resolved by speaking of the quality of the product and the effectiveness of the process in producing quality products' (1993: 104). Obviously, different perceptions and perceptual screens are used in assessing quality and effectiveness. Despite the caveats mentioned above, for the purposes of this chapter the quality of a variable may be defined as the extent to which it is perceived to meet expected standards.

Additional aspects of resolution of the 'quality debate' were provided by the Higher Education Council (1992a: 69) in these statements:

> Any individual judgement of quality requires very careful consideration against a range of variable factors such as geographic location, community expectation, resource base, institutional role and objectives, the type and style of university management, the type and quality of student intake, the quality of academic staff and the quality of facilities and equipment.

> Quality in higher education is multi-faceted and for this reason it is better to consider a 'quality profile' than a single quality standard. There can be no one measure of quality of a university or a school, department, course or individual teacher. It is meaningless to add scores of different and unrelated characteristics of a profile.

The content presented above led to the conceptual model in Figure 4.1. It incorporates a systems approach with inputs, processes, outputs and feedback; examples of criteria by which the quality of selected aspects can be evaluated; perceptual screens which are involved in this evaluation; and the relationship between evaluation of the quality of individual aspects and the overall graduate programme. Two major messages that this model presents are that quality relates to many programme aspects as well as to the programme overall, and that assessments of quality depend on perceptions of particular stakeholders.

Support for use of such a systems model is found in the literature, especially that from Australia. The Department of Employment, Education and Training (1993) discussed relationships between inputs, processes and outcomes in higher education. Also, the Higher Education Council (1992a: 7, 13) stated that all activities of an institution – teaching, administration, research, and professional and community work – 'contribute to its development and are reflected in its graduates' and that evaluation of quality in universities involves evaluation of all programme processes – 'quality of the teaching and learning, the teaching methodologies, the student assessment methods, the equipment and physical plant, and so on'. An additional comment by the Committee for Quality Assurance in Higher Education (1994: 9) is relevant: 'The existence of demonstrably good processes is likely to deliver, over time, good outcomes.'

Input issues

In this section and those that follow some of the major quality issues are identified and discussed.

Purposes of postgraduate education

What are the main purposes of postgraduate education? Does agreement exist on these purposes? For Europe, de Wied *et al.* (1991) described two different conceptions of PhD programmes: (a) emphasis on development of a set of discrete instrumental and/or methodological research skills, which are frequently discipline-specific; and (b) emphasis on the contribution to knowledge and subjecting this contribution to assessment by scholars. They noted that 'the prevalence of these two views differs from discipline to discipline and from country to country' (1991: 39). For example, problems in the natural sciences tend to be more clearly demarcated and research methods more standardized than in the social sciences. For the UK, Elton and Pope (1989: 268) concluded that 'there is no general agreement on what constitutes a PhD, what is its purpose and what may be its value'.

However, general agreement does seem to exist that postgraduate programmes should expose students to advanced academic content, have them analyse and reflect on this content, synthesize concepts and ideas related to selected issues and practices, and improve their academic skills. The term 'postgraduate education' now legitimately includes both academic/research preparation and professional qualification/upgrading. The latter involves coursework master's programmes (e.g. MBA, MEd and MEng) and doctoral programmes (e.g. EdD and DPharm). Conrad *et al.* (1993) showed that substantial growth has occurred in US master's programmes and that these have successfully fulfilled a need. In Australia, Canada and the UK, the greatest postgraduate enrolment increases for more than a decade have been in professional master's programmes, especially in business administration and education.

The purpose of the research component and how postgraduate students should conduct their research have often been discussed. One point of view is that postgraduate degrees should be awarded only to those students who can, with little assistance, produce a substantial original thesis which makes a major contribution to our knowledge. The other view is that the post-graduate research experience is really an 'apprenticeship' in which students have much to learn about research methods and the conduct of a research project, and that supervisors therefore must offer a great deal of guidance during the thesis experience. This second viewpoint also sees the thesis as the first research product in a career, and not necessarily as a land-mark document. Nevertheless, both views see merit in including coursework in both master's and doctoral programmes. Some courses in research methods and subject matter are common in North America, although the number of courses varies markedly across disciplines.

Bowen and Rudenstine (1992: 283) suggested that ways be sought 'to encourage students to begin to engage the reality of serious dissertation-related research during their first and second years, so that the transition from traditional course-work to intensive original research is less abrupt and paralyzing for many students'. This is, of course, not an issue when coursework is not required in doctoral programmes, as in many UK and Australian universities.

University organization

The responsibility for postgraduate education is typically shared among a central body (graduate faculty/school/committee), the dean's office in discipline faculties, and departments. The following functions/roles were identified by Gordon *et al.* (1990: 3) as necessary for graduate schools to fulfil their primary purpose, which is 'to define and support excellence in graduate education, and the research and scholarly activities associated with it':

- articulate a vision of excellence for the postgraduate community;
- provide quality control over all aspects of postgraduate education;
- maintain equity across all academic disciplines;
- define what postgraduate education is;
- bring an institution-wide perspective to all post-baccalaureate education;
- provide a cross-university perspective;
- enhance the intellectual community of postgraduate students and faculty;
- serve as an advocate for postgraduate education;
- emphasize the importance of training future college and university teachers;
- develop ways for postgraduate education to contribute to undergraduate education;
- support and further the non-academic interests of postgraduate students;
- serve as an advocate for issues and constituencies critical to the success of postgraduate programmes.

Postgraduate faculties/schools are far more common in North America than in other countries. Within North America, some disagreement exists over whether individual faculty members should be accredited by the graduate dean as members of 'the graduate school', and thereby be approved supervisors of graduate students, or whether all full-time tenure-track faculty members should automatically be eligible to serve as supervisors. Those who favour the former approach perceive that accrediting by the graduate dean is an essential prerequisite to the provision of high-quality supervision.

Research environment

The research environment is obviously part of the essential infrastructure for postgraduate studies. With respect to provision of a high quality research training environment in the natural sciences, de Wied *et al.* (1991) listed these aspects: opportunity of regular formal and informal interaction with peers, scholars and researchers; proper facilities and equipment; network of international contacts; coherent and integrated research; and sufficient size. Obviously some of these aspects are important in all discipline areas. Bowen and Rudenstine (1992: 70) also noted the importance of a 'reasonably substantial "critical mass" in order to create the conditions for excellent graduate work'.

Funding

Funding of postgraduate education involves two major aspects: (a) infrastructure – administration, teaching staff, library, computing, research facilities, etc.; and (b) student support – scholarships, fellowships, assistantships, research expenses and loans. Canadian graduate deans were particularly concerned about funding of students, although the extreme variability across departments was noted. The best doctoral students in the natural sciences and engineering in Canadian universities received scholarships in 1996–7 of about £7500 per annum, which may be supplemented by extra awards or payment for instruction or other services. But many postgraduate students receive little or no university support, and some faculties have no teaching assistantships to offer. Those in the humanities and some social sciences are particularly affected. For example, the Canadian graduate coordinators in 1992 reported that the following percentages of full-time doctoral students received at least C\$7000 (£3200) per annum through the university: physical sciences 90 per cent, biology 83 per cent, and engineering 82 per cent, as compared with humanities 61 per cent and education 40 per cent.

National research councils provide financial support for some postgraduate students in Canada, Australia and the UK. However, in all three countries, the total amount available for fellowships from the research councils was assessed by virtually all respondents to be insufficient. Parry and Hayden (1994) emphasized the need for some external funding of individual students, but noted that this approach can generate concerns about intellectual property. In Sweden and Germany, a majority of those who are pursuing a doctorate are funded through their employment as researchers or research assistants.

By far the greatest concern in the interviews held with presidents of Canadian graduate students' associations (GSA) was inadequate funding of graduate students, especially for those in the humanities and social sciences (Holdaway *et al.*, 1995a). 'Well below the poverty level' was a commonly held view. The most frequently identified 'greatest concerns' of postgraduate students on the questionnaire to GSA presidents were funding (23 out of 28 identified this), quality of supervision (12), quality of facilities (nine), lengthening time to completion (eight), fee increases (five), quality of educational programmes (four), cost of living (two), cost of equipment and books (two), need for an improved health plan (two), and intellectual property rights (two). Financial matters were obviously the most dominant concerns that these GSA presidents identified. One GSA president made this statement: 'As a result of the serious lack of funding, many postgraduate students are forced to take part-time jobs. Others have to quit for short periods of time to make money. The consequence is that postgraduate students do not complete their degrees in a timely fashion.'

Process issues

Supervision

Many experts consider that effective supervision is the key to the overall quality of postgraduate education. What are the essential elements of effective supervision?

Quality

Questionnaire comments provided by (a) Canadian postgraduate coordinators and experienced supervisors and (b) interviewees from various categories of personnel in Canada, Australia and the UK revealed substantial concern about the quality of postgraduate supervision provided by some faculty members (Holdaway *et al.*, 1995b). However, in both Germany and Sweden, the close working relationships between 'postgraduate students' and their supervisors who are embedded in a research culture resulted in very little concern about the quality of supervision. Canadian graduate deans commonly observed that the quality of postgraduate supervision is highly variable, both within and between departments. Some students, especially in the humanities, were perceived to be left alone too much during their research and thesis activities. One Canadian research administrator stated that we must get humanities faculty members to feel that 'students are not a nuisance in their research'. Many individual Australian universities now hold training workshops and provide written guidance to supervisors. In 1994, the University of Melbourne intended to require all new faculty members who wish to be supervisors of postgraduate students to attend workshops on effective postgraduate supervision.

Committees

Whereas in Canada postgraduate students typically have a primary supervisor and other members of a supervisory committee, postgraduate students in Australia and the UK usually have one supervisor and no supervisory committee. However, use of committees in those countries is becoming more common. Some Australian and UK interviewees favoured the use of co-supervisors or supervisory committees, as did the Australian Vice-Chancellors' Committee (1990), considering that these practices would improve the quality of postgraduate students' experiences. Others concluded that this would result in an unnecessary increase in workload.

Experience

For master's thesis-route students, 74 per cent of the experienced Canadian supervisors who responded believed that only faculty members who are active in research and publication should be assigned as their primary supervisors; for doctoral programmes, the figure was 94 per cent. Such people would improve the quality of students' research activities. The strongest support for this position was obtained at the master's and doctoral levels from coordinators in biology, engineering, physical sciences, health, business and humanities, and the least support in the social sciences and education. One experienced supervisor provided this comment:

> The fact that certain professors who engage in no research activity are authorized to direct master's and doctoral students seems to me to be nonsense. This situation, along with the lack of relationship between the thesis subjects and the areas of interest of the directors, explains a large part of the problems related to abandonment or the excessive length of studies at the doctoral level.

Monitoring

Several Canadian graduate coordinators stated that removal of an inadequate supervisor is a difficult but necessary task. A commonly held view in universities in Canada, Australia and the UK is that department heads are responsible for ensuring that supervisors are supervising effectively. Use of an annual or biannual evaluation form on which supervisors describe the progress of their graduate students appears to be universal in both British and Australian universities, but not in Canada. The Australian Vice-Chancellors' Committee (1990: 6) concluded that 'written reports from the student and the supervisor are an important and formal means by which any problems concerning the candidature can be identified'.

Workload

Effective supervision of postgraduate students can be very time-consuming. In Canada, Australia and the UK a common concern was that postgraduate supervision is often added to a full undergraduate teaching and research load. Many respondents expressed views which were consistent with the following comment: 'The other problem is a crushing and increasing workload caused by underfunding. Supervisors who have to do their own typing, data entry, heavy teaching, heavy administration, just don't have time to supervise as well as they might. Most are [extremely] stressed.' The number of postgraduate students supervised at any one time is an important aspect of supervisory workload and can obviously affect the quality of the students' experiences.

Research and independence

Supervisors were asked to indicate how frequently students' thesis research projects were an integral part of or closely related to their supervisor's research activities. The overall means for master's and doctoral programmes were 3.65 and 3.86, between Often (3) and Usually (4). The highest level of this relationship occurred in biology, engineering, physical sciences and health, and the lowest in humanities, education and social sciences. Three supervisors provided these comments:

> It seems clear that different constraints operate in the humanities vs. sciences owing to financial requirements of sciences. Students in science must work on projects of their supervisor's origin with relatively limited room for digression, relative to what is possible in other disciplines.

> It is most important to provide a balance between supervisors' direction and students' independence. It is not up to the supervisor to provide the incentive for the student to finish a project, but it is up to the supervisor to set reasonable deadlines and return work promptly with appropriate recommendations.

> In the humanities at least, the doctoral program – courses, comprehensives, and thesis – should be treated as a single overall process, rather than sequential, as often happens now. The thesis topic should be isolated and developed with the supervisor at the beginning of the program, and work in courses and preparation for examinations should be regarded as a whole, with frequent crossovers.

Effectiveness
The 10 practices perceived by experienced Canadian postgraduate supervisors to be the most important in assisting doctoral students to successfully complete their theses and pass the final oral examination in an appropriate period of time were, in order of overall means, as listed below. (The response scale was 1 = None, 2 = A little, 3 = Some, 4 = Considerable and 5 = Great.)

- provide prompt feedback (mean = 4.47);
- provide balance between supervisor's direction and student's independence (4.35);
- hold regular progress report meetings (4.34);
- assign supervisors who are expert in the students' specific research fields (4.30);
- help students revise research design if unforeseen problems require such revision (4.28);
- ensure that the thesis does not grow excessively (4.26);
- ensure that students continually make progress (4.16);
- provide settings for students to present progress reports for feedback (4.16);
- provide a detailed student handbook (4.14);
- assign supervisors at the beginning of students' progammes (4.00).

Many of these aspects have also been identified by other authors as assisting completion (e.g. Council of Graduate Schools, 1991; de Wied *et al.*,

1991; Salmon, 1992; and Parry and Hayden, 1994). Also, Ballard and Clanchy (1993: 61) posited that 'skillful supervision of graduate students always involves a blend of academic expertise and the skillful management of personal and professional relations.'

Institutional culture

A commonly mentioned theme in the interviews was that postgraduate students tend to feel that they are treated as if they are not an integral part of the university. Several in the UK and Australia used the term 'marginalized' to describe this feeling. They are frequently quite isolated and have inadequate facilities. On the other hand, postgraduate students are often very supportive of each other.

The extent to which postgraduate students are integrated into academic departments is highly variable. In the Ontario universities with the smallest postgraduate enrolments, postgraduate students commonly are treated as junior faculty members. The way that postgraduate students are viewed and treated also depends upon their age, work experience and attendance patterns. Obviously, a supportive institutional culture can heavily influence the effectiveness and quality of many aspects of postgraduate programmes.

External partnerships

To what extent should external agencies be involved in partnerships with universities to provide elements of postgraduate programmes? Most of the literature addresses partnerships with industry, and OECD has found that university–industry interaction is increasing in most countries (Powles, 1994: 1). The National Board of Employment, Education and Training (1992) noted these points: (a) PhD training in Australia is not usually suited to the needs of industry; and (b) the approach to industrial R & D training needs to be reassessed.

The different cultures in different types of organizations must be taken into account when discussing external partnerships. In this regard, Powles (1994: 69–70) observed that postgraduates have 'to bridge the two cultures and to negotiate two different modes of professional socialization' and proposed that 'convivial research environments, informed supervisory practice, clear expectations and effective communication between supervisors and students – all critical elements in traditional university-based research education and training – are all the more complex in the three-way relationship'. Powles was mainly considering industry, but similar benefits and concerns could be assumed to be associated with partnerships involving postgraduate students doing thesis research in business, government and human service agencies. Such work in external organizations can improve the quality of the thesis research experience by providing different perspectives, establishing new contacts, and using different equipment and subjects.

Development of teaching skills

Should doctoral students receive assistance in developing their teaching skills? Concern has surfaced in several countries that emphasis on development of research competence has led to neglect of developing teaching competence. Smith (1991: 59–60) reported that 'today's problems [with university teaching] will perpetuate themselves since there is no requirement that teachers of tomorrow learn anything about teaching' and concluded that 'the opinion in the university community seems to be that research technique takes years to learn but teaching simply comes naturally'.

Greenwood and Sunell (1993) were equally critical of the current neglect of developing teaching competence in the USA. They advocated development of teaching and communication skills, teaching of professional standards and ethics, and making postgraduate students aware of the impact of changes in demography on classroom climate in order to ensure that future postsecondary instructors will be well prepared for undergraduate and postgraduate teaching.

Output issues

Completion

Two interrelated issues are relevant to completion. First, what are reasonable maximum times for completion of master's and doctoral programmes for full-time students? Second, what percentages of incoming cohorts should be expected to complete?

Completion times and completion percentages are the two output variables that have received by far the most attention by national bodies, for example, the Higher Education Council (1990) in Australia; the Canadian Association for Graduate Studies (1995); the Association of Graduate Schools in the Association of American Universities (1990) in the USA; and UK research councils, especially the Economic and Social Research Council (e.g. 1990).

Concerns about slow time-to-completion relate to the commitment of staff and other resources for extended periods, the desirability of concentrating graduate studies in a reasonable time period, the possibility that information obtained in the research may become obsolete before completion of the thesis, and delays in researchers moving on to other projects. Yeates (1991a: 17) concluded that 'there is no quick fix [to attrition] because the entire research funding, student support, faculty reward, and employment environment influence the graduation rate and the time it takes to complete a degree.'

The graduate deans in Canada commented that percentages completing are lower than they would like, but that this aspect varies among departments. The humanities have often been identified as having a particular problem with completion, resulting partly from lack of financial support and a high degree of independent research activity. In Australia, the natural sciences (including biological sciences), engineering, economics and medicine tended to have the shortest time-to-completion and the highest completion percentages.

One Canadian graduate student president provided this relevant reaction:

> The length of time to complete a degree particularly in humanities and social sciences is a concern. There are many students in their 5th–6th year of what should be a 4-year PhD program. Despite the fact that funding only covers four years, the majority of students still haven't defended by then. At that point, funding is terminated and job seeking or other pursuits can then interfere with thesis writing and/or revisions.

Not all respondents agreed that faster completion should be forced. The 'strait-jacket of time' was considered by some UK interviewees to be undesirable because graduate research activities often have unpredictable aspects, such as difficulties with equipment and cooperation with field subjects. Several proposed that better supervisory practices and reduced expectations about the scope and complexity of theses would help to improve both completion rates and times.

One of the most notable disciplinary differences in data provided by Canadian postgraduate coordinators occurred in the responses concerning the influence of 'lack of financial support' on the prevention of completion: 71 per cent of humanities coordinators identified this as a reason as compared with a range of 22 per cent to 47 per cent for seven other discipline areas. Coordinators and supervisors supplied many illuminating comments on their questionnaires:

> Our longest programs are due to candidates who complete their course requirements, leave to take a job, and procrastinate in thesis writing.

> Theses that take years to complete are usually the last pieces of substantial research that these students undertake, instead of being, as they should be, the first. The statistics on my own students convince me that the faster they have completed their doctoral programs, the more productive and original scholars they are likely to be.

Theses

The Council of Graduate Schools (1991: 6–7) drew this conclusion about doctoral theses: 'Although there is general agreement that a doctoral research project should be original, substantial, significant, and independently carried out, disciplinary differences emerge when one seeks to define the terms.' This Council also stated that doctoral research should be 'theory-driven investigation characterized by rigorous methodology' and that the type of thesis may also depend upon whether the function of doctoral education is preparation for a research career or for practice.

Criteria/evaluation issues

How should the quality of postgraduate programmes be evaluated and what criteria should be used in this evaluation? Many of the criteria are implicit in the variables listed in Figure 4.1.

Programme reviews

The Council of Graduate Schools (1990: 6–7) identified these key characteristics of programme review. It is:

- usually initiated and administered by universities;
- evaluative, not just descriptive;
- directed towards improvement and makes specific recommendations;
- based on only academic criteria;
- as objective as possible;
- independent of reviews for other purposes;
- followed by action.

The Council also identified some examples of criteria that should be used: (a) Is the department advancing the state of the discipline or profession? (b) Is the teaching useful and effective? (c) Does the programme meet the profession's needs? The following statement encapsulates the Council's position (1990: 3): 'The primary purpose of all program reviews is the improvement of graduate programs, as measured by the quality of the faculty, the students, library and other educational resources, the curriculum, available facilities, and the academic reputation of the program among its peers.'

The Ontario Council on Graduate Studies (Yeates, 1991b: 2–3) reviews all graduate programmes in 15 autonomous universities over seven-year cycles, using two final categories: 'good quality' or 'not approved'. If 'not approved', the particular university must not admit more students to the programme. During the reviews, these matters receive particular attention: (a) whether the work is 'demonstrably more advanced, rigorous and integrative' than undergraduate studies; (b) whether resources are focused on selected areas; and (c) whether scholarship is apparent as evidenced by 'critical analysis of existing ideas and knowledge'. In Australia and the UK, reviews of postgraduate programmes are part of the formal reviews of universities and of the research activities of departments.

In 1994, the University of Alberta (1994) began a series of external reviews which uses these six factors and relevant measures to evaluate the quality of postgraduate programmes and research:

- excellence of the students in the programme and the graduates from the programme (e.g. number of major scholarships won by students);
- excellence of the faculty members (e.g. number of awards and honours);
- quality and impact of the research and creative work done by faculty and postgraduate students (e.g. quality and number of books and publications);
- quality of the research environment (e.g. availability of infrastructure for research);
- quality of instruction of postgraduate students (e.g. student course evaluations);
- management of postgraduate programmes (e.g. time to complete postgraduate degrees).

Quality assurance and quality improvement

The Federated Australian University Staff Association and the Union of Australian College Academics (1992: 41) observed that 'quality assurance measures do not necessarily lead to quality improvement. Often quality assurance can impede quality improvement.' These bodies recommended that a quality improvement approach is more likely to be productive. Peer review is seen by most academics to be the only valid means of assessing quality, although, as the Australian Vice-Chancellors' Committee (1992) stated, it may be supplemented by other approaches such as self-evaluation and performance data. Also, peer review may emphasize 'internal' variables while de-emphasizing or ignoring the aspect of *value* of outputs – including the skills and knowledge of master's and doctoral graduates – to 'external' stakeholders, especially employers.

Master's programmes

After conducting extensive interviews in the USA, Conrad *et al.* (1993) identified four dimensions as attributes of high-quality master's programmes:

- *culture* – unity of purpose of participants and a supportive learning environment;
- *planned learning experiences* – core courses, activity-centred learning, immersion, individualization, out-of-class activities and tangible product;
- *resources* – institutional and departmental support;
- *leadership and the human dimension* – strong programme leadership, faculty involvement, committed students with diverse backgrounds, and faculty with non-university workplace experience.

Interviewees generally believed that these dimensions were more important than were the traditional variables of high-quality staff and students, resources, a thesis requirement, comprehensive examinations, stringent admission procedures and full-time attendance. Conrad *et al.* (1993: 295) provided three caveats in connection with their list of attributes: (a) the attributes were often expressed differently across programmes; (b) the combination of many attributes contributed to the quality of students' experiences; and (c) the list is not a 'cookbook' for planning and evaluating master's programmes.

Doctoral theses

With respect to assessing the quality of doctoral theses, Salmon (1992: 9) considered that this activity should use the criteria of originality and contribution to knowledge. She noted that these criteria seem to be 'straightforward and unproblematic' but 'in practice, they often prove ambiguous and slippery'. Further, Phillips (1994: 137) identified the aspects that examiners look for in a good thesis: depth of dealing with issues; competence in facing up to all involved aspects; means of handling contradictions in evidence; how problems were sorted out; and whether conceptual understanding, critical ability and well-structured argument are evident.

Suggestions for addressing quality issues

As discussed earlier, 'quality' in postsecondary education has different meanings to different stakeholders. Also, to some it has an absolute value whereas to others it has meaning only in a relative sense. In postgraduate education, 'quality' and 'effectiveness' can apply to individual input, process and output aspects of programmes (Figure 4.1), as well as to programmes overall.

Inasmuch as the aspects identified in Figure 4.1 are often interrelated, university departments should pay attention to all these aspects and adopt a systems orientation. They should also recognize that an inadequate or inferior input or process aspect, e.g. funding of students or supervision, can have a disproportionately negative affect upon output variables such as completion percentage or thesis quality. Departments should assess the quality of their outputs and make appropriate adjustments in the quality of their inputs and the effectiveness of their processes.

Based on personal reflection of issues provided above, I recommend that these actions be undertaken to improve the quality and effectiveness of postgraduate programmes:

- universities should examine ways to increase financial support to full-time postgraduate students;
- coursework should be supportive of both completion of the thesis and acquisition and development of appropriate knowledge and skills;
- supervisors should normally approve only doctoral research projects that full-time students can complete within four years;
- placement of some postgraduate students in human service organizations to conduct their thesis research should be encouraged;

- the nature and purpose of master's and doctoral theses should be carefully assessed by postgraduate councils/committees at each university;
- appointment as a primary supervisor of postgraduate students should be dependent upon having an active record of research and scholarship;
- new staff members and first-time supervisors should be required to attend a workshop on effective supervisory practices;
- postgraduate supervision should be formally recognized as part of the workload of faculty members;
- annual reports on progress and activities of each postgraduate student should be prepared;
- universities and departments should develop policies about intellectual property after appropriate consultations.

Finally, universities are encouraged to initiate continuing research projects about procedures that affect the quality and effectiveness of postgraduate programmes. Over the last decade such research has gained momentum, but more comprehensive studies need to be conducted. Two potentially useful approaches could be to examine the effects of *individual* input and process variables upon the quality of output variables, and to assess the *interactive* effects of these individual variables, such as student funding and programme requirements, in identifying quality issues.

Acknowledgements

These contributions are gratefully acknowledged: the Social Sciences and Humanities Research Council of Canada, which provided a research grant for 1991–4; my co-investigators, Drs Claude Deblois and Ian Winchester; the staff and graduate students of universities and other organizations who provided materials, completed questionnaires, participated in interviews and assisted in several other ways; Dr Joe Fris, Dr Alexander Gregor, Mrs Colleen Judge, Mrs Georgie Kwan and Mrs Christiane Prokop, who assisted in preparation of this chapter.

References

Association of Graduate Schools in the Association of American Universities (1990) *Institutional Policies to Improve Doctoral Education*. Washington, DC: AGSAAU.
Australian Vice-Chancellors' Committee (1990) *Code of Practice for Maintaining and Monitoring Academic Quality and Standards in Higher Degrees*. Canberra: AVCC.
Australian Vice-Chancellors' Committee (1992) Quality in the Australian university system, in Higher Education Council (ed.) *The Quality of Higher Education*. Canberra: Australian Government Publishing Service.
Ballard, B. and Clanchy, J. (1993) Supervising students from overseas. In D. J. Cullen (ed.) *Quality in PhD Education*. Canberra: Australian National University.
Bowen, W. G. and Rudenstine, N. L. (1992) *In Pursuit of the PhD*. Princeton, NJ: Princeton University Press.
Bulmer, M. (1992) *Overview of the ESRC Training Board Research into Training Programme*. London: London School of Economics and Political Science.

Canadian Association for Graduate Studies (1995) *Statistical Report 1995.* Ottawa: CAGS.

Committee for Quality Assurance in Higher Education (1994) *Report on 1993 Quality Reviews.* Canberra: Australian Government Publishing Service.

Conrad, C. F., Haworth, J. G. and Millar, S. B. (1993) *A Silent Success: Master's Education in the United States.* Baltimore, MD: The Johns Hopkins University Press.

Council of Graduate Schools (1990) *Academic Review of Graduate Programs.* Washington, DC: CGS.

Council of Graduate Schools (1991) *The Role and Nature of the Doctoral Dissertation.* Washington, DC: CGS.

Cullen, D. J. and Allen, M. (1993) Retrospective: Quality and 'efficiency and effectiveness'. In D. J. Cullen (ed.) *Quality in PhD Education.* Canberra: Australian National University.

de Wied, D., Aubert, G., Ehrhardt, H., Friedenson, P., Jespers, P. G. A., Kasse, M., Rinnooy Kan, A. H. G., van den Berghe, H., Blume, S. S., Spierts, L. J. V. and Muller, A. M. E. (1991) *Postgraduate Research Training Today: Emerging Structures for a Changing Europe.* The Hague, Netherlands: Ministry of Education and Science.

Department of Employment, Education and Training (1993) *National Report on Australia's Higher Education Sector.* Canberra: Australian Government Publishing Service.

Economic and Social Research Council (1990) Postgraduate Training: The Green Paper Response, *Social Sciences,* 5(1).

Elton, L. and Pope, M. (1989) Research supervision: The value of collegiality, *Cambridge Journal of Education,* 19, 267–76.

Federated Australian University Staff Association and Union of Australian College Academics (1992) Quality in higher education, in Higher Education Council (ed.) *The Quality of Higher Education* (pp. 31–49). Canberra: Australian Government Publishing Service.

Gordon, R. E., Baker, M., Croft, R. A., D'Arms, J. H., Dimminie, C. B. and Sheridan, J. D. (1990) *Organization and Administration of Graduate Education.* Washington, DC: Council of Graduate Schools.

Greenwood, M. R. C. and Sunell, L. A. (1993) The graduate school in the modern university or the academy of the 21st century: Changing, reforming or just plain scared? *Communicator,* 26, 3–5, 9, 12.

Higher Education Council (1990) *Future Directions for Australian Graduate Studies and Higher Degrees.* Canberra: National Board of Employment, Education and Training.

Higher Education Council (1992a) *The Quality of Higher Education.* Canberra: Australian Government Publishing Service.

Higher Education Council (1992b) *Achieving Quality.* Canberra: Australian Government Publishing Service.

Holdaway, E. A., Deblois, C. and Winchester, I. S. (1995a) *Organization and Administration of Graduate Programs.* Edmonton, Canada: Department of Educational Policy Studies, University of Alberta.

Holdaway, E. A., Deblois, C. and Winchester, I. S. (1995b) Supervision of graduate students, *Canadian Journal of Higher Education,* 25, 1–29.

Maclean's (1996) The sixth annual ranking – universities 1996. Special issue, 25 November, 109, 18–76.

Moses, I. (1994). *The Graduate Research Experience and Supervisory Practices – An Australian Perspective.* Paper presented at the SSHRCC National Conference on

Graduate Research and Studies in the Social Sciences and Humanities, Ottawa, Canada, November.

National Board of Employment, Education and Training (1992) *Productive Interaction.* Canberra: Australian Government Publishing Service.

Parry, S. and Hayden, M. (1994) *Supervising Higher Degree Research Students.* Canberra: Australian Government Publishing Service.

Phillips, E. M. (1994) Quality in the PhD: Points at which quality may be assessed, in R. G. Burgess (ed.) *Postgraduate Education and Training in the Social Sciences.* London: Jessica Kingsley.

Powles, M. (1994) *Postgraduates as Partners in University–Industry Liaisons.* Canberra: Australian Government Publishing Service.

Rivers, J. (1996) Building for the future – consider the NZ experience. *Campus Review Special Report* (p. 15) [Australia], 4–10 September.

Salmon, P. (1992) *Achieving a PhD: Ten Students' Experiences.* Oakhill, Stoke-on-Trent: Trentham Books.

Smith, S. L. (1991) *Report: Commission of Inquiry on Canadian University Education.* Ottawa: Association of Universities and Colleges of Canada.

Times Higher Education Supplement (1987) The mystery of quality, 2 January.

University of Alberta (1994) *Evaluation of Graduate Programs and Research.* Edmonton, Canada: Faculty of Graduate Studies and Research, University of Alberta.

Yeates, M. (1991a) *Doctoral graduation rates in Ontario universities: A discussion paper.* Toronto: Ontario Council on Graduate Studies.

Yeates, M. (1991b) *The Graduate Appraisal Process in Ontario.* Toronto: Ontario Council on Graduate Studies.

Part 2

Lifelong Learning

5

Lifelong, Postexperience, Postgraduate – Symphony or Dichotomy?

Chris Duke

Perspectives and context

This discussion of postgraduate and postexperience education (PGE and PExpE respectively) from the perspective of lifelong learning is informed by living and working in the United Kingdom higher education (HE) system and, for 16 years to 1985 and again very recently, within the Australian system. The comparative perspective which this affords is stimulating yet manageable: close enough to allow real comparison, different enough to foster sharp reflection. Over the three decades that I have consciously exercised this comparison the two systems have both emulated and leapfrogged each other: Australia ahead with one innovation (or response to environmental exigencies), the UK ahead with another.

I should declare a further interest and consequent perspective. I have worked in these two systems for some 30 years as a Continuing Education (CE) scholar, teacher, administrator, policy analyst, lobbyist and apologist. Throughout this time the dominant terms of discourse have changed continuously: adult, extension, extramural and continuing education, CVE, CPD, recurrent, permanent, and now increasingly, lifelong education or learning. Attention-seeking soundbites and name changes have become common, demonstrating that this has become territory worth contesting. More recently I have worked in senior management in a UK university as a pro-vice-chancellor concurrently with exercising my CE brief. I now work in a management position in an Australian university. I have no distinct responsibility for CE but still combine with the requirements of general institutional management an abiding commitment to the 'accessible university'.

It is from these two perspectives in particular – international comparativism based mainly in two national systems but more widely informed, and central management with long experience of institutionally provided CE – that the subject is examined. Sustained attention has recently gone to credit recognition and transfer in the UK, and to the standardization and widening of forms of accreditation, mostly at undergraduate level (Robertson, 1994). That debate has been entangled with issues of curriculum – academic or vocational – convergent, twin-track or dichotomous. These are pertinent also to postexperience education. I was tempted to take as the theme of this chapter 'Credit Where Credit's Due'. Instead I have chosen to conclude with a comment on the implications of 'lifelong learning' at postgraduate levels and postexperience stages also for the undergraduate level – itself increasingly a post- as well as a pre-experience matter.

One aspect of the social context of higher education particularly relevant to this analysis is the new demography and political economy in which it exists. High unemployment persists; jobless growth is recognized as a possibly abiding condition. The economically inactive proportion of the population is high and rising. Rising longevity presents formidable problems for health, social security and welfare planning (as well as for individuals' budgeting and life planning). Tendencies towards smaller government arise naturally from a need to contain these costs. Welfarism is being curtailed, redefined and repositioned with greater emphasis on self-reliance and private provision. The dominant trend and the imperative behind it (especially following the collapse of the Soviet system and the discrediting of State socialism) is likely to remain common ground to all mainstream political parties in all the highly industrialized and knowledge-based societies.

In this context the 'new higher education' is moving through a 'mass' phase towards a 'universal' condition in these societies. Recently and even now, still, it is or has been virtually free as a right for those able to gain entry. Élite higher education has thus been an individually inexpensive and exclusive privilege enjoyed by a few young people who reproduce and reinvigorate the socio-economic élite. Its rapid expansion, coinciding with the new ageing demography and low employment economy, largely explains the 'crisis in higher education' which is often couched in somewhat reactionary and self-interested ways as decline in standards and threat to quality. There is near-universal recognition (a) that the expansion of initial higher education will continue and (b) that the costs will be reallocated so that the individual student and/or parents will pay significantly more.

For HE systems and institutions the crisis manifests itself in identity questions for individual universities and in fragmentation and segmentation internal to the system. It implies a reappraisal of core mission and of modes of management (Shattock, 1996), and fosters the creation of groups, sets and leagues within HE, characterized as 'Ivy League', 'research-led', 'world class', and in Australia as 'sandstone' and Go8 (Group – or Gang – of Eight). Calls for diversity of mission and function are often couched, and more often heard, in self-seeking terms. No sooner are HE systems 'unified' than new hierarchies clamour for recognition. The Harris Report, which appeared about the same time in Britain in 1996, illustrates a tendency, coded or overt, to define out and support more exclusively and expensively, especially in terms of public research funds, a set of leading or 'world class' universities. The public debate occasioned by the 1996–7 UK Dearing Inquiry into Higher Education (and exemplified par excellence in the pages of the *Times Higher Education Supplement*) provides ample evidence. This chapter makes no attempt to critique these reports or engage with the Dearing debate, which will have moved on well before this book is published. The point of contextualization is to locate issues about postgraduate and postexperience education very firmly in an immediate context but in such a way that their broader significance is also clear. Inevitably reports about the location of and support for postgraduate education and the public funding of research are read in the political environment of Quality and Excellence, Diversity and Standards, Research and Teaching-only universities, feeder colleges, etc. The urge to compete and excel, with relatively diminishing public resources and increasingly transparent and publicized public indicators, and the excitement of public contest for position, mean that the longer-term significance to society of expanding PGE and PExpE may be obscured. In recognizing the way the growth of education beyond the undergraduate level is part of immediate political knockabout we also need to ask where this growth is leading the HE system and its parent society.

Learning in the context of 'postmodern times'

I made reference earlier to the changing discourse of continuing and recurrent education and lifelong learning. Let us put aside the familiar confusion and sometimes calculated obfuscation between education, provided by increasingly various forms of teaching and study support, and the learning that education is intended to foster but which can and often does also occur without deliberate educational intent. We need an operational understanding of 'lifelong learning' in the context of 'the learning society' and reinforced by 'learning organizations' to be able to see how PGE and PExpE relate to lifelong learning. 1996, the European Year of Lifelong Learning, saw something of a climax to the rhetorical debate on these matters. To some extent the old European debate of the early 1970s on recurrent and permanent education is coming together with and being reinvigorated by new interest in the learning organization and learning society. Underpinned as this has been by more solid work on the nature and nurturing of the 'learning organization' it would be premature to claim any clarity or fixity of value and intent to lifelong learning, despite its universal acclaim. The Harris Report (Harris, 1996, especially pp. 27–8) is typical in its acknowledgement of lifelong learning. The assumptions informing much of the debate at postgraduate as at undergraduate level, however, reveal how shallowly the 'lifelong learning paradigm' has yet taken root. For PGE in particular the dominant pre-experience paradigm prevails, much as the attitudes and assumptions of many who lead and manage universities remain those of the 18-year-old finishing school (Duke, 1992).

We can see how shallow is our grasp of the potential of 'lifelong learning' for initial graduate and undergraduate education by recalling the serious debate which occurred during the early years of recurrent education discourse fostered by the OECD and others, about lowering the school-leaving age and redistributing educational opportunity much more widely throughout life, for instance in the deliberations of the Association for Recurrent Education in the UK and in Australia. The proposition became problematic, and to a degree fudged and confused, by economists' unresolved differences about return on educational investment to society and individuals, initially and in later life. It was more comprehensively swept aside by the fact of high unemployment, and very high youth unemployment. This created a new imperative to hold young people back from the labour market. Rising and widening middle class aspirations completed the work of raising the age participation rate (APR) for initial higher education following an upper secondary participation rate approaching 100 per cent in many regions. Alternating paid youth employment with education seems implausible when youth unemployment is very high. Only recently has the mood shifted again somewhat towards work experience for young people. Even so the stress is on training for useful if low-paid occupations with work experience as a component of this, rather than any lifelong learning recurrency principle. The vocational and general continue to be separated, partly on class and status lines.

Mass higher education is still normally identified and measured in terms of the APR, despite long-standing recognition of the 'adultification' of higher education and the attainment of an 'adult majority' (Abrahamsson, 1986 and later studies; Campbell, 1984). So dominant is this paradigm at undergraduate level that the perspective offered by lifelong learning (LLL) on learning needs is only slowly penetrating the revision of curricula and teaching–learning methods. Indeed the LLL perspective is mainly called to service, it must be said, to validate changes in teaching strategies dictated by financial constraint and worsening staff–student ratios in a labour-intensive industry. Self-directed learning and its synonyms finds a cogent rationale in LLL but its genesis is more often a matter of the bottom line!

In summary: we have moved a long way in terms of adopting the slogan of lifelong learning, but not far in grasping its meanings and implications for curriculum and forms of provision within higher education. The idea of the learning society is still less well formed: it often means little more than the teaching, educating or training society, whereas in its full reach the concept encompasses the capacity of a society to reflect upon its experience and renew itself, supporting and enabling its members to contribute to this process as active citizens. The level intermediate between learning society and individual lifelong learner, the learning organization, has been more fully developed as a 'learningful working environment' although it too is easily reduced to mean no more than 'the company that trains'. There are implications from each of these full, as distinct from reductionist, meanings as we turn to the connections between LLL and PGE/PExpE. The fuller understanding helps us to ask how far postgraduate and postinitial curricula respond to the needs of individuals and organizations in such a society; and how far our institutions and their working assumptions have also really altered to meet these needs. Because higher education institutions (HEIs) are diverse, the answer will be varied; but in the two systems with which I am most familiar the answer has to be 'rather little' in recognition, though further in reality.

'Graduateness' and beyond

Concerns about quality, standards and excellence dominate especially the UK HE agenda, although they are probably nowhere absent from the HE debate. The Higher Education Funding Council of England (HEFCE) exercises quality assessment regimes for both teaching and research, while the Higher Education Quality Council (HEQC) has been charged with quality assurance institution-wide. The Harris Committee was required by its commissioning Council HEFCE to consider, inter alia, 'the quality of postgraduate training, and current arrangements for monitoring this' (Harris, 1996: 75). Rapid expansion and much slower growth, then absolute reduction, in public expenditure provides an obvious explanation, behind which lurk less overt political and professional agendas. Australia arrived later at a national politically driven quality assurance system and has worn it more lightly, but it may be predicted that the semiprivatizing instincts of the 1996 Liberal (conservative) Administration which replaced the more expansionist Labour reforms will not exclude tight quality accountability of some kind.

As the refrain about declining standards swelled in Britain, the then Secretary of State for Education John Patten charged the HEQC with assuming responsibility for comparability of standards across institutions of the honours degree. The Council responded in part by building the question into its Auditors' template for institutional visits, also by launching a 'graduateness' project to investigate what was distinctive, or unique, about undergraduate education. At about the same time the National Institute of Adult Continuing Education in its second HE policy paper (1995) raised the slightly different, and better, question: what was 'higher' about higher education? HEQC also seeks to build into its audit visits specific consideration of both graduate and partnership (franchised and validated) programmes. While this is all relevant to our consideration of contemporary PGE and PExpE, the concept of graduateness is particularly important, and latently antithetical, from the perspective of lifelong learning.

'Graduateness' also compels us to confront the difference between PGE and PExpE. PGE, the further formal and accredited education of those who have already graduated, is understood to mean a higher level and traditionally more specialized study, requiring and building on what went before. Traditionally it is also seen as a continuation of postinitial 'front-end-loaded' full-time education taken by the 'brightest' graduates, often and as desired by their teachers in order that they move on into research and academic teaching positions. Ageism has been rampant in this area, and research scholarships have often traditionally been legally or practically inaccessible to many who have taken any significant break from full-time education.

This simplified sketch of a monolithic PGE system is now a stereotype. The familiar system has crumbled. Even the classified honours degree system is being questioned. None the less the attitudes, assumptions and culture still widely flourish. Postexperience education has always been more complex. Its differentiation from PGE as part of the core business of the university raises issues that 'graduateness' intriguingly and innocently comes to confront. If a student-learner can undertake graduate-level study without any undergraduate qualification, much less one in the field in which the graduate study is undertaken, the concept of graduateness, if not of the graduate in itself, begins to unravel. From a LLL perspective this is all to the good. The terms graduate, bachelor and most obviously master have a fixity which sits awkwardly with the realities of rapid technological change and the obsolescence of knowledge and skills. The 'first class Oxford man' is – was – a social artefact rather than a life-time guarantee of 'learnability'. Such a degree still carries considerable social cachet and economic value, but its pertinence to lifelong learning and coping with change is more doubtful. It may not be long before the first degree is treated as having a limited useful lifespan other than as a record of high-level general preparatory education. Mandatory renewal or updating is not uncommon in those areas where qualifications relate to ability to perform in employment.

On the vocational side, defining and operationalizing competencies at high levels of intellectual and professional attainment is proving frustratingly, and predictably, unattainable. Similarly, on the 'academic side', to adopt the familiar dichotomy, beyond very general 'transferable skills' it proves difficult to capture, define, judge and evaluate what produces 'generic graduateness' across disciplines, programmes and institutions. HEQC's quest will in the end be no more easily satisfied than NVQs at 'level 5'. Why is this relevant to a consideration of PGE and PExpE?

Post-experience (higher) education is a loosely defined and shadowy concept, without clear boundaries. It will remain so, and become increasingly diffuse and hard to pin down, as modes, partners, locations, curricula and learning objectives continue to proliferate. Within HE systems the larger part of PExpE is also PGE: taught master's degrees, credit-bearing short courses, units or modules, at the least 'continuing education units' or courses leading to professional and managerial qualifications which have some validity and transferability into graduate-level academic currency. Much graduate research study (research master's through to doctoral degrees) is also now postexperience – often also part-time and concurrent with employment. At the very least it is vocational training for the academic profession. But increasingly PGE, research as well as taught programmes, is a form of postexperience education for other occupational groups employed in organizations sensing their way to becoming learning organizations.

In other words there is no convenient, easily workable distinction between PGE and PExpE, conceptually, administratively or indeed pedagogically. Even within universities, let alone outside them, there may continue to be substantial PExpE programmes not subsumed or credited into PGE. But an increasingly large proportion of university PGE is already in fact PExpE; and that high proportion will continue to rise, as formally supported and accredited lifelong learning becomes ever more widespread. The postexperience education of youngish as well as older students will become still more usual. More people without first degrees will find their way into graduate programmes (PGE as well as other PExpE), at least in the broad social sciences and probably humanities as well as some professional disciplines.

The status of graduate and the concept of graduateness will thus become less and less useful. An exception will remain the more abstract, mathematically based and linear science disciplines, including those at the core of hard, high cost and big science which tends to set the terms of debate for all university research and graduate education. In research budget and status these areas will continue to exercise influence; numerically they will represent an increasingly small proportion of PGE and PExpE as indeed of undergraduate education. A small minority can still exercise hegemonic ascendancy, and there are good reasons for the linear hierarchy of qualification and attainment to persist in such areas, with little if any time out for students from sequential, sustained and continuing study and training.

We should however recognize the small size of this minority in scanning for emerging lifelong learning paradigms of postinitial and graduate education. There may otherwise persist an unjustified and in a sense now illegitimate tendency to treat graduate education as essentially (a) advanced preparation for the academic professional and (b) the next stage of economic and social selection after the first degree, the social function of which is to discriminate out that small élite whom undergraduate education selected out in earlier times. Such a further extension of initial 'front-end' higher education into master's levels and beyond is a natural phenomenon, given institutional inclinations to select lazily, and individuals' imperatives to separate themselves out to compete in a mass HE world.

Such postgraduate education will increasingly be privately funded in the future. That apart, its utility for the nurturance of lifelong learners in a learning society is problematic. It is far more sensible from an individual as well as a societal perspective to redistribute most such postgraduate learning opportunities throughout more of adult life, and find another way to match graduates to labour market and societal needs rather than using the postgraduate master's as a finishing and selecting year, as is already happening very obviously in the UK and less markedly as yet in Australia. We will need to move beyond the concept of graduateness, and beyond the widening reach of the graduate finishing school, to develop a higher education fitted to post-20th century needs.

The dichotomous nature of the 'master's degree'

The pivotal point for emergent postgraduate education and burgeoning post-experience education is the English and Australian, as distinct from Scottish or continental, taught master's degree. The established research master's is the first step on the graduate road to an academic position (whether taken out or converted to a higher, usually doctoral, degree), whereas the taught master's has become the quasi-mandatory post-honours fourth year which allows the more ambitious and perhaps wealthy to distinguish themselves from the other 30 per cent or more coming through initial higher education, with significantly higher job prospects at the end – a natural answer to graduate unemployment for the first generation in mass higher education. Also, the taught master's provides a postexperience qualification of a partly vocational kind for those who wish to update, upgrade or diversify into new occupational fields. The MBA suffers a status stigma in traditional academe because classically it plays this part: 'is it a *real* master's degree?' is the question one hears asked. Fittingly for a degree that is taken at early to mid-career rather than as part of initial higher education, it is commonly available in a greater diversity of modes than most programmes: full-time, part-time, external or distance of whichever generation, mixed-mode, company partnership, consortium, joint-institutional, work-based learning and so on.

The distinction between taught master's and research master's can only in part be aligned with a distinction between PExpE and PGE. Some taught master's can be located in the arena of advanced knowledge transmission: application of advanced concepts and insights to diverse operational settings in business, manufacturing systems, education and social work. The research master's requires, albeit modestly, some originality of enquiry and product: a step towards new knowledge creation. In reality the distinction quickly breaks down. I am familiar with very large (especially full-time overseas student) one-year taught master's degrees, which constitute a form of high-level selective finishing school and which are not postexperience. I have been caught up in a process of cannibalization and a conflictual contest to redefine and reshape one home-student oriented part-time and work-based postexperience taught master's into just such a pre-experience programme for young overseas clients.

However, I have also seen significant numbers of postexperience taught master's students using this degree as a way into a research degree – usually MPhil converting to PhD. This has happened over the years with an old-style MEd and more easily still with the refurbishing of that degree into a taught MA with a research methods component. The distinction between master's (T) and master's (R) has partly dissolved with curriculum development, and because the clientele itself chooses to treat the educational offering in a different way. Postexperience taught master's have become the first step to postgraduate research, also postexperience, within a lifelong learning paradigm. Significantly, such later-life researchers using the (taught) master's route are characteristically employed in high-rate-of-change sectors where the 'learning organization' is being fostered and to some extent fashioned, whether or not it is acknowledged as such.

This means that at the critical first level after the undergraduate first degree, the tidy picture of recent times has become blurred. Conventionally there was a vocational preparation path for the next generation of academics. One view of the university, as creator and preserver of knowledge, is that this is its essential teaching task. This route took bright young graduating students (first and upper seconds full of the quality of 'graduateness') through a research master's to a doctoral degree and on, perhaps via a postdoctoral fellowship (PDF), into an academic career. Alongside this, but usually terminating if not at first degree level then after it with a master's degree or other graduate-level professional qualification in uneasy alliance with a professional body, was the preparation and (partial) qualification to practise in another occupational field. Postexperience vocational education (PEVE) or continuing professional or vocational education (PCE or CVE) was, (stereo)typically, short courses taken for professional updating on a part-time, in-service, commonly evening or weekend, basis, but not usually for academic or even professional credit. A typical CVE programme would comprise a mix of open or closed (negotiated, 'tailor-made') day conferences, short courses and workshops for different one-off or repeat-business clienteles. It was if not literally then certainly in other senses off-campus and off the core curriculum and core business of the university.

Table 5.1 summarizes the traditional position and the much more confused present position. The taught master's degree recently sat at the pivotal point in a relatively dichotomous system following the taught undergraduate degree, i.e. top-up 'taught finishing school' (and quasi-professional qualification) leading to a job *or* postexperience master's of doubtful academic standing (MEd, MBA) *versus* research master's doctoral for academic/science career (taught master's rarely a stepping stone). It is now utterly 'promiscuous' in the way it is defined, treated and used.

The duality of diversity

A glorious postmodern confusion thus characterizes the taught master's degree. Institutions have played imaginatively with the given level and framework (120 'M level' CAT – credit accumulation and transfer – points) to produce all kinds of qualification-bearing learning opportunities. Some are approached piecemeal by students (or clients who really do not define themselves as 'students') to build up to a taught master's. Some prove a springboard to planned-for or unanticipated research degrees. Some are the final year of the new 'advanced English honours system', to coin a phrase. Some remain more conventional steppings stones to professional careers (rather than within professional careers); or they assist career change; or they deliberately test and screen students to go on to a research programme.

Table 5.1   PGE and PExpE: Traditional and current positions

	PGE	PExpE
Traditional	Normally immediately following first degree Route: MA/MSc; MPhil; PhD; PDF; an academic or scientific career *or* graduate diploma or other vocationally oriented training for employment (PGCE, as teacher legal workshop as lawyer, etc.)	Normally after workforce experience Route: non-award-bearing short courses; enhanced professional competence
Present-day	Normally on graduation or often at any time throughout life Route: graduate diploma/taught master?; MA/MSc; MPhil; PhD; PDF (sometimes now part-time/ partly distant, possibly work-based); often other than academic careers	Normally after workforce experience (but sometimes very little) Route: a wide variety of courses, very often carrying credit towards a master's or other qualification; including experience-based R degrees, many and diverse MBA-type degrees, a growing portfolio of taught doctorates (EdD, DBA, DEng, DTech, etc.)

This is the *plurality* of diversity, from a learner and course-opportunity perspective. In terms of institutional definitions there is a tendency, rather, by institutions of high prestige to polarize, or dichotomize, into a clear *duality*. This redivides postgraduate and postexperience work along research-focused, or practically and professionally oriented, lines. It is often expressed as research(-led) and teaching(-only) universities, and hotly contested for its rigidifying tendencies by those likely to be, and maybe stay, in the latter category. Much of the mid-1990s HE policy debate in Australia, as well as in the UK and no doubt elsewhere, hinges on this attempt to resegregate out a super-international, ivy, or sandstone league of research universities.

It will be clear from this account of the evolution of PGE and PExpE that a simple 'dualizing' of the HE system cuts clumsily across the more spontaneous and very vigorous evolution of graduate and postexperience programmes. This evolution displays increasing diversity of formats, teaching modes and learning styles, places of provision, locations and resource bases (such as work-based learning or WBL), including the capacity to build up elements towards a higher qualification in a more individually customized way, and to move through mixed teaching-and-research graduate levels to the highest, doctoral, awards. These may appear to be dualistic – research-only or taught – yet they do themselves represent a broad continuum with partly taught doctorates ever more common.

In short, instincts to 'refreeze' the system into a 'research-only' or 'teaching-only' dualism run counter to the instincts of teachers and their departments and of course teams, as well as of students and behind them employers and the community. They would also, incidentally, have prevented the emergence to remarkable eminence of my former university, Warwick, among the nation's research leaders, with one of the higher proportions of both postgraduate and postexperience students in the system. To align postgraduate with research(-led) and postexperience with teaching-(only) would contravene the evidence of both market demand and institutional behaviour. The PGE/PExpE perspective suggests that such dichotomous strategies would not well serve either HE system, community, or ultimately élite university interests.

Student-to-learner perspectives

Another way of looking at the quite remarkable and recent change in the character of PGE and PExpE is to see these as merging together in an immensely rich and diverse postinitial higher education lifelong learning tapestry, in which the PGE–PExpE distinction is progressively less sharply defined, with the partial exception of the 'big-science-hard-science-mathematics' end of the spectrum. 'Lifelong learning' implies fusion and diffusion of the student role into other roles throughout life: the roles of worker and citizen in learning organizations and a learning society. The academic tribes will still attempt to occupy traditional tribal lands. Those that can so afford may wish to retain a pure vein of academically oriented PGE research students, warding off other tendencies. Yet in as traditional a subject as Classics, salvation is found in the postexperience market. It is not that aspiring later-life classicists have the career plans typically connected with a PExpE clientele, for the motivation is essentially intrinsic. Many now studying classics at university, and less conspicuously ancient history, local history, archaeology and a range of other of the liberal humanities and social sciences, do so purely for interest and personal development, though they may become accomplished scholars and published (amateur) researchers in consequence.

The focus of public and official debate about lifelong learning is essentially economic. It concerns national competitiveness, the obsolescence of jobs, and the rate of technological change. The public and official UK position is especially narrow in this respect. It has been criticized for its narrowness even beside the agenda of the European Commission, which encompasses social inclusion or exclusion as well as economic considerations. The transition from student to lifelong learner in fact extends far wider than just into vocational (or, to be more precise in language, occupational) motives and curricula, as analysis of the mature age postexperience clientele of most modern universities shows.

The actual profusion of graduate-level learning opportunities – rather than the archetypal 'graduate programme(s)' with which administrators may still build from institutional perspectives – shows how much the inherited linear essentially pre-experience university has changed. It has been comprehensively invaded by all kinds of postexperience learners taking all kinds of award-bearing programmes. They are no longer cordoned off into zones and activities branded as extramural, continuing, non-award-bearing, non-traditional, industrial, or even liberal and vocational with the special connotations these words have carried. Much of the work is indeed 'extension' or 'extramural' in place or mode of delivery but the new discourse – partnership, work-based, self-directed and mixed mode, even flexible and alternative delivery – suggests a break from the earlier dichotomous condition.

Not that the old dualities do not survive in attitude and assumption. We have noted an institutional inclination (which I have called ill-advised in terms of long-term self-interest) for élite research universities to sustain and recreate a duality. This might steer 'postexperience' work into modern universities in seeking to pull back more pure research PGE work exclusively to the élite. It is hard to see any other stakeholder, least of all the growing army of lifelong learners, warming to this. Even though the friends and alumni of traditional academe may rally to protect this sterile version of 'the diversity of HE' from misguided loyalty to an Alma Mater or a wish to contain public expenditure, the losers will include the research universities themselves.

Stakeholders and purchasers

Most stakeholders in the HE enterprise now employ the rhetoric of lifelong learning. They include a wide variety of employers and their organizations, professional bodies, government departments and agencies as well as politicians, European government as well as national. The societal interest, and the 'communities' that constitute society, are in one sense represented by elected government. In the UK this has certainly adopted 'lifelong' although the official version is, a little idiosyncratically, called lifetime learning. It is also common currency in the broadsheet press. Parents as parents are more concerned with initial end-on than recurrent through-life education, but are probably also increasingly aware of the options and advantages of deferred initial higher education. At PGE and PExpE level parents, as parents, have a less clear interest. Student-learners are shifting towards lifelong from once-only in their perception and consumption of HE opportunities, and moving in the process more into the role of purchasers of HE.

The shift towards lifelong learning alters the balance between stakeholders specifically as purchasers of higher education. The main debate in the mid-1990s is about who pays for initial higher education. The 'continuing education and access community', loosely defined, has sustained a campaign on behalf of the adult part-time student, still essentially at undergraduate and 'first time-second chance' level and status, in Britain. As Britain moved towards adopting an Australian HECS-type (higher eduction contribution scheme) solution to the funding of mass higher education in 1996, HECS itself in Australia lurched into crisis with political change following a federal election and a decision to shift the balance between public (State) and private (via HECS) contributors.

There has been less attention to the funding of postgraduate education in the UK. It has however been seeping into consciousness that the 'fourth year' end-on taught master's that is growing up in several disciplinary domains for home as well as full-fee overseas students is becoming virtually a privately funded selecting and selective finishing year. UK universities are being forced to re-examine their taught master's fee structures and significantly raise the price to reduce internal cross-subvention. Thus one changing dimension of PGE is the appearance of privately funded selectivity which gives social and labour market advantage but has little to do directly with lifelong learning. More negatively still, the impact of a higher-fee regime on self-financing master's students in the PExpE mode could lead to substantial contraction in lifelong learning opportunities. In Australia the 1996 government-induced crisis in higher education includes the prospect of most master's coursework programmes being squeezed out of the State-funded (HECS) category into a full-fee regime within two years. Again, the impact on continuing self-directed master's-level recurrent education for lifelong learning could be substantial.

The general presumption is that initial school education is a right, and that access to initial higher education is also a right, but that some of the benefits of the latter (though not of upper secondary education as it moves to quasi-compulsory status) should be paid for by the student-beneficiary in later life by one means or another. The debate has become one of means rather than principle. For postexperience education, which is increasingly indistinguishable from and part of postgraduate education, the presumption is that the cost should be borne by the learner and/or by another stakeholder-cum-beneficiary, usually an employer. PExpE as a major component of PGE becomes a through-life private or enterprise good to be bought by one or other of these. The government's (and thus the 'community's') interest in lifelong learning is not deemed to extend beyond limited and selective subvention. In the debate over sharing or redistributing the cost of initial (pre-experience, front-end-loaded) education in an ageing society unable to create full employment, let us not lose sight of this other reality: as PGE becomes progressively more co-extensive with PExpE outside the initial master's phase it, like the 'finishing master's', is moving more firmly into the privately funded sector. In other words, the key stakeholders and funders of PGE, the bulk of which is coming to be PExpE, are coming to be not the (Welfare) State but the individual and the private sector. As more and more of HE becomes PExpE, so the level of 'privatization' rises.

Implications

We have noted a central conclusion and implication: that the rise of life-long learning through PGE/PExpE involves a significant system shift towards privately funded HE, as the proportion of postexperience and through-life education of the 'adult majority' rises. The 'typical' pre-experience young student around whom the whole university enterprise and paradigm still tend to be constructed becomes less and less typical. Similarly the 'typical' postgraduate research student who remains the professor's ideal type becomes an ever-diminishing proportion of the research, and more so of the gradu-ate, student population. This has exploded numerically within expanding mass higher education and massively diversified in character and mode of study. The typical PG student is becoming a PExp student. For this student, increasingly, the student role is shared and fragmented within other life roles and distributed through quite long periods of adult life. It is ironic that mass HE is still commonly measured by an APR which reflects but a minority of the HE clientele.

Returning to the temptation to dichotomize universities in the name of diversity as between research and teaching institutions, note first that the 'research enterprise' is becoming much more widespread, dispersed and democratized with the recognition and spread of the 'learning organiza-tion'. We are moving from 'reflective practice' to research on and in prac-tice continuously to inform practice. In this kind of world research and knowledge-creation spill out ever more widely beyond the walls of univer-sities (research-only and other). So does the activity, guidance, support and even formal supervision of PG students in their now increasingly normal part-time student PExpE mode. The very notion of the learning organ-ization draws research into the management and practice of businesses like health, education and welfare as well as industry and commerce. I am familiar with mature age knowledge creators completing part-time work-based doctoral degrees in sectors such as further education and nurs-ing because their employers want to use the knowledge generated in their workplaces as well as to raise the competence as researcher-practitioners of those whom they are supporting in their studies. Engineering and business schools have similar experiences. So do a widening range of other univer-sity science and social science departments.

From the perspective of lifelong learners who have been through an initial higher education universities offer opportunities for a study base and reference point. They enable contact with fellow-scholars, both from within the institution and, like themselves, from outside. They facilitate and provide a structure for systematization and assessment of study. Formal, public, accredited recognition of attainment offers intrinsic and extrinsic rewards. Insofar as their study and research findings are available back in their community or workplace as well as in enhancing their understand-ing, knowledge and skills, they are contributing to a significant new role for the modern university: economic, social, organizational and community development. It is likely that the research agenda for such students, universities and regions will be written, or rewritten, from new perspectives to answer new questions and meet new societal and organizational learning needs (cf. Gibbons *et al.*, 1994).

There are thus implications arising from the reshaping of PGE alongside and increasingly within PExpE for the processes of knowledge creation and its utilization, as well as for skills renewal. The new-look lifelong learner undertaking postgraduate study (part-time, fragmented, maybe modular with an element of employer or other agency commissioning as well as university guidance and assessment) will be generating new kinds of knowledge in new ways from diverse 'laboratories of life'. Again, this will be less common in the pure sciences, though not entirely absent, and more common in the technologies and the social and human sciences. It is likely progressively to re-anchor research and scholarship in the world from which universities draw nurturance and, over time, to create a new basis for their valuing.

Finally, this discussion has naturally concentrated on the changes affecting postgraduate and postexperience education from a lifelong learning perspective. However, many of the conclusions and implications drawn out at the postgraduate level may be applied with considerable if not quite equal force at the undergraduate level. There is an increasing number of postexperience undergraduates. Some are just 'deferrers' taking a year or a few years out, others are 'sustained deferrers' or late developers coming to university perhaps eight or ten years after leaving school. Others again are 'second chance' or 'equity and access' students (the language varies according to time and place) at this or a much older age.

Such students, especially in the subjects and courses to which they tend to gravitate, connect study with life beyond the institution and are often in the knowledge-creation business, albeit in modest and limited ways. Teaching–learning methods, running back into and through the secondary curriculum and beyond, also seek (back-to-basics backlashes notwithstanding) to foster enquiry, investigation, a researching mind, the connection of formal study with 'real life'. The undergraduate thesis is part of the accredited learning experience of students in many systems. It has even become a marketable commodity to at least one enterprising European publisher. Without exaggerating or glamorizing what is often mainly a pragmatic response to loss of resources, masquerading as self-directed learning, it is not too fanciful to see the knowledge-creating (and utilizing) tendencies of postexperience postgraduate students reflected back from undergraduate pre-experience and, especially, from among older postexperience undergraduate students.

The regenerating effects of lifelong PGE and PExpE student learners at the postgraduate level may be increasingly replicated more widely in the institution. This will assist the redefinition and refocusing of the 21st-century university. In this sense postgraduate education, rapidly growing yet still curiously marginalized in teaching discourse and involved mainly, and rather misguidedly, in the battle for élite research status, will increasingly define the future essential character of higher education. PExpE incorporating much of PGE will then be in harmony with lifelong learning, and no longer disjointed.

References

Abrahamsson, K. (1986) *Adult Participation in Swedish Higher Education*. Stockholm: Almqvist and Wiksell International.

Campbell, D. (1984) *The New Majority: Adult Learners in the University*. Edmonton: University of Alberta Press.

Duke, C. (1992) *The Learning University: Towards a New Paradigm?* Buckingham: Open University Press.

Gibbons, M. *et al.* (1994) *The New Production of Knowledge*. London: Sage.

Harris, M. (1996) *Review of Postgraduate Education*. Bristol: Higher Education Funding Council for England.

National Institute of Adult Continuing Education (1995) *An Adult Higher Education*. Leicester: NIACE.

Robertson, D. (1994) *Choosing to Change*. London: Higher Education Quality Council.

Shattock, M. (1996) *The Managerial Implications of the New Priorities*. Paper presented at the Thirteenth OMAHA General Conference, September. Paris: Institute for the Management of Higher Education, Organization for Economic Co-operation and Development.

6

Lifelong Learning and European Universities: Rhetoric or Future Reality?

Barbara Merrill

> Education is a public service constituted to enable an educated and educating public domain – open, just and democratic, respecting and involving the capacities of all citizens. The organization of education can facilitate or frustrate the creation of an open, learning society.
>
> (Ranson, 1994: 113)

Situating lifelong learning: context and issues

Discussions about the need for learning to continue throughout a person's life now centre on the following terms: lifelong learning, learning organizations and a learning society. Adult education language in the past talked about recurrent education, lifelong education and continuing education. Lifelong learning is largely assumed to be about adults learning, residing in the domain of adult and continuing education. Despite the changes in trends in adult education terminology the issues and perspectives essentially remain the same except for a growing interest in vocational education. What is also different is the growing interest of the state and industry in adults learning, albeit in a particular form of adult education. Traditionally adult education, since its origins in the 19th century in Britain, has functioned with minimal support or interference from the state, offering mainly liberal adult education, workers' education and community education. More recently Access course provision, and other initiatives, have widened opportunities and opened the door to undergraduate degree programmes in further and higher education institutions. At postgraduate level the modularization of the curriculum, availability of part-time programmes and the growth of continuing vocational education (CVE) courses offer increasing opportunities for lifelong learning.

European higher education institutions (HEIs) are experiencing a period of expansion and change. Economic, social and political factors are forcing universities to reassess their policies and mission. No longer can HEIs remain isolated 'ivory towers'. Increasingly universities are having to forge partnerships at regional and national level with industry and other groups in the community. Establishing such partnerships creates, potentially, the mechanisms for opening up universities as centres for lifelong learning. Unlike Sweden, for example, formalized educational provision in the UK was and is limited to initial education which 'meant that there never was a feeling that the provision of adult learning facilities was a human right which every government must guarantee' (Bell, 1996: 156). However, there is now a growing concern with lifelong learning, which is not confined to the UK. Economic and demographic changes have forced European governments to consider the merits of lifelong learning almost to the extent of viewing lifelong learning as essential to the survival of society. At the same time with a growing ageing population the time available for learning has expanded. 1996 was also the European Union's year for promoting lifelong learning across Europe, which resulted in a plethora of publications and conferences engaged in debates on lifelong learning in Europe.

This chapter examines lifelong learning from a European perspective. My interests lie in adult education and the access of adults, particularly non-traditional adult students to universities within a comparative European perspective. Working with European colleagues in this field has revealed cultural differences in adult education policies and practices across Europe. The current climate favours lifelong learning, but how are different European countries responding to this in practice within higher education and education in general? To what extent will good intentions of policy be translated into resources and good practice? Will access and opportunities be available to all adults who want to participate in learning or will the policies and structures favour those from élite groups who have already benefited from the education system. This raises equality issues. Lifelong learning needs to be concerned with including those social groups, such as women, 'working-class' people and minority ethnic groups, who have traditionally been excluded from education, particularly higher education. Inevitably an examination of the concept of lifelong learning necessitates a discussion on the nature of education in society. Antikainen *et al.* (1996: 99) situate it in the following way:

> The learning society is a new programme of education reform after the social-democratic project of the 1960s and 1970s, as well as the new liberal or right project of the 1980s.

In examining the nature of lifelong learning within Europe it is important to understand the ideological, political and cultural forces behind the current interest in and promotion of lifelong learning. This process necessitates the clarification of the concept of lifelong learning. However, defining lifelong learning and associated concepts is problematical because the language has become part of a political discourse within Europe. Different groups and organizations, nationally and internationally, claim ideological ownership of a particular concept. In broad terms, the concepts of lifelong learning, lifelong education and learning society imply that learning occurs throughout life. The dichotomy between initial and adult education is broken down as learning is viewed as a process which continues, regardless of age. A closer examination reveals that these concepts are also used in a political sense. They originate largely from policy makers in national governments and organizations such as the United Nations Educational, Scientific and Cultural Organization (UNESCO), the Council of Europe and the Organization for Economic Co-operation and Development (OECD). UNESCO's report, *Learning to Be* (Faure *et al.*, 1972), advocated governments to provide lifelong educational opportunities as a human right while stressing the economic benefits of such a policy. The European Commission's (1995) White Paper, *Towards the Learning Society*, stresses the need for lifelong learning to combat rising unemployment and social exclusion within Europe. Although economic in its intentions (Field, 1996) the European Commission's policy also recognizes the social advantages of lifelong learning:

> There is a need to whet society's appetite for education and training throughout life . . . Everyone must be able to seize their opportunities for improvement in society and for personal fulfilment, irrespective of their social origin and educational background.
>
> (European Commission, 1995: 2, 3)

While appearing liberal, and even radical, the policy of lifelong learning is none the less linked to the economic and political values and needs of a market economy:

> Policy makers such as the European Commission . . . have spoken of a learning society as an ideal state, in which individuals and organisations acquire and apply new skills in order that they keep pace with the changing environment. Usually this view rests largely upon economic grounds, and the learning society is envisaged as a means of sustaining competitivity in the future.
>
> (Field, 1996: 2)

This has also been the case in Britain. The concepts of lifelong learning and the learning society are used to promote a specific economic policy, which was put into practice by the former Department of Employment. In political terms these concepts relate to the needs of the economy and industry through the provision of vocational education. In educational terms, therefore, the policy translates into a narrow view of learning and education for adults. In 1994 the Economic and Social Research Council (ESRC) launched a research initiative entitled 'The Learning Society' which provided scope for adult education research. An examination of its aims and objectives reveals an interpretation of lifelong learning that favours vocational and accredited learning.

The current interest in and emphasis on vocational education stems from a changing economic system within Europe. The structure of employment is being transformed throughout Europe. Individuals can no longer be certain of having a job for life. The pattern of working life may now include periods of short-term contracts, part-time work or unemployment. In common with other European countries, Britain's rapidly changing industry and technology requires different types of skills from its workforce and more frequent upskilling if the economy is to survive and advance. A changing economy also demands workers to be more flexible and multiskilled. Implicit in this is the expectation that individual workers will retrain throughout their working lives. Interest in lifelong learning by governments is closely linked to the economic and technological needs of postindustrial society. A consultation document by the Department for Education and Employment (DfEE), using the term lifetime learning rather than lifelong learning, is dominated by such values:

> Creating a culture of lifetime learning is crucial to sustaining and maintaining our international competitiveness . . . The skill levels of the workforce are vital to our national competitiveness. Rapid technological and organisational change mean that, however good initial education and training is, it must be continuously reinforced by further learning throughout working life. This must happen if skills are to remain relevant, individuals employable, and firms able to adapt and compete.
>
> (Department for Education and Employment, 1995: 3, 4)

Responsibility for learning, however, is firmly placed upon the individual. Recognition of the social benefits of lifelong learning is acknowledged as 'vital' to a 'free and civilised society'. A study commissioned by the German Federal Ministry of Education, Science, Research and Technology to correspond with the EU's year of lifelong learning argues that learning is essential if we are to cope with the rapidly changing economic, technological and social world:

> it will become increasingly necessary for people affected by change to pursue lifelong learning in order to develop consistent comprehension, interpretation and behaviour patterns that will enable them to cope adequately with changing situations and to maintain a stable identity.
>
> (Dohmen, 1996: 4)

In several northern European countries cohesive policies and practices on lifelong learning have been the norm for many years. The tradition of lifelong learning has been embedded, for example, within the Swedish culture since the 19th century through folk high schools and study circles. About 50 per cent of the adult population engage in some form of adult education each year. Abrahamsson (1996: 170) explains that the idea behind the policies of the 1970s in Sweden 'was to promote adult learning in a lifelong perspective by alternating periods of work, education and leisure activities'. In southern European countries, such as Spain and Italy, adult education is linked more closely to social movements and the idea of education for social transformation rather than state-led policies and initiatives.

Lifelong learning, learning organization and the learning society: bridging concepts

Conceptually, lifelong learning is related to two other concepts, learning organizations and learning society. Lifelong learning can only be a reality in a society whose educational values and structure enables its members to return to learn at different ages throughout their lives and where to do so is regarded as the norm. In Britain, and many other European countries, the 'front-end' model of education still prevails. Education for life is provided by initial education. Schuller is critical of such an approach:

> A primary concern in the work has been with access to learning opportunities throughout the lifecourse, powered by a belief that the traditional identification of education with schooling and pre-adulthood is both inefficient and inequitable.
>
> (Schuller, 1996: 186)

Within the UK and many other European countries a dual system of initial and adult education or andragogy has developed with little relationship between the two sectors. The term adragogy is referred to here in a broad and general sense to mean the teaching and learning of adults. Andragogy is used by Knowles (1970, 1984) and other adult educators to make a distinction between the processes of learning by adults from those of children in initial education. Within this is an assumption that adults have different learning needs to children.

Drawing on the work of Giddens (1991), Schuller questions the need for the dividing of life into three distinct cycles: schooling, work and retirement, and instead calls for 'a more pluralistic modelling of the lifecourse' (1996: 187). Lifelong learning and the creation of a learning society requires a fundamental shift in the attitudes, values and culture of a society. In Scandinavian countries the boundaries between initial and adult education are less distinct. For example, in Denmark 'because of high participation rates among adults in all forms of education it is considered "normal" for adults to study' (Cooke, 1995: 88). In such a learning society the concepts, mature student and non-traditional adult student become less significant than in Belgium, Spain and the UK, for example.

The attitudes of many adult learners are still shaped by the traditional front-end model rather than the lifelong view of education. A study of mature undergraduate students at Warwick revealed that they perceived the opportunity to return to learn and study for a degree as 'completing their education' (Merrill, 1996). The adults shared a narrow view of education: studying is associated with gaining specific qualifications. For many, postgraduate study was viewed as being outside of their domain, 'something younger students did'. Implicit in this model is the assumption that there is a finality to education. However, as they immersed themselves in the learning process and culture and as their degree studies neared completion, attitudes changed as several contemplated participating in postgraduate degrees or postgraduate professional studies.

Lifelong learning is frequently discussed as an aspect of adult education rather than applying to the whole spectrum of education. Implicit in this assumption is the notion that educational innovation and change is only required in relation to adults but not schools. Faure *et al.* in the UNESCO report, *Learning to Be* (1972), argued that lifelong learning should be used as a strategy to reform all levels of education. Conceptualizing lifelong learning is problematical because, as Knapper and Cropley (1985: 15) point out, 'the term is used in various ways by different writers'. Confusion also arises because lifelong learning is often used interchangeably with lifelong education. Knapper and Cropley offer a general interpretation:

> One way of looking at lifelong education is to regard it as a rationalisation of a number of existing trends in contemporary educational theory and practice . . . At least to some extent, lifelong education can also be thought of as encompassing a philosophy or model of education. In this sense, the term is used to refer to: (a) a set of goals for education; (b) a set of procedures for realising these goals; (c) a set of values.
>
> (Knapper and Cropley, 1985: 17)

Drawing on the work of the European Lifelong Learning Initiative (ELLI) Longworth and Davies present a definition which centres on the individual learner:

> Lifelong learning is the development of human potential through a continuously supportive process which stimulates and empowers individuals to acquire all the knowledge, values, skills and understanding they will require throughout their lifetimes and to apply them with confidence, creativity and enjoyment in all roles, circumstances, and environments.
>
> (Longworth and Davies, 1996: 22).

Lifelong learning implies that learning not only takes place throughout a person's life but also in a variety of learning situations, both formal and informal:

> the idea inherent in the concept of lifelong learning, namely that links between educational processes and everyday practice, between formal and informal learning.
>
> (Alheit, 1996: 4)

Literature in the field overwhelmingly refers to learning for adults in formal educational or work environments on accredited courses. Learning which takes place informally within leisure, family and community also needs to be taken into account within the context of lifelong learning. For adults in formal education the dialectics between their life experiences and theory are an important part of their learning process. Brookfield (1994) points out that in the USA adult educators in community colleges have promoted the inclusion of life experiences within formal learning. In some areas of adult education, particularly in the UK, there is a growing recognition of the value of informal learning through Accreditation of Prior Experiential Learning (APEL). A learners' prior learning in the workplace or home is documented as a portfolio in which the student outlines their learning processes in a critical and reflective way. APEL is used either as advanced standing to gain exemption from part of a programme or is accredited as part of a course. In some UK university departments, having a first degree is not always a prerequisite for entry onto a master's programme, particularly those that are vocational in content. In continuing education, for example, several years of work experience in the field and the ability to work at postgraduate level may be accepted as entrance requirements. The acknowledgement that learning taking place outside an educational institution is valid is an important step forward. However, it also appears to be contradictory in that informal learning is subject to assessment and accreditation and hence institutionalizes informal learning. Lifelong education calls for a synthesis between formal and informal learning (Brookfield, 1994; Dohmen, 1996).

The policy and practice of lifelong learning will only succeed within a learning society if both complement each other. Lifelong learning requires a fundamental shift in the values and practices, not only of educational institutions but society as a whole if adults are to be given the right to learn throughout their lives. Education is no longer viewed as a once only activity confined to young people in schools. All institutions, not just educational ones, therefore, need to become learning organizations within a learning society.

Learning organizations are primarily associated with business organizations and the 'empowerment of the workforce and, through this, the need for a complete reorientation of a company's total strategy towards learning as a means of doing this' (Longworth and Davies, 1996: 74). It should be noted, however, that empowerment is antithetical to the philosophy and ideology of many managers. In Britain, Ford and Rover are cited as examples of learning organizations. The learning organization concept has been most fully developed by organizational theorists. Charles Handy, for example, defines a learning organization as:

organizations which encourage the wheel of learning, which relish curiosity, questions and ideas, which allow space for experiment and for reflection, which forgive mistakes and promote self-confidence, these are learning organizations.

(Handy, 1990: 199)

Within the last few years the concept has been applied to the context of universities (Duke, 1992; Barnett, 1996). Duke (1992: xii) asks, 'how far universities may, as key teaching and learning institutions, practically speaking adopt the new paradigm of lifelong learning?' This relates to questions of the accessibility and flexibility of universities in their mission and practice for adult learners.

A learning society requires a culture of learning from the cradle to the grave. In such a society people would internalize values that motivate and provide both formal and informal learning. For Barnett:

> The learning society is, by definition, a society which takes learning seriously. Its members come to understand that learning is not fully accomplished by any age or biographical point but is a responsibility to be fulfilled more or less continually through the lifespan.
>
> (Barnett, 1996: 14)

Husen (1974), an early advocate, identifies a number of prerequisites for a learning society:

- people have an opportunity for lifelong learning,
- formal education extends to the whole age group,
- informal education – such as adult studies – is in a central position and self-study is widely accepted,
- other institutions and organizations support education which in its turn depends on them.

> (Husen, in Antikainen *et al.*, 1996: 10)

Critics argue that the notion of a learning society is a Utopian or mythical one (Hughes and Tight, 1995). For others (Duke, 1992; Ranson, 1994) the development of a learning society is a necessity if democratic, postindustrialist societies are to survive. Visions of what a learning society should be vary between the economic/market forces perspective at one end of the spectrum to the social equality/citizenship perspective at the other.

Lifelong learning and universities: a contradiction or a possibility?

European universities have traditionally been élite institutions (Scott, 1984; Duke, 1992). However, British universities, for example, also have a history of promoting adult education through extramural departments and, more recently, continuing education departments. Until recently liberal adult education was the mainstay of university adult education. External policy changes have resulted in such courses being transformed into accredited courses. The past 10 years have witnessed an expansion in British higher education to the point whereby the word mass, rather than élite, is applied to universities (Trow, 1989). Not only has there been a growth in the number of 18-year-olds entering the system but also in the number of adult students. At postgraduate level adult students are most noticeable on part-time programmes. In 1993–4 62.9 per cent of students studying on a part-time research programme were adults over the age of 25, and on taught part-time courses adults constituted 90.3 per cent. Fewer adults study by the full-time mode at postgraduate level: 37 per cent on research degrees and 9.3 per cent on taught courses (Higher Education Statistics Agency, 1994). British universities are characterized by institutional variations in terms of embracing lifelong learning. However, it is easier for adults, particularly non-traditional adult students, to enter higher education in the UK than in some European countries such as Spain and Belgium. (By non-traditional adult student I mean those adults who may lack the traditional entry qualifications, who have been out of the education system for a number of years and/or who are members of under-represented social groups in universities such as 'working-class' people, women and minority ethnic groups.) Currently a period of consolidation in the UK is preventing further growth although there is still scope for expansion in the area of part-time study.

To become centres for lifelong learning, universities must adapt and change. The ivory tower needs to be penetrated, disintegrated and replaced with a mission that is more community oriented. Longworth and Davies outline their vision of a lifelong learning university:

> Instead of an institution for educating an elite of highly intelligent undergraduates and researchers, it becomes a universal university, open to all irrespective of background, qualification, age, or subject. If we believe in the power and the value of learning, and if we can create the sort of society in which learning is natural and pervasive, that is the way the traditional university must go.
>
> (Longworth and Davies, 1996: 107)

Changes in the state funding of universities have, to a certain extent, forced institutions to reassess their role and purpose in society:

> Universities are thus beginning to learn that to survive they must function as much more open systems, with regular traffic permeating throughout all the porous membrane which has replaced the ivory walls.
>
> (Duke, 1996: 76)

Continuing education has a key role to play in facilitating lifelong learning within universities. For Duke, 'continuing education is at the cutting edge as universities become more fully "learning organisations"' (1992: 4).

Lifelong graduate learning: is it applicable to European universities?

Over the past four years I have been working closely with continuing education colleagues in universities in Belgium, Germany, Spain and Sweden (Peter Alheit, University of Bremen; Etienne Bourgeois, University of

Louvain; Agnieszka Bron, University of Stockholm; and Ramon Flecha, University of Barcelona). The focus of this work has been a comparative study on the access of adults to universities. Learning about each other's education system, and in particular the higher education system, was not always an easy task because of cultural variations in education structures and cultural differences in the interpretation of key concepts such as 'access' and 'non-traditional adult student'. One of the problems is that there is no common definition of what age a person becomes an adult student. In Britain at postgraduate level students are classified as adult if they are aged 25 years and over, but in Belgium there is no such definition. This section looks at the extent to which lifelong learning at university level is a reality for adults in these four countries and the UK. This raises the question how accessible are universities to adults, particularly non-traditional adults? Is there uniformity or discrepancy in policy and practice across Europe?

Sweden

Sweden is often cited as the epitome of a learning society as adult education provision is widespread at all levels. In terms of higher education specifically, 'Sweden is a unique country in Europe, because it was here where the doors of higher education institutions became open for adults' (Agelii and Bron, 1997: 1). Education is highly valued and not considered as something that ends with schooling. The aims of Swedish adult education are to 'promote greater equality and justice, . . . contribute towards the development of a democratic society' and 'to help achieve full employment'(Abrahamsson, 1996: 172). Abrahamsson maintains that equity issues have been at the heart of governmental adult education access policy as 'a high level of knowledge and education benefits both the individual and society' (1996: 175). The concern for equality is also reinforced by the fact that non-university adult education, such as study circles, has its roots in popular movements.

Adult education policy has not remained static. Rubenson (1993) identifies five distinct policy periods between 1960 and the early 1990s of significance for higher education. The act established the practice of recurrent education which encouraged movement between work, leisure and education. Greater interaction between higher education and working life was established through the introduction of vocational courses. A wider range of courses were introduced in the day time and evening, particularly short courses, which attracted large numbers of adults. Abrahamsson (1986) referred to this process as the 'adultification' of higher education.

Agelii and Bron maintain that 'the "adultification" of Swedish students is not only the result of access policy, but also of the law of 1965 allowing adults educational leave without losing their job' (1997: 3). This included postgraduate study. Together with the introduction of state grants and loans, these laws removed the economic constraints for adults wanting to study enabling those with a first degree to return to university for postgraduate or vocational courses. The policy priority enjoyed by adult education was eroded by a new conservative–liberal government in the early 1990s. Financial cutbacks were announced in 1992. Public protests managed to reduce the amount of money to be cut from the adult education budget but it became clear that the education of young people was the focus of attention for the new government (Abrahamsson, 1996; Bron, 1996). In relation to higher education, Bron maintains that recent policy has limited access to certain groups:

> Higher education policy for the 90s in Sweden differs again from the European policies by slightly closing its open access system for non-traditional students and giving more opportunity for traditional ones by creating more places for them.
>
> (Bron, 1994: 10)

On the other hand, Abrahamsson (1996) argues that policy changes have led to a growth in adult education, at least in relation to employment training schemes. 'In spite of the various efforts to limit the role of adult education it has, paradoxically enough, expanded significantly in the last year' (Abrahamsson, 1996: 177).

An important outcome of legislative changes in the 1990s has been the decentralization of higher education. Each university and department now has their own admission requirements, the number of single courses has increased but study programmes will disappear. Adult access will be dependent upon the policy of individual universities. Potentially this could enable universities to be more flexible in terms of admissions policies for adults. Certainly in relation to non-university adult education Abrahamsson (1996: 181) has noted that 'the strong and bureaucratic state intervention is withdrawing, thereby opening up new options at the local and community-oriented level'. At the same time the Government has axed an important entry route for adults. Before 1993, adults who were aged 25 years and over and who had four years' work experience could apply to university. Entering higher education as an adult is now dependent upon passing a university test. In reflecting upon the recent policy changes, Abrahamsson summarizes that:

> It is not easy to anticipate the impact of these new conditions on the notion of a lifelong education society. From a Swedish perspective, it is possible to conclude, however, that the 'grand plan' of a coherent strategy of recurrent education has seen its best days ... Today there is more focus on finding matching areas connecting individual needs and sets of incentives to stimulate and facilitate active adult learning projects. With some oversimplification, it is possible to conclude that Sweden is taking a big step from recurrent education to recurrent learning and is thereby getting closer to the concept of lifelong learning used in many UNESCO settings.
>
> (Abrahamsson, 1996: 181)

Despite the policy changes, Sweden has an ethos and climate that encourages adults to participate in university adult education and adult education generally. Most importantly, the state provides the opportunities and structures to do so. Belgium and Spain, in contrast, are more closed in relation to adult access to universities, while the UK lies between the two models.

Belgium

Understanding the Belgian system is problematical because of the cultural division between the Flemish-speaking and French-speaking communities (there is also a small German-speaking community). Research data generally refers to either the Flemish or the French community rather than a unified whole. Higher education in Belgium has a low participation rate of adults because it is difficult to enter without the appropriate school qualification; the DAAES. As a result, the lack of alternative access routes for adults at undergraduate level therefore means that there are very few opportunities for adults to study at postgraduate level:

> on the other hand, it is highly selective in the sense that it is quite difficult for people without the formal qualifications required ['non-traditional' students] to gain access, especially to non-university long-cycle and university education.
>
> (Bourgeois and Guyot, 1995: 66)

Consequently the numbers of adults in universities is small: those over the age of 30 in 1990–1 constituted 8.2 per cent of the student population. Unlike the UK, part-time postgraduate courses are not available. Gaining postgraduate qualifications are associated with entry to an academic career. Teaching posts in universities are not open to those over the age of 30. Studying at this level is viewed as occurring in a linear fashion without breaks between undergraduate and postgraduate levels thus offering little possibility for lifelong learning.

The Belgian degree programme is divided into three levels or cycles; the *candidatures* (two to three years), the *licence* (two to three years) and the *diplomes d'études approfondies ou spécialisées* (one year). Part of level two and level three encompasses postgraduate work. More adults can be found in the non-university higher education sector, mostly on short-cycle programmes despite being three years in length. Non-university higher education offers vocational and professional programmes in areas such as agriculture, education and social work. Qualifications gained in this sector also provide a route into university through a bridging admissions policy. In this situation a non-university higher education degree is used to gain entry to the second university cycle, the *licence*. Adult students who opt for this route may have to take additional courses at the university from which students could continue to graduate studies. However, few adults choose this pathway.

Compared to Sweden and the UK, the Belgian system is very difficult to access for adults who do not possess the formal qualifications. Those who

enter are mostly traditional adult students who have prior educational qualifications and who enter university for vocational or professional updating:

> In conclusion, the Belgian higher education system is relatively open
> to the extent that there is virtually no selection of students at entry
> other than formal qualifications.
>
> (Bourgeois and Guyot, 1995: 75)

Although the possibilities for lifelong education are limited through the university system other channels for learning are open. Lifelong learning provision has traditionally been outside of the formal education system. Labour
organizations in particular have been key providers offering mostly non-
accredited courses with the aim of furthering the social and cultural development of workers. However, continuing vocational courses run by private
and state organizations are becoming a growing sector. Such programmes,
following the pattern of other European countries, are in response to an
increasing rate of unemployment and a deteriorating economic situation.

Spain

In Spain the historical context has determined the nature of adult education. The current system is largely a mixture of policies from the period
of the Franco dictatorship and those from the democratic era of 1978
onwards. After the transition to democracy there was an interest in popular
participation:

> One of the subjects which rapidly gained importance was adult educa-
> tion; different proposals were made on how to solve the problem of
> illiteracy, encourage practical adult education and link non-formal
> educational activity with the objectives of the social and cultural involve-
> ment of the people.
>
> (Lopez, 1992: 2)

The government of the education system is divided between the state, the
Autonomous Communities and the universities. Lifelong learning opportunities for adults in universities are limited. Adults consisted of only 12 per
cent of the higher education student population in 1987–8 (Osborne, 1995)
but this is still higher than Belgium. The priority for adult education in
Spain is adult basic education (literacy and numeracy). The substantial
expansion of universities since the late 1970s has not provided an increase
in learning opportunities for adults.

It is possible for adults to enter postgraduate programmes after several
years' break from studying but the possession of a first degree is essential.
Master's programmes are not common in Spain (the first degree is five to
six years in duration). Recent developments place greater significance and
priority on vocational programmes and CVE short courses than on academic ones. A small amount of postgraduate teaching occurs in Official
Adult Education Schools:

In its formal adaptation, it [Official Adult Education Schools] usually embraces six steps: literacy, new readers, certificate, undergraduate, graduate and postgraduate . . . Usually the adult education centres also have activities of socio-cultural awareness.

(Flecha, 1992: 194)

The curriculum of both the Popular and Peasant Schools is similar but their historical origins are political: they developed in opposition to the educational structure of the dictatorship.

A recent development has been the introduction of laws on adult education by some of the Autonomous Communities such as Andalusia, Galicia and Catalonia. The laws have been developed in conjunction with the Federation of Associations of Adult Education in Spain (FAEA) and in consultation with local people. One effect of the law in Catalonia, for example, has been the promotion of community development:

The main emphasis on adult education is moved from the school system to educational concerns in community development. Thus, this law is not a regulation of formal education, but a common orientation to different kinds of adult education.

(Flecha, 1992: 197)

In Spain the adult education movement was strongly influenced initially by the theory and practice of Freire and, since the 1980s, Habermas and the theory of communicative action and transformative perspectives. The priority for adult education in Spain, therefore, is adult basic education to tackle the high rate of illiteracy and unemployment through community development rather than access to higher education, particularly postgraduate education.

Germany

Higher education students in Germany tend to be on the whole older than in other European countries because of the length of the degree studies (seven years). In 1991, for example, 35 per cent of students in western Germany were aged 26 and over (Davies and Reisinger, 1995).

The academic tradition remains strong in German universities. However, recent pressure from industry and a changing economic situation has resulted in policy changes in 1992 allowing limited study at universities. Opposition to widening access through the acceptance of vocational and professional qualifications has been voiced by the universities who fear a decline in quality and standards. Concern about quality echoes the situation regarding widening access in the UK in some quarters. Postgraduate distance learning courses are expanding within Germany mostly within the field of vocational education. For example, the German Academic Society for Adult Continuing Education (AKAD) have developed integrated distance learning models rooted in the self-directed learning of adults in vocational education. All are short-cycle programmes on business management, business-related information technology and industrial engineering. Entry is possible for adults lacking appropriate qualifications provided they complete and pass a foundation course. Teaching approaches are student-centred but assessment is by examination. However, students are encouraged to become independent and autonomous learners. The distance learning courses rely heavily on the adults having access to various forms of media and technology which may exclude certain groups. AKAD's objective is to promote closer cooperation between industrial firms and educational institutions. This they view as essential for lifelong learning within a learning society.

The University of Bremen has initiated a transnational distance learning European MBA programme aimed at managers. Six European universities participate in the project. The distance learning element is supplemented by video-conferencing, fax, e-mail and telephone and are regarded as an essential component for lifelong learning and the trend towards a European Information Society.

In contrast Roskilde University in Denmark has launched an adult education open university programme in Continuing Education at master's level. The programme is part-time (three years) and aimed at adult students who have some academic and/or professional experience. The aim of the programme is to 'connect practical milieus with academic research' (Olesen, 1996). Most students are professionals in education, health education or social work and many are women. The adults study in self-managing work groups and are encouraged to reflect critically upon their professional practices.

Britain

Britain is not as far along the road to a learning society as Sweden. Educational and class inequalities ensure that participation in adult education is mostly by those in the higher socio-economic groups. However, since the 1980s a number of factors have interacted to facilitate the widening of access for adults to higher education, primarily at undergraduate level, creating greater opportunities at postgraduate level. Importantly:

> The urge to change higher education admissions and curriculum practices in the quest for wider access comes to some extent from within higher education itself, where there have always been those who, even before Robbins, accepted the principle that education at any level should be available to all those who can benefit from it. It has seemed to them to be a simple, incontrovertible question of social justice.
>
> (Parry and Wake, 1990: 1)

'Adultification' in British universities is limited to certain institutions and departments even at postgraduate level. The Open University has for a number of years provided an important, flexible alternative to traditional universities for adult learners wanting to study at postgraduate level, particularly those in full-time employment.

The development of lifelong learning at postgraduate level has been more visible in relation to CVE short courses. As a research-led university Warwick makes an interesting study as it has committed itself to promoting lifelong learning opportunities for non-traditional adult students and links with the local community. However, the notion of a learning university has not penetrated all corners of the University, as the 'academic tribalism' (Becher, 1989) enacted by some departments encompasses resistance to widening access for local adults. The participation rate of adults on master's programmes, for example, varies between departments and faculties. Most adults are found on social science master's programmes, particularly sociology and continuing education. Adults are largely absent in the sciences such as biological sciences. This stems partly from the attitudes, beliefs and culture surrounding scientific knowledge.

Continuing vocational education has become a growth industry in many universities. Warwick is no exception, offering a variety of short CVE courses, often in partnership with external organizations. Accessibility, however, becomes problematical when courses are delivered in conjunction with, for example, employers, as the opportunity for lifelong learning is restricted to employees of those companies. Biological sciences at Warwick provides an updating course for the Institute of Environmental Health Officers, which is recognized by a professional body. Although it is a specialized CVE course the delivery is flexible. The Department also offers a programme designed in partnership with a local water authority. It is non-assessed but restricted to employees of the company.

The Local Government Centre works with a research consortium of local governments to research recent changes in local government. Short courses are available to assist managers in local government to manage change. This is an example of a research-led CVE course, applying the research findings to an organizational setting. In contrast the Warwick Manufacturing Group directs a programme to help managers of small businesses to adopt the best practices with the aim of contributing directly to regional economic regeneration. This course is relatively open within a specific client group as no prior educational qualifications are required. A broader CVE programme is delivered by the Language Centre for both members of the public and businesses. Most of these courses are accredited. At present a flexible and accessible vocational business language centre is being developed. The final example of a CVE programme at Warwick is the MBA offered by the Business School. A recent development to the programme is to provide a knowledge update system for those who have completed an MBA whereby adults can tap into seminars, latest research and research bulletins. It is an important model of lifelong learning as it links adult students into the University on a long-term basis and reflects the current policy of the European Union expressed in the Leonardo programme.

The openness of CVE courses depends upon the extent to which a university has exploited the model of modular master's programmes, enabling individual learners to study particular modules. Within CVE there is the dilemma of having to respond to market needs at the expense of individual learners' needs. However, with increasing employment insecurity there is a greater need for professionals to assume responsibility for their own learning. In such an economic situation transferable and generic skills become important.

The expansion of European universities in the 1980s and early 1990s has now largely stopped and many countries are now facing a period of consolidation. Although universities have opened their doors to more students, both young people and adults, they continue to be the preserve of the young and those from the higher socio-economic groups. In most countries and most institutions the number of adult students in higher education remains low, particularly at postgraduate level and restricted largely to the 'low status' universities and non-university higher education institutions. In all the European countries discussed economic imperatives are resulting in demands from industry and governments for an increase in vocational programmes and work-based learning. However, most universities in Europe have moved only slightly on the compass towards becoming learning organizations providing lifelong learning opportunities for both young students and adults.

Lifelong learning: visions, ideology and futures

An analysis of the role of higher education as a mechanism for and provider of lifelong learning needs to be examined within the wider macro context of society. The image of what an ideal learning society should be varies according to different ideological perspectives. The ideological differences pivot on issues related to equality, the nature of a curriculum and the construction of knowledge for lifelong learning, formal and self-directed learning, individualism versus collectivism and the outcomes for the individual, group and society. Underlying these are political, economic, social and moral arguments. This raises the question of what type of social order is necessary for the Europe of the future? Barnett, for example, situates the discourse within the individualistic/society axis:

> At one extreme, 'the learning society' can stand for a society in which its individuals took learning seriously, understood that they had responsibilities for their own continuing learning through their life-span so that they might be able to contribute continually and effectively to the productivity of society and its capacity to maintain or enhance its place in the global competitive environment. This sense of the learning society is not to be downvalued; but it is a limited notion. At the

other extreme, 'the learning society' can stand for a society which is intent on developing its understanding at the societal level. This might mean: . . . That society can, in a meaningful sense, come to understand itself and even critique itself.

(Barnett, 1996: 20, 21)

Education as a marketplace with learners as consumers and individuals choosing and taking responsibility for their own learning is now a dominant view within education, stemming from the ideology of the new right. Within this framework:

A 'learning society' so defined is a society which systematically increases the skills and knowledge of all its members to exploit technological innovation and so gain a competitive edge for their services in fast-changing global markets.

(Ainley, 1994: 155)

The notion of collectivity and society has been fragmented and subsumed to the needs of the individual. In contrast, educationalists such as Ranson (1994) call for the reassertion of a democratic society. Ranson advocates the social and civic benefits which lifelong learning can bring to a democratic society:

The challenge for the time is to create a new moral and political order that responds to the needs of a society undergoing a historic transition . . . The creation of a moral and political order that expresses and enables an active citizenship within the public domain is the challenge of the modern era. The task is to regenerate or constitute more effectively than ever before a public – an educated public – that has the capacity to participate actively as citizens in the shaping of a learning society and polity.

(Ranson, 1994: 105)

The concept of citizenship and a specific political structure are central to Ranson's vision of creating both a learning and democratic society. In such a society individuals and groups would be actively involved in shaping the future of their communities:

The conditions for a learning society are, in the last resort, essentially political, requiring the creation of a polity that provides the fundamental conditions for individuals and the communities in which they live to develop their capacities and to flourish . . . The connection between individual well-being and the vitality of the moral community is made in the public domain of the polity: the good [learning] person is a good citizen. Without political structures that bring together communities of discourse, the conditions for learning will not exist . . . The preconditions of the good polity are justice, participative democracy and public action.

(Ranson, 1994: 110, 111)

In order to achieve the goal of a learning society Ranson (1994: 113) argues for the reform of government and education, outlining his strategies in terms of 'organizing principles for democratic governance'. Implicit in this approach to lifelong learning are notions of equality and equal participation in society. While Ranson offers a critique of class in the current educational structure there is little explanation of how citizens in a learning democracy will overcome the structural inequalities of class, gender and race.

More recently Alheit (1996) put forward his innovative and interesting Utopian vision of lifelong learning at a European conference. Alheit himself refers to his ideas as 'a provocative proposal'. The core of his thesis calls for 'a progression from a labour society to a learning society' (Alheit, 1996: 3). It is the recognition of a European society in transition; a longer lifespan, mass unemployment and shorter working hours. For Alheit these are critical questions, which need to be addressed:

> What is needed, instead, is a European debate on 'macrosolutions'. This would be an appropriate way to tackle the pending educational reforms, and a necessary step given the severe socio-political problems that exist.
>
> (Alheit, 1996: 4)

Three key ideas dominate Alheit's debate:

- the concept of a second, non-commodified sector of activity;
- the idea of a citizen's wage for socially essential activities;
- the idea inherent in the concept lifelong learning, namely that links be established between educational processes and everyday practice, between formal learning and informal learning.

> (Alheit, 1996: 4)

The 'socially essential activities' would include 'social, environmental and cultural services' and participation in lifelong learning initiatives such as self-learning centres or study groups. Involvement in the civil sector (a two-year period) would be a citizen's duty, financed by a 'citizen's pay'. The outcomes of this model of a learning society would be the development and rediscovery of public-spiritedness and communitarianism in which people 'learn how to learn'. Alheit (1996: 4) also proposes that those previously excluded or alienated from educational activity would participate in 'self-organised educational practice'. What role higher education and other educational institutions would play is not discussed.

Higher education and lifelong learning: a conclusion

Establishing a system of lifelong learning in which everyone has the entitlement and right to participate in learning, both formally and informally, is not an easy process. Lifelong learning can only be a reality within a learning society. To achieve lifelong learning, society has to be transformed by challenging inequalities and values on education. The process of lifelong learning raises fundamental questions about what being a citizen means and what type of society is desirable. Universities in Europe have always been perceived as centres of knowledge in society. However, the transmission of such knowledge has been the preserve of a privileged, élite minority. What indications are there that universities are changing and becoming learning organizations? Field argues that 'the university needs to reappraise its traditional role and purpose' (1996: 10), while Duke maintains that as learning organizations develop:

> we may look to the university to provide some leadership, by examples as well as by precept, in the quest to evolve political, social and civic forms which will move us closer to being learning societies.
>
> (Duke, 1996: 76)

With expansion European universities have undergone changes and to a certain, but limited extent, the doors have been opened to a more diverse group of young and adult students. The discussion of higher education systems in Europe in this chapter reveals the diversity of practices and policy in relation to access and learning opportunities for the socially excluded. Those in university continuing education have an important role to play in moving universities towards becoming centres for lifelong learning for a learning society.

In discussing the structures, ideologies and strategies required for lifelong learning it is easy to forget the learner. University life, in those institutions which have opened up, albeit modestly, does have a profound effect upon the lives of adult students (Pascall and Cox, 1993; Merrill, 1996). Many become 'hooked' on learning, their lives transformed by access to knowledge. The value, enthusiasm and the enjoyment of learning as experienced by mature students demonstrates the importance of the need to move towards a situation whereby lifelong learning becomes a reality to all, not just to a minority:

References

Abrahamsson, K. (1986) *Adult Participation in Swedish HE*. Stockholm: Almqvist and Wiksell International.

Abrahamsson, K. (1996) Concepts, organization and current trends of lifelong education in Sweden, in R. Edwards, A. Hanson and P. Raggatt (eds) *Boundaries of Adult Learning*. London: Routledge/Open University Press.

Agelii, K. and Bron, A. (1997) Mature Students' Access to Stockholm University, in S. Hill, *Access, Equity, Participation and Organizational Change*. European Society for Research on the Education of Adults (ESREA), Leamington Spa. Department of Continuing Education, University of Warwick and the Université Catholique de Lourain.

Ainley, P. (1994) *Degrees of Difference: Higher Education in the 1990s.* London: Lawrence and Wishart.

Alheit, P. (1996) A provocative proposal: from labour society to learning society, *Lifelong Learning in Europe,* 2, 3–5.

Antikainen, A., Houtonen, J., Kauppila, J. and Huotelin, H. (1996) *Living in a Learning Society.* London: Falmer Press.

Barnett, R. (1996) Situating the learning university, *International Journal of University Adult Education,* XXXV(1), April, 13–27.

Becher, T. (1989) *Academic Tribes.* Buckingham: SRHE/Open University Press.

Bell, B. (1996) The British adult education, in R. Edwards, A. Hanson and P. Raggatt (eds) *Boundaries of Adult Learning.* London: Routledge/Open University.

Bourgeois, E. and Guyot, J. L. (1995) Belgium, in P. Davies (ed.) *Adults in Higher Education: International Perspectives in Access and Participation.* London: Jessica Kingsley.

Bron, A. (1996) *Definition of Non-Traditional Adult Student in the Swedish Context.* Stockholm: University of Stockholm.

Brookfield, S. (1994) Lifelong education in the US, *International Journal of University Education,* 1, April, 23–48.

Cooke, A. (1995) Denmark, in P. Davies (ed.) *Adults In Higher Education: International Perspectives in Access and Participation.* London: Jessica Kingsley.

Davies, P. and Reisinger, E. (1995) Germany, in P. Davies (ed.) *Adults in Higher Education: International Perspectives in Access and Participation.* London: Jessica Kingsley.

Department for Education and Employment (1995) *Lifetime Learning – a Consultation Document.* London: HMSO.

Dohmen, G. (1996) *Lifelong Learning: Guidelines for a Modern Education Policy.* Bonn: Federal Ministry of Education, Science, Research and Technology.

Duke, C. (1992) *The Learning University: Towards a New Paradigm.* Buckingham: SRHE/Open University Press.

Duke, C. (1996) What has the 'learning university' learned? *International Journal of University Adult Education,* XXXV(1), April, 74–7.

European Commission (1995) *Towards the Learning Society.* White Paper on Education and Training. Brussels: EC.

Faure, E. *et al.* (1972) *Learning to Be: The World of Education Today and Tomorrow.* Paris: UNESCO.

Field, J. (1996) Universities and the Learning Society, *International Journal of University Adult Education,* XXXV(1), April, 1–12.

Flecha, R. (1992) Spain, in P. Jarvis (ed.) *Perspectives on Adult Education and Training in Europe.* Leicester: National Institute of Adult Continuing Education.

Giddens, A. (1991) *Modernity and Self-Identity.* Cambridge: Polity Press.

Handy, C. (1990) *Inside Organizations.* London: BBC Books.

Hughes, C. and Tight, M. (1995) The myth of the learning society, *British Journal of Educational Studies,* 43(3), 290–304.

Husen, T. (1974) *The Learning Society.* London: Methuen.

Knapper, C. and Cropley, A. (1985) *Lifelong Learning and Higher Education.* London: Croom Helm.

Longworth, N. and Davies, W. K. (1996) *Lifelong Learning.* London: Kogan Page.

Lopez, V. A. (1992) Popular universities in Spain, *International Journal of University Adult Education,* XXXI(2), July, 1–7.

Merrill, B. (1996) 'Gender, Change and Identity: Mature Women Students in Universities'. Unpublished PhD thesis.

Olesen, H. S. (1996) *Adult Education Open University – New Agendas for Lifelong Learning*. Paper presented at Conference on Lifelong Learning, Bremen.

Osborne, M. (1995) Spain, in P. Davies (ed.) *Adults in Higher Education: International Perspectives in Access and Participation*. London: Jessica Kingsley.

Parry, G. and Wake, C. (1990) *Access and Alternative Futures for High Education*. London: Hodder and Stoughton.

Pascall, G. and Cox, R. (1993) *Women Returning to HE*. Buckingham: SRHE/Open University Press.

Ranson, S. (1994) *Towards the Learning Society*. London: Cassell.

Rubenson, K. (1993) Adult education policy in Sweden, 1967–91, in R. Edwards, S. Sieminski and D. Zeldin (eds) *Adult Learners, Education and Training*. London: Routledge/Open University Press.

Schuller, T. (1996) Modelling the lifecourse: age, time and education, in S. Papaioannou, P. Alheit, J. F. Lauridsen and H. S. Olesen (eds) *Community, Education and Social Change*. Roskilde: Roskilde University.

Scott, P. (1984) *The Crisis of the University*. Beckenham: Croom Helm.

Trow, M. (1989) The Robbins trap: British attitudes and the limits of expansion, *Higher Education Quarterly*, 43(1), 55–75.

7

Postgraduate Education and Lifelong Learning as Collaborative Inquiry in Action: An Emergent Model

Susan Weil

Prelude

> We live in both/and worlds full of paradox and uncertainty where close inspection turns unities into multiplicities, clarities into ambiguities, univocal simplicities into polyvocal complexities.
>
> (Lather, 1991: xvi)

As we approach the beginning of the next millennium, higher education is faced with a host of external pressures to defend and renegotiate its identity, purposes and value. A new and harsher world does not accept these as 'givens', to be asserted by those who 'know'. New questions are focused on the authority and role 'of the don', like that of most professionals. This is an age where the rhetoric of accountability and efficiency savings is given overriding importance by politicians and other pundits leaping into the affray (Weil, 1995a).

Within the walls of academe there is also a 'legitimation crisis' (Barnett, 1985). Long-held assumptions about knowledge and 'good science' are being found wanting, paradoxically, on the back of scientific progress, such as in biology or physics. So too are the traditions and practices these assumptions support (Gergen, 1994). Disciplines are co-mingling, as the boundaries between them collapse. And the validity of sanctity afforded to the notion of the independent detached objective world being 'in here' and the subjective under-theorized world being 'out there' has also been placed at issue. Such shifts in the world within and the world beyond higher education requires institutions to engage in new forms of transaction and mediation with adult learners at boundaries that are no longer fixed.

I am a child of this world. So too is the alternative model to postgraduate education and lifelong learning explored in this chapter. It was conceived in appreciation for the polyphonic character of the emergent culture. It respects its potential for empowering voices long silent, and new forms of relationship with learners and communities. At the same time, I have evolved this model with a critical eye to the cacophonous and manipulative dimensions of imposed change by government policy makers. This needs continual deconstruction and redefinition. For example, the social costs of the mechanistic over-'managerialized' paradigm, to which UK public services, higher education included, are being subjected, demand new forms of intervention. They need challenging from alternative expert perspectives (e.g. Hutton, 1995). Such concerns will be seen to be integral to the model's origins, aims, values and processes.

Key features of the model – an introduction

a pedagogy that would collapse the distinctions separating teaching, research and art might also have the power to guide transformation of the lived social world.

(Ulmer, 1985: 27)

I introduce the model by identifying some of its key characteristics in terms of:

• its remit and values;
• its focus and concept, including those whose learning needs it is intended to meet;
• the alternative pedagogical and research assumptions that underpin it;
• its connections to emergent social needs and challenges.

Key dimensions and principles of the model are highlighted in this exploration:

• The model has been developed to meet the postgraduate and post-experience development needs of people who are first and foremost concerned with the challenges of social change. This includes those with interests in, for example, urban regeneration, changes in health and social care, inter-agency working, community development, new forms of professional education and development, community safety, housing, local government effectiveness, equal opportunities, partnership schemes and so on.
• In particular, the model takes into account people in positions of responsibility for stimulating and supporting new kinds of learning and change processes within and across organizations and communities. For example, it is intended to benefit people such as managers, development specialists, consultants and other kinds of 'change agents' in public service, voluntary, not for profit and community organizations: people who work 'in the service of the public'.
• The model makes it possible to bring together an integrated set of alternatives for learning and development at postexperience/postgraduate

levels. The model therefore allows for multiple points of entry to and engagement with an interrelated programme of lifelong learning, career development and research opportunities. These include, for example: non-award-bearing short courses, seminars and forums, postgraduate cohort-based programmes (to diploma, MPhil and PhD levels), funded consultancy and research.

• The model is focused on processes of transformative and effective cultural change in complex living systems (Wildemeersch, 1996). In particular, it seeks to support the critical examination of assumptions and the creative and collaborative evolution of alternatives to dominant models. Within public services, these tend to be mechanistic and reductionist, operating within assumptions of prediction and control. The limitations of these 'hand me down' concepts from the private sector, and 'quick fix' structural solutions in the context of pressures for short-term political gain and efficiency savings have both intended and unintended effects. These remain under theorized and under researched (e.g. Pattison, 1991; Hutton, 1995; Weil, 1995b, 1995c; Pollitt, 1996; Public Management Foundation, 1996).

• Real world dilemmas associated with social and organizational change – not disciplines – provide the starting point for learning and inquiry. 'Local theories in use' (Argyris and Schön, 1974) and the processes, contexts and circumstances of those participating in collaborative inquiry form the hard core of research in this model.

• The model brings reflection and action into new forms of relationship (Argyris and Schön, 1974; Schön, 1983; Flood and Romm, 1996). This enables the testing of assumptions about effective learning and change processes (one's own and others) and the creation and review of alternatives that may have greater meaning and impact within the social, cultural and historical circumstances of *particular* contexts (Alasuutaari, 1996).

• The model places an emphasis on participatory action research and action-based collaborative inquiry into such areas (Oja and Smulyan, 1989; Reason, 1994a, 1994b; Zuber-Skerritt, 1996). Research is conceptualized as a social and reflexive process that generates new understandings that are continually tested, deepened, revised and challenged in action. In the undertaking itself, research becomes a learning and change process. The model embraces a notion of research *as* social change, rather than *on* social change and as a process that is carried out *with* people, not *on* people. It has the empowering aim of making a difference in the lives of people, organizations and communities. (See also Fals-Borda and Rahman, 1991.)

• The implementation of the model is itself to be understood as an action research project (Peters, Gaddis and Marchel, 1997). A key question becomes the implications of inquiry that starts with alternative epistemological and ontological assumptions. For example, it legitimates understandings of knowledge creation that differ from traditional science.

Such inquiry challenges the validity of value-free research, detached observation, and generalizable universal truths. These alternative starting points – which can be defined as 'post positivist' – inevitably require new criteria for quality, ethics and rigour (e.g. Lincoln and Guba, 1985; Lather, 1991; Gergen, 1994; Reason, 1994a, 1994b; Lincoln, 1996). Notions such as 'critical subjectivity' and reflexivity become central to such endeavour (e.g. Ashmore, 1990; Hatch, 1996).

• This inherently social constructionist model is concerned with living systems, and the interconnectedness of the individual, the group, the organization and the wider context. The model encourages research students to function as co-researchers and co-theorists, engaging in different forms of reflexivity, both organizational and individual. As Giddens (1993: 33) argues, 'the reproduction/transformation of systems is implicated in a whole variety of day to day decisions and acts'.

• The model therefore encourages research students to move between different disciplines and structures, and communities. It allows for different related theoretical perspectives (such as postmodernism, poststructuralism, critical systems thinking, feminism, deep ecology) and thinking and practice from different fields (such as from health, arts, humanities, cultural studies, hard sciences, biology) to be brought to bear on action-based inquiry. Therefore, the model encourages what Gregory calls 'discordant pluralism' (Gregory, 1996). It 'legitimates similarities *and* differences' of perspectives (theoretical and methodological). It fosters 'critical appreciation' and aims to transform organizations and communities through 'understanding of self and others' (1996: 622). This leads to the possibility of transdisciplinarity in the production of knowledge, while shifting the responsibility of university staff and introducing a wider range of stakeholder interests into the process.

• The principle of creative and fluid partnerships – internally, regionally, nationally and internationally – is key. The structure and processes of the model allow for different kinds of mutually beneficial relationship, with access to many opportunities for learning and development.

• The notion of multiple partnerships at the heart of this approach to postgraduate education can operate in service of a diversity of aims. For example, dehumanizing processes of change often have high social costs (despite claims for financial savings). Liberatory social aims can be served through the generation of alternatives. A model that is so deeply rooted in commitments to participatory action research and collaborative inquiry further develops a humanizing research paradigm. Such aims are strengthened through collaboration across the growing international community of scholars in this area (Reason, 1994a, 1994b; Lincoln, 1996). Organizational development aims are served through the participation of internal 'change agents' in the varied development programmes. Different forms of participation can create collaborative learning and collective benefit within single organizations. As programme participants become programme contributors/facilitators, career development is facilitated.

They have the opportunity to become part of a 'real world workshop' where managers, practitioners and development specialists can think and work together.

For me, it is legitimate for postgraduate research and lifelong learning to have genuine meaning and impact within clients' lives and careers, their organizations and the society of which we are all a part. We also make a difference by placing real life dilemmas at the heart of collaborative inquiry, and not confining research students to traditional faculty or disciplinary 'boxes'. The model therefore integrates that which has usually been kept separate. In turn, we create new transactions between higher education institutions and communities in relation to things that *matter*. At the same time, alternative understandings of quality and rigour in an expanded system of postgraduate education and research can be developed. (In the penultimate section of this chapter, I explore conditions and benefits relating to implementation in further detail.)

A dance around possibilities and contradictions

[in] the rhetoric of 'quality' is a new found importance attached to higher education by modern society [expressing] the closer relationship between the two now demanded. It is also a reflection of the sense within the host society that higher education has not sufficiently adjusted to the demands of the age.

(Barnett, 1992)

This innovation has been conceived at the same time as traditional boundaries in higher education have begun to crumble. The large influx of new kinds of students has demanded less entrenched ways of thinking about processes and structures for teaching and learning (Schuller, Tight and Weil, 1988; Fulton, 1989). Paradoxically, this model is being developed at a time when government policy and funding strategy seems to be making risk taking virtually taboo.

This is being felt most acutely in the UK within the former polytechnic and college sector. Throughout the first half of the 1990s, this sector generated new understandings of quality, diversity of mission, lifelong learning, continuing professional development, career and overall student development, community regeneration through partnership, and 'relevant' educational processes (Watson, 1989; Harrison, 1995; Slowey, 1995; Webb, 1995; Weil, 1995b). Much innovative capacity was unleashed by initiatives such as Enterprise in Higher Education, the Partnership Awards and the Royal Society of Arts' Higher Education for Capability (Stephenson and Weil, 1992; Weil, 1992), and new understandings of 'responsiveness to employers and society evolved, without recourse to narrow vocationalism' (Duke, 1992; Elton, 1992).

Internally, received wisdom about knowledge creation and quality in scientific inquiry is being challenged. Few disciplines are exempt from such debates or the disarray and despair they engender. Certainties that have underpinned a complex range of implicit intellectual and cultural values are slowly and relentlessly unravelling. On the surface, the questions posed, for example by postmodernism, may seem to be different from those confronting the physical sciences. However, the questions raise common themes and issues (Lather, 1991; Gergen, 1994).

My model rests on a belief in the value of collaborative and collective learning in action processes in a 'risk society'. Discontinuities and uncertainty are rife. These are generating needs for new forms of social learning and participatory action research:

Social learning has to do with the learning of groups, organisations and communities in conditions which are new, unexpected, uncertain and hard to predict. It is aimed at the solution of unforeseen context problems, and is characterised by an optimal use of the problem solving potential of which a group, institution or community disposes. Social learning is action and experience oriented, it is critically reflective. In other words, it is based on the questioning of assumptions and taken for granted problem definitions; it is interactive and communicative, which means that the dialogue between the people involved is of foremost importance, and finally, it is interdisciplinary, as the solution of relatively complex issues presupposes the collaboration of a diversity of actors.

(Wildemeersch, 1996: 3)

Surely, higher education has a responsibility to give meaning to these developments. We need new forms of pedagogy and cross-disciplinary inquiry that remain connected to responsible action in the face of pressing social problems.

Inevitably, forces of conservatism and control militate against innovations that take account of such social developments (Barnett, 1992, 1997). Resources, quality criteria and publication protocols continue to favour traditional models and traditional assumptions about what constitutes quality and effectiveness in research and education. Sameness and mediocrity in higher education are at risk of becoming entrenched values, as a consequence of inappropriate forms of accountability and control at institutional and government levels (e.g. see Harrison, 1995; Madron, 1995; Webb, 1995).

This model is located within postgraduate and postexperience education because this is where the space for innovation is currently available. This is an arena where the aims and values of the model can be fully expressed. (How long the capacity for innovation at postgraduate level will be available to the entire sector remains to be seen.)

A tangled tale

I fell asleep, and while sleeping, I dreamed that I was a butterfly. But when I awoke, I was uncertain whether I was a man [*sic*] dreaming that I was a butterfly, or whether I was a butterfly dreaming that I was a man, dreaming that I was a butterfly.

(Old Chinese proverb)

The ontological and epistemological frames for this model cannot be separated from my own history. My own career has enabled me to look at usual practices in higher education in ways that are not accessible to those who are immersed within that culture. Moreover, they must work within assumptions and incentives that are favourable to their careers within that world.

I came to Britain from a rare position of being at the cutting edge of innovation in American higher education. I worked for one of the first consortia of universities in the USA that comprised the Universities of Loyola, Tulane, and Xavier, Delgado Community College and St Mary's Dominican. I was appointed to conduct research into the feasibility of a human service development degree specifically in the area of 'multi arts therapy'. This study was conducted at a time when government funding was favourable to innovation – structural, cross-cultural and educational. Not unlike UK higher education in the 1990s, resource issues were at play. There were concerns with excessive duplication of offerings and the sheer number of institutions in cities and regions. Entry for non-traditional students was high on the political agenda, in the wake of the riots and student unrest during the 1960s. There were pressures to keep costs of higher education down. The events of the earlier decade had spawned a sober yet earnest consideration of taken for granted policies and practice in higher education. Processes of professional education and development were also being looked at afresh.

The first phase of the feasibility study revealed the value of developing a programme that was complementary to, rather than competitive with, existing degree programmes. This would allow high levels of innovation, with less risk of marginalizing students and programme processes. Programme development took account of needs that are equally relevant to the model at issue in this chapter, such as needs for:

- complementarity and interdisciplinarity;
- collaborative inquiry;
- multifaceted responsiveness, to changing professional, organizational and social needs;
- opportunities for 'boundary crossing' within and across institutions and the wider community.

The pilot implementation stage of the project had enabled programme features such as:

- self and group assessment;
- contract-based learning, with individually negotiated reading, community placements and individual learning aims kept under continual review;
- the use of reflexive journals as an integrative learning process and an assessment tool;
- exposure to a variety of disciplinary perspectives and professional values and practices;
- an emphasis on the values of integrating experiential and propositional knowing (e.g. Weil and McGill, 1989);
- exploration of implicit theories in action (Argyris and Schön, 1974);
- breaking down the theory practice hierarchy and split;
- multiprofessional collaborative learning;
- an overall principle of student autonomy.

This radical and unusual form of socialization into the academic world was influenced by radical thinkers in humanistic psychology and education, such as John Holt, Carl Rogers, Ivan Ilich, Neil Postman, and A. S. Neil, and the earlier work of those such as William James.

Students could not wall off their experience in this programme from their experience of their traditional degree programmes. This inevitably led to questions being asked of the usual approaches to professional development. This created problems for myself, students, staff and other contributors to this programme. Regular reflection and review sessions across related disciplines and the participating institutions focused on what was 'fixed' and what was 'mutable' in their own practice. These consultations were an essential part of the process and politics of this innovation. Only committed and progressive staff participated in these sessions, but they represented a start on the wider organizational/professional development goals that this innovation supported. Such issues will be seen to be integral to questions about maintaining 'value coherence' and the institutional and leadership conditions that would allow a model such as this to be given life and sustained in the current climate.

Cross-cultural transpositions and disjunctions

> Unless educators expose themselves to the popular culture across the board, their discourse will hardly be heard by anyone but themselves.
> (Freire, 1996: 107)

After two years at the Consortium, I was offered a place at Harvard to do postgraduate study, related to my interests in development and change in higher and professional education. My creation of this programme dovetailed Argyris and Schön's (1974) groundbreaking research at Harvard and MIT. However, life often happens while you make other plans. A family illness brought me unexpectedly to the UK, forcing me to give up this place.

The work and thinking around innovative models for professional development undertaken in America seemed to have little social, cultural or educational meaning in this new context. I confronted a system that at the time had no understanding of postgraduate study in areas that had not been pursued at undergraduate level. Despite having received highest academic honours from a university recognized by the US Department of Education and Science as 'excellent', my experiential learning also had no 'credit value' (formally or otherwise) in this very different world.

I became discouraged by what seemed insurmountable barriers to anything analogous to what I had planned to do in the USA. I focused my attention on opportunities outside the academy, in communities and professional organizations, where there was scope to evolve alternative approaches to teaching, learning and change. During the intervening period, despite my involvement in pioneering work related to professional development, and social and institutional change, I nevertheless absorbed the message that, without credentials, my learning from this experience 'did not count'. I became more and more uncertain about finding a course of postgraduate study that would relate to my experiences of engaging in new approaches to learning and change in a variety of contexts. I had command of no 'one' literature, no 'one' discipline. Indeed any 'one' approach would have felt unreasonably constricting. From an academic perspective, I felt myself to be both a misfit and a mongrel.

My re-entry into the system occurred when the University of London allowed me to sit postqualifying exams to progress on to postgraduate study. This opening arose as the result of access and continuing education being forcefully injected into the higher education agenda (Schuller *et al.*, 1988). It was to be some time, however, before I could truly value my alternative journey as one that opened my eyes to other understandings of learning that would later prove to be important.

An alternative stance: not a matter of choice?

our arguments and counter-arguments in support of rival paradigms may not be conclusive. We can appreciate how much skill, art, and imagination are required to do justice to what is distinctive about different ways of practising science and how 'in some areas' scientists 'see different things'.

(Bernstein, 1983: 92–3)

It was through my doctoral research that I was able to start to make sense of my experience. I explored my research questions through the life stories of people who had returned to higher education, either after leaving school at 16 with no qualifications, or as postexperience/postgraduate students, after years as practising professionals. Their expectations about what constituted meaningful learning were shaped as much by their often negative experiences of former education as by their alternative engagements within the 'world' – as self-discovered capable adult learners. Their decision to re-engage with formal education often brought these different constructions of learning and being a learner into sharp contrast with those of their lecturers. The extent to which instrumental learning seemed to be valued often proved demotivating and indeed, profoundly distressing (Weil, 1986, 1988). The disjunctions this gave rise to could be either enabling and disabling, depending on the nature and quality of relationships and dialogue within that learning context (Weil, 1986, 1988, 1989; Weil and McGill, 1989; hooks, 1994; Savin-Baden, 1996).

This research suggested that there may be many capable former graduates and experientially qualified candidates for postgraduate education who may not be prepared to deny their own values, experience and commitments. To abandon their 'learner identity' and values (Weil, 1986, 1988) – gained outside the academy – merely for the sake of a paper qualification or 'getting on' can feel like a major compromise in integrity. (See also Usher and Bryant, 1989.)

Those whose lives have been spent entirely within the academic tradition rarely understand the purposes and meanings for 'learning' that those whose lives have been spent outside bring with them. To dismiss these as inferior is no solution. The struggles that go on amidst the process of re-engagement with what can be seen as narrowly defined academic meanings of learning often remain invisible (Weil, 1986, 1988). This is changing. More academics are now engaged in 'border negotiations' between alternative kinds of learners and the 'rituals' of traditional academic tribes and territories (Becher, 1989). They often come to recognize the unsustainability and inauthenticity of many traditional attitudes, practices and assumptions within higher education (Fulton, 1989; Stephenson and Weil, 1992).

Through this research, I became alert to the implications of different research paradigms. Working within a traditional psychology department, I confronted many epistemological and ontological premises that were taken as 'givens'. I was unsettled by the extent to which, within the traditional paradigm, I was expected to set aside core personal values from my work as an adult educator, such as collaboration, authenticity, and dialogue in learning. Instead, donning the role of the impersonal objective observer was not seen as problematic. It was just a matter of 'putting on new clothes'. Issues of integrity and relationship, and how these may relate to the quality of the data generated, seemed to be of no importance. I became increasingly interested in the literature that set out these 'positivist assumptions' in contrast to those that were associated with a postpositivist and social constructionist paradigm. This went deeper than debates about 'quantitative' or 'qualitative' methods.

In reviewing this growing literature, I questioned notions deriving from the separation of researcher and researched, such as value-free inquiry, research on rather than with people, or the idea that generalizations could be divorced from their historical and cultural context. These were the assumptions that shaped what was seen as 'valid' in research and pedagogical terms. I was working within as 'emergent paradigm' that explored research as an encounter with the world and with people that could not be understood objectively, but rather was shaped by our own constructions. This alternative sensibility towards research was being generated as much by scientists as by social scientists (e.g. Varela *et al.*, 1991; Denzin and Lincoln, 1994; Reason, 1994a, 1994b; Heron, 1996).

I began to see that demands for rigour within the new paradigm were far more searching than those of traditional research. As Hutcheon argues, the kind of research in which I was engaged 'makes its biases part of its argument', and therefore, 'arises as a new contender for legitimacy' (Hutcheon, 1989: 4). The challenges of this reflexive approach forced me to unearth, review and abandon many of my own basic assumptions. In a more traditional study, I could easily have left these untouched (e.g. Lather, 1991; Lincoln, 1996; Reason and Lincoln, 1996; Weil, 1996). My earlier 'humanistic' leanings gave way to a far more critical theory of action perspective. I had to recognize that there was no longer the promise of 'truth' through method. But I was discovering that there was significant space within which to explore the potential of alternative research assumptions for emancipatory projects.

Making connections: positivist assumptions and change in public services

The more managers try to direct others, we see the more unpredictable is the outcome and the greater the resistance. Indeed it could be argued that resistance is a consequence of applying . . . change management thinking and is why so many organisations feel paralysed . . . Seeing something differently is to re-interpret its significance and meaning from within an existing frame of reference. The 'I' observing remains secure. Seeing differently brings imagination to bear, and in the process, transforms the observer. What was previously an observed event becomes an experience involving oneself. Before Einstein showed the limitation of space and time, for example, it was not recognised that they were relative concepts. That recognition shook some of the most fundamental assumptions of scientific enquiry. The enquiry itself was seen to shape what was seen.

(Pidgeon and Knight, 1995: 8)

By the time of the 1988 Education Reform Act, I had become part of national debates on issues of higher education policy, managerial practice and institutional reform (e.g. Weil, 1992) I was increasingly alarmed by unquestioned assumptions about efficiency, learning and change in the public services. For example, the notion that one could 'manage' change and learning through breaking 'it' down into its 'constituent parts' prevailed. So too did the possibility of managerial control, through top-down strategies, which could be arbitrarily enforced, as if those on the receiving end were passive recipients, rather than clever 'meaning making' social actors. I began to see that these assumptions derived directly from the same ontological and epistemological assumptions that dominated academic research and pedagogy. I became fascinated with their deep-rootedness in society. Those who held these seemed blinded by their unacknowledged theory, as well as to the disjunctions and frustrations they generated in the face of complex social challenges. Their instrumental efficacy was dogmatically asserted, as if this were enough.

In the everyday world of practice, management effectiveness was seldom construed as being willing to test assumptions, or to examine implicit 'theory'-in-practice (Argyris and Schön, 1974). Actively testing out alternative ways of realizing change *with* others, such as professional groups, in support of pressures for financial savings and alternative understandings of effective social outcomes, was all too rare. Moreover, 'participatory' approaches seemed to be used in increasingly instrumental and manipulative ways (Weil and McGill, 1989). Management was often portrayed or lived out as what you did *to* people, in support of controlling their movement from 'here to there' – as if this could be predetermined, and 'fixed' obstacles could be removed.

I subsequently joined an organization established to challenge the limitations of much of the private sector thinking that was now being assumed to be good medicine for the public services. This organization was set up to appreciate the complexity of public service management, and its need to manage multiple bottom lines (Parston, 1993). In my new role, I was able to challenge and offer alternatives to existing understandings of professional, executive and organizational development throughout the public services, while specializing in higher education. Senior managers and professionals in mixed public service groups who worked with me over months, would often provide, in confidence, examples of how dysfunctional and damaging they were finding the dominant paradigm and its assumptions. We began to support each other's action based inquiries into alternatives – and, out of this work, the model discussed here began to emerge.

Increasingly, I wanted to create an alternative approach to postgraduate research and education that could enable those who were actively struggling with these dilemmas to become co-inquirers, co-researchers, learn through action at and across the boundaries of various domains. Herein lay the promise of tackling complex social issues through seeing and acting differently.

Tilting against the culture

To argue for transformation in the concept of social knowledge is to tilt against the major institutions of the culture . . . they raise significant questions regarding the division of knowledge by distinct departments, the reliance on lectures and texts as pedagogical practices, the use of examinations to test student knowledge and the existence of highly select colleges and universities. To extend these to the culture more generally, we find the broad array of assumptions derived from the Enlightenment, and informing virtually all our public institutions, thrown into question. Assumptions of objectivity, rationality, truth, individual freedom and progress are all placed in jeopardy.

(Gergen, 1994: ix)

The key characteristics of my model, as set out in the first section of this chapter, provides an alternative to postgraduate education that has implications for action in the 'real world'. It resonates with the counter academic culture emerging out of the 'death' of positivism, modernism and structuralism. However, as is made evident above, although influenced by them, the model was not borne directly out of these disciplinary struggles. I was also not being driven by the usual incentives and norms to which most academics are subject. This made it easier for me to interrelate areas that for many would be treated separately. The model further reflects my incapacity to ignore the critical insights that my alternative pathways generated. My commitment to integrity and authenticity with respect to my experience made it impossible for me to retreat to traditional academic assumptions, conceptions and paradigms. To me, these were *not* merely an alternative set of clothes.

In summary, the model legitimates postgraduate research and career development that brings into active relationship, each with the others, the following:

- the generation of social value in public/voluntary service organizations and communities;
- processes of learning from interaction with continuous change in complex human systems;
- processes of managing, organizing and inquiry to support social and organizational learning from engagements with continuous change;
- processes of building capacity for responsiveness, to internal and external changes – in individuals, groups, organizations and communities;
- processes of post-positivist inquiry, and in particular participatory forms of action research, and emergent criteria for quality, rigour and ethics;
- processes of collaborative inquiry that begin with the dilemmas of social change and make a difference in the lives and contexts of those who participate in that complex human system;
- implicit assumptions and processes in action as content to guide critical engagement, and revised action.

But such a vision only has meaning and authenticity within a learning community of co-inquirers and co-researchers.

There are many forces that might make such an innovation difficult to sustain. At the same time, there are as many that make it timely and appropriate. As Lather asserts:

> questions of how to do 'good' openly value based inquiry can [now] be seriously entertained, a discourse unheard of outside marginalised circles such as Feminist and Freirean Participatory Research until very recently . . . This is a both exciting and dizzying time in which to do social inquiry.
>
> (Lather, 1991: 14)

The challenge of value resonance

> The problem of value resonance is simply this: To the extent to which the inquirer's personal values, the axioms undergirding the guiding substantive theory, the axioms underlying the guiding methodological paradigm, and the values underlying the context are all consistent and reinforcing, inquiry can proceed meaningfully and will produce findings and interpretations that are agreeable from all perspectives. But, to the extent that they are dissonant, inquiry proceeds only with difficulty and produces findings and interpretations that are questionable and noncredible.
>
> (Lincoln and Guba, 1985: 178)

By its very nature, such a model focuses on collaborative inquiry, reflexive practice, and commitments to 'discordant pluralism' (Gregory, 1996) – and above all, what it means to live these in action. Disjunctions between what is espoused, and what is experienced will always be at issue, if such a model is to be given life within a higher education institution in the current context. The very tensions associated with quality, ethics, power and the crisis of representation in new paradigm research will be mirrored. So too will issues in debates about organizational learning that take account of postmodernism and complexity theory (Wheatley, 1992; Lincoln, 1994, 1996; Boje *et al.*, 1996; Stacey, 1996). The implementation of such a model would face questions such as:

- How do you allow for diversity and multiple realities, without losing the parameters within which meaningful and responsible action can be carried out?
- How do you hold basic assumptions open to continual revision and question, without becoming entrapped in short-term instrumentalism or pressures to achieve consensus?
- How do you create self-organizing systems that can generate and sustain innovation and learning, and operate 'at the edge of chaos' in institutions in a context that still places emphasis on the metaphor of the organisation as a machine (Morgan, 1986)?

This model embodies particular assumptions regarding the nature of knowledge, the methods through which that knowledge can be obtained, as well as a set of root assumptions about the nature of the phenomena to be investigated. This point is elaborated by Morgan and Smircich as follows:

Once one relaxes the ontological assumption that the world is a concrete structure, and admits that human beings, far from merely responding to the social world, may actively contribute to its creation, the dominant methods become increasingly unsatisfactory, indeed, inappropriate.
(Morgan and Smircich, 1980: 498)

The interconnectedness of assumptions about organizing, researching and learning in the model are based on post-positivist assumptions. However, the world still operates largely on the basis of an alternative epistemology and ontology, which is largely positivist. This continues despite a powerful emerging academic culture that is slowly dismantling its authoritative power, and the intellectual and cultural practices its assumptions have generated.

The legitimation crisis (Barnett, 1985) of 'old against new', of new against old, can generate retreats to absolute traditionalist models of 'quality pedagogy and research'. Practices and their evaluation could become unreflexively routinized. Alternatively, we can create space within our institutions to explore in action the implications of new forms of engaged pedagogy and research (hooks, 1994). These might respond more effectively to needs within society to learn to live with ambiguity, paradox and contradiction; and continuous change, without resorting to instrumental means–ends controls and narrowly reductionist problem solving. Alternative approaches can begin to address the challenges of being in and acting on and learning through our interaction with cultures in transition, as actors who too are part of this and whose biases, positions and actions warrant ongoing critical scrutiny (Weil, 1997). The assumptions underlying traditional models perpetuate our biases in the name of objectivity: they are self-limiting, unable to take account of the complexity of change, the real challenges of responsible action, and the ways in which we co-constitute our worlds.

But what if the spaces for evolving alternatives become marginalized enclaves, continually under assault from fixed and traditionalist understandings of quality in pedagogy and research. The resulting dissonance, as suggested by Lincoln and Guba (1985) in the earlier quotation can result in inquiry that is neither 'here' nor 'there'. Trustworthy by no set of standards, it could become entrapped by the very forces it seeks to challenge. We run the risk of falling between giving life to the values inherent in the model and succumbing to the pressures of dominant academic and political norms. A whole new territory needs to be carved out in the higher education sector, to legitimate a more participatory paradigm that integrates responsive dialogue and compassionate action, while redefining new forms of rigour, quality and ethics in research. Otherwise, innovations such as this will wither and die.

Making it real: considerations and potential benefits

Saying is one thing and doing is another.

(Montaigne, *Essays*)

Certain conditions become essential if such a model is to be implemented successfully. At the very least, it would require an institution's senior managers and professionals to provide leadership in taking their institution through:

- the risks and the potential of adopting this innovative stance;
- the participatory action research/collaborative inquiry focus, that stresses research with, not on, people and research as, not about, social change;
- the structural, cultural and logistical implications of evolving a genuinely interdisciplinary model;
- the involvement of internal and external staff in the generation of capacity and impact through diverse activity, in ways that go against the grain of tradition;
- the management of a complex web of external and internal relationships, in terms of remuneration, recognition and support;
- the blurring of part- and full-time distinctions at postgraduate research levels;
- new attitudes and ways of working to support the development of the quality and impact of the model to full potential;
- the ongoing support and development needs of those directly involved in the implementation, given the multiplicity of activity and demand that potentially can be generated.

With such leadership, the organization could enhance its:

- capacity for responsiveness to changes in higher education policy and funding;
- profile and reputation for innovation and excellence in an emergent form of research at traditional boundaries between higher education and communities, thereby building new capacity within the institution, particularly with staff working in applied areas;
- ability to develop and sustain new forms of *external* partnership that strengthen the position and influence of the institution;
- scope for generating income from multiple sources and forms of activity;
- image as an institution attuned to emergent social and community challenges and capable of devising educational and research processes that do justice to their complexity while providing practical support on difficult issues;
- contribution to the value and impact of social and public services within its immediate community;
- role as an honest broker in developing and bringing together managers, policy makers, practitioners and service users, to anticipate and respond to social change.

Sustainability, particularly in the early stages, would also require a recognition of multiple bottom lines. There could be risks in going for short-term returns on investment. As with any public service, the different kinds of return such a model can yield cannot be reduced to merely a financial bottom line (Parston, 1993).

Junctures of possibility

If you are really preparing for groundlessness, preparing for the reality of human existence, you are living on the razor's edge, and you must become used to the fact that things shift and change. Things are not certain and they do not last and you do not know what is going to happen. My [best] teachers [are those who] have always pushed me over the cliff . . .

(Chodron, in hooks, 1994)

Pressures on higher education to generate new forms of postgraduate research, career development and lifelong learning opportunities will not go away. Changes within and beyond institutions demand alternative kinds of transactions. There are many potential candidates for postgraduate and postexperience education. They constitute a diverse and sizeable group of adult learners and former graduates. All of these can benefit from new forms of relationship with academic institutions and many have the desire to do so. However, as they dance close to the borders, they can confront sterile dualities, such as between theory and practice, objectivity and subjectivity, discipline purity and problem centredness, universalized and contextualized truths. For such candidates, the psychological and social costs of re-engaging with the assumptions, practices and traditions of the formal system – merely for the sake of a qualification – may be too great to warrant investing time, energy and spirit. (See also Weil, 1986, 1988, 1989.)

The model explored in this chapter offers one way of redefining these terrains and boundaries. It suggests integrating engaged criticality and reflexivity with action. Ultimately, it is what we do that is important. As the increasing diversity at undergraduate level works its way through to postgraduate level, we cannot ignore the importance of new models, nor the need for them. We need managers and professionals to be aware of their leadership responsibilities in higher education, to be willing to take risks, and to provide the space and support required for innovations of the kind set out in this chapter.

Questions of rigour, quality and standards would in no way be compromised. They just become different. A genuinely diverse system of higher education no longer allows this dilemma of quality to be treated as a status issue – relegating innovations like this to the bottom of a hierarchy. The existing hierarchy is maintained only through allegiance to a paradigm that itself is crumbling.

So I close with some 'quality questions' that, in the new world of post-graduate education, must be addressed.

• At what *cost* do we shy away from the opportunities for learning and repatterning that innovations such as suggested by this model potentially offer?
• At what *risk* do we maintain a system of incentives and practices that rest on an obsolete world view?
• What forces collude with our resistance to enlarging our worldviews of pedagogy and research?

We can no longer promise truth through method. We can and must generate alternative models for learning and change to breathe new life into – to reanimate – our social processes and institutions.

Acknowledgements

I would like to thank Bob Burgess, Carlis Douglas, Annette Karseras, Judi Marshall, John Peters, Peter Reason, Donald Schön and all at Nene College for the encouragement and support that have made this chapter possible. I am especially grateful to Bob Burgess, Mike Daniel and Roy Madron, for their assistance with earlier drafts.

Note

The model being presented here began to be implemented at Nene College of Higher Education, Northampton in June 1996. The opportunity to do so arose from my long professional association with the College, culminating in our joint decision to establish the SOLAR Centre, a postgraduate action research and development centre to support, 'Social and Organizational Learning and Reanimation' with people working in the service of the public. No other institution offered the strength of commitment I encountered amongst the Deans and Senior Management. Their willingness not only to invest in this innovation, but to establish it as a genuinely collaborative and interdisciplinary, cross-institutional venture was not something that other universities with interest in the model could offer, and was a key factor for me in deciding to locate SOLAR at Nene.

References

Alasuutaari, P. (1996) Theorizing in Qualitative Research: A Cultural Studies Perspective, *Journal of Qualitative Inquiry*, 12(4): 371–84.
Argyris, C. and Schön, D. (1974) *Theory in Practice: Increasing Professional Effectiveness.* London: Jossey-Bass.
Ashmore, M. (1990) *The Reflexive Thesis.* Chicago: University of Chicago Press.
Barnett, R. (1992) *Improving Higher Education: Total Quality Care.* Buckingham: SRHE/ Open University Press.

Barnett, R. A. (1985) Higher education: legitimation crisis, *Studies in Higher Education*, 10, 241–56.

Barnett, R. A. (1997) *Higher Education: a Critical Business*. Buckingham: SRHE/Open University Press.

Becher, T. (1989) *Academic Tribes and Territories*. Buckingham: SRHE/Open University Press.

Bernstein, R. J. (1983) *Beyond Objectivism and Relativism*. Oxford: Basil Blackwell.

Boje, D. M., Gephart, R. P. and Thatchenkery, T. J. (eds) (1996) *Postmodern Management and Organisation Theory*. London: Sage.

Denzin, N. and Lincoln, Y. A. (eds) (1994) *Handbook of Qualitative Research*. London: Sage.

Duke, C. (1992) *The Learning University*. Buckingham: SRHE/Open University Press.

Elton, L. (1992) Research, teaching and scholarship in an expanding higher education system, *Higher Education Quarterly*, 46, 252–68.

Fals-Borda, O. and Rahman, M. A. (eds) (1991) *Action and Knowledge: Breaking the Monopoly with Participatory Action Research*. New York: Intermediate Technology/Apex.

Flood, R. and Romm, N. (1996) *Triple Loop Learning*. Chichester: John Wiley.

Freire, P. (1996) *Pedagogy of Hope*. New York: Continuum Publishing Company.

Fulton, O. (1989) *Access and Institutional Change*. Buckingham: SRHE/Open University Press.

Gergen, K. J. (1994) *Toward Transformation in Social Knowledge*, 2nd edn. London: Sage.

Giddens, A. (1993) *New Rules of Sociological Method*, 2nd edn. Oxford: Polity Press.

Gregory, W. (1996) Discordant pluralism: a new strategy for critical systems thinking?, *Systems Practice*, 9(6), 605–25.

Harrison, M. (1995) Change and stability: from poly to varsity, in S. Weil (ed.) *Introducing Change 'From the Top' of Universities and Colleges*. London: Kogan Page.

Hatch, M. J. (1996) The role of the researcher: an analysis of narrative position in organization theory, *Journal of Management Inquiry*, 5, 4.

Heron, J. (1996) *Co-operative Inquiry: Research into the Human Condition*. London: Sage.

hooks, bell (1994) *Teaching to Transgress: Education as the Practice of Freedom*. London: Routledge.

Hutcheon, L. (1989) *The Politics of Postmodernism*. New York: Routledge.

Hutton, W. (1995) *The State We're In*. London: Jonathan Cape.

Lather, P. (1991) *Getting Smart: Feminist Research and Pedagogy with/in the Postmodern*. London: Routledge.

Lincoln, Y. S. (1994) *The Sixth Moment: Emerging Problems in Qualitative Research*. Paper presented at the annual meeting of the Society for Studies in Symbolic Interaction, Urbana, Illinois.

Lincoln, Y. S. (1996) Emerging criteria for quality in qualitative and interpretive research, *Qualitative Inquiry*, 1(3), 275–89.

Lincoln, Y. S. and Guba, E. G. (1985) *Naturalistic Inquiry*. London: Sage.

Madron, R. (1995) Performance improvement in public services, *The Political Quarterly*, 66(3), 181–94.

Morgan, G. (1986) *Images of Organisation*. London: Sage.

Morgan, G. and Smircich, L. (1980) The case for qualitative research, *Academy of Management Review*, 5, 491–500.

Oja, S. N. and Smulyan, L. (1989) *Collaborative Action Research: Developmental Approach*. London: Falmer.

Parston, G. (1993) *A New Framework for Public Management.* London: Office for Public Management.

Pattison, S. (1991) Masters of change, *Health Service Journal,* October.

Peters, J., Gaddis, R. and Marchel, C. (1997) *AR²: Action Research on Action Research.* Paper delivered to the 10th Annual Conference on Qualitative Research in Education, Athens, Georgia, January.

Pidgeon, H. and Knight, A. (1995) *Seeing with New Eyes – Enhancing the Responsiveness of Your Organization.* Berkhamsted: Ashridge Consulting Limited.

Pollitt, C. (1996) Business approaches to quality improvement: why they are hard for the NHS to swallow, *Quality in Health Care Journal,* 5, 104–10.

Public Management Foundation (1996) *The Glue That Binds: The Public Value of Public Services.* London: Public Management Foundation/MORI.

Reason, P. (ed.) (1994a) *Participation in Human Inquiry.* London: Sage.

Reason, P. (1994b) Three approaches to participative inquiry, in N. Denzin and Y. Lincoln (eds), *Handbook of Qualitative Research.* London: Sage.

Reason, P. and Lincoln, Y. (eds) (1996) Special issue: quality in human inquiry. *Journal of Qualitative Inquiry,* 2, 1.

Savin-Baden, M. (1996) 'Problem Based Learning: a Catalyst for Enabling and Disabling Disjunction Prompting Transition in Learner Stances?' Unpublished PhD thesis, University of London.

Schön, D. A. (1983) *The Reflective Practitioner.* London: Maurice Temple Smith Ltd.

Schuller, T., Tight, M. and Weil, S. W. (1988) Continuing education and the redrawing of boundaries, *Higher Education Quarterly,* 42(4), 335–53.

Slowey, M. (ed.) (1995) *Implementing Change from Within Universities and Colleges.* London: Kogan Page.

Stacey, R. (1996) *Complexity and Creativity in Organisations.* San Francisco: Berrett Koehler.

Stephenson, J. and Weil, S. (1992) *Quality in Learning.* London: Kogan Page.

Ulmer, G. (1985) *Applied Grammatology: Post(e)-pedagogy from Jacques Derrida to Joseph Beuys.* Madison: University of Wisconsin Press.

Usher, R. and Bryant, I. (1989) *Adult Education as Theory, Practice and Research: The Captive Triangle.* London: Routledge.

Varela, F., Thompson, E. and Rosch, E. (1991) *The Embodied Mind.* Cambridge: MIT Press.

Watson, D. (1989) *Managing the Modular Course.* Buckingham, SRHE/Open University Press.

Webb, A. (1995) Two tales from a reluctant manager, in S. Weil (ed.) *Introducing Change 'From the Top' of Universities and Colleges.* London: Kogan Page.

Weil, S. (1986) Non-traditional learners within traditional higher education institutions: discovery and disappointment. *Studies in Higher Education,* 11(3), 219–35.

Weil, S. (1988) From a language of observation to a language of experience, *Journal of Access Studies,* 3(1), 17–43.

Weil, S. (1989) 'Influences of Lifelong Learning on Adults' Expectations and Experiences of Returning to Formal Learning Contexts'. Unpublished PhD dissertation, University of London.

Weil, S. (1992) Creating capability for change in higher education, in R. Barnett (ed.), *Learning to Effect.* Buckingham: SRHE/Open University Press.

Weil, S. (1993) Access: towards education or miseducation?, in M. Thorpe, R. Edwards and A. Hanson (eds), *Culture and Processes of Adult Learning,* London: Routledge.

Weil, S. (ed.) (1995a) *Introducing Change 'From the Top' of Universities and Colleges.* London: Kogan Page.

Weil, S. (1995b) Management and change in colleges and universities: the need for new understandings, in S. Weil (ed.), *Introducing Change 'From the Top' of Universities and Colleges.* London: Kogan Page.

Weil, S. (1995c) Bringing about cultural change in colleges and universities: the power and potential of story, in S. Weil (ed.), *Introducing Change 'From the Top' of Universities and Colleges.* London: Kogan Page.

Weil, S. (1996) From the other side of silence: new possibilities for dialogue in academic writing, *Changes*, 14(3), 223–31.

Weil, S. (1997) Social and organisational learning and unlearning in a different key: an introduction to principles of critical learning theatre and dialectical inquiry, in F. Stowell *et al.* (eds) *Systems for Sustainability.* New York: Plenum Press.

Weil, S. and McGill, I. (eds) (1989) *Making Sense of Experiential Learning.* Buckingham: SRHE/Open University Press.

Wheatley, M. J. (1992) *Leadership and the New Science: Learning about Organization from an Orderly Universe.* San Francisco: Berrett-Koehler.

Wildemeersch, D. (1996) Social Learning for Reconstruction and Development: Perspectives on Experiential Learning for Social Transformation. Paper presented at the fifth ICEL conference, Cape Town, South Africa.

Zuber-Skerritt, O. (1996) *New Directions in Action Research.* London: Falmer Press.

Part 3

Careers

8

Mass Higher Education: Mass Graduate Employment in the 1990s

Keith Dugdale

The creation of a mass higher education system in the UK has led to a fundamental change in the structure of the graduate labour market. The concept of a graduate job has been redefined, the ways in which graduates enter the labour market have become increasingly diversified and the gap between success and failure more polarized, while the range of employers who recruit graduates is far wider in the mid-1990s than ever before.

This chapter reviews this fundamental restructuring of the graduate labour market. The introduction focuses on the expansion of higher education at both undergraduate and postgraduate level as a major driver for change. It then examines the supply and demand for graduates in the 1990s and analyses the current graduate destination data to provide a commentary on career opportunities for graduates.

The debate on 'graduateness' and the need for graduates to offer different skills to match the needs of this new labour market is then examined from both the graduates' and employers' perspectives. Finally, the chapter summarizes the key points and provides an overview of potential developments to the millennium.

The impact of mass higher education

Although the overall growth in higher education in the last decade has been well documented (Smithers and Robinson, 1995, 1996) it is important, none the less, to emphasize a number of key characteristics of the nature of this growth.

As Table 8.1 shows, enrolments in higher education in 1995 topped 1.6 million with dramatic rises in both full-time and part-time numbers.

This growth was largely fuelled by an increase, to over 30 per cent, in the age participation rate. As a result, even within a mass HE system, we have

Table 8.1   Enrolments in higher education

Provision	Thousands		
	1986	1995	% change
Full-time			
First degree	428.0	860.5	101.1
Postgraduate	69.1	134.6	94.8
Certificate/diploma	98.9	111.6	12.8
Part-time			
First degree	96.4	174.1	80.6
Postgraduate	52.0	182.2	250.4
Certificate/diploma	200.4	162.0	−19.2
Total	944.8	1625.0	72.0

Note: Does not include 34,400 students writing theses or on sabbatical.
Source: HESA, 1996.

a familiar picture of entry to university dominated by academic qualifications accounting for 74 per cent of first degree admissions. Within this overall growth, important structural changes have taken place, including:

• *the impact of the new universities.* The rapid expansion of the new university sector has shifted the traditional balance in HE away from more academic towards more vocational subjects and more part-time and sub-degree courses (Smithers and Robinson, 1996).

• *male : female ratios.* Women now form the majority in higher education (51.5 per cent), although they remain under-represented in a number of significant subject areas, including engineering and technology, computing and the physical sciences.

• *mature student growth.* 29 per cent of students are now 21+ on entry, in the new universities this has risen to 34.2 per cent. 62 per cent of part-time students are aged 31 or over compared to only 10 per cent on full-time courses (Connor *et al.*, 1996).

• *ethnic minorities.* The percentage of students from ethnic minorities continues to rise slowly. 13 per cent of total entrants are now from these groups although they remain concentrated in a small number of institutions, in particular in the new universities.

• *postgraduate growth.* In recent years, postgraduate numbers have grown even more rapidly than at undergraduate level. Between 1992–3 and 1994–5 there was an 11 per cent growth in postgraduates compared with 7 per cent for undergraduate students (Higher Education Funding Council, 1996). Not only the size but the shape and composition of the postgraduate sector has also been fundamentally transformed in the 1990s. For example, nearly 60 per cent of all taught postgraduate students are now studying on a part-time basis (Higher Education Statistics Agency, 1996).

Table 8.2 All first degree graduate destinations, 1990–4*

Category	1990	1991	1992	1993	1994
Permanent UK employment	52.0	44.7	41.9	43.9	47.0
Short-term UK employment	5.2	5.7	6.4	7.0	7.0
Further academic study	9.7	11.3	12.1	12.0	11.1
Teacher training	3.7	4.5	4.8	4.7	4.4
Other training	7.5	7.8	7.8	7.0	6.6
Employment overseas	2.7	3.0	2.7	2.5	2.4
Overseas students leaving UK	5.4	6.7	6.9	7.0	7.3
Unemployed	8.1	11.5	12.9	11.7	9.7
Not available	5.5	4.7	4.4	4.2	4.4

Notes: Data based on total known destinations. *After 1994, responsibility for the production of these statistics passed to the Higher Education Statistics Agency (HESA). It introduced a number of significant changes making comparisons with earlier years impossible. Comparative data can therefore only be included up to 1994.
Source: Higher Education Careers Services Unit (1989–94).

Such rapid expansion in a traditionally conservative system within less than a decade has produced a more diverse student population entering higher education with an increasingly broad range of qualifications and choosing to study, at both undergraduate and postgraduate levels, a wider range of subjects in more flexible patterns and modes. Not surprisingly, as these products of a mass HE system move through into the labour market, the jobs and employers they join after graduation reflect this new diversity.

The changing graduate market

The rapid expansion of higher education coincided with the economic recession of the early 1990s. As Table 8.2 shows, the result was a substantial rise in graduate unemployment, a dramatic fall in permanent employment and a significant increase in the percentage of students moving on to post-graduate study or training at the end of their degree.

It is noticeable that the increase in graduates moving directly on to further academic study, teacher training and other forms of training, all peaked at the height of the recession in 1992. This suggests that a major factor encouraging larger numbers of graduates to remain in higher education was the lack of opportunities in the job market.

A comparison between the old and new universities over the period 1990–4 (Figure 8.1) shows a marked difference in employment patterns. For the old universities the fall in permanent employment and rise in unemployment levels was not nearly as substantial as for the polytechnic/new university sector. This suggests that in a period of economic recession larger recruiters focused their activities on their more traditional recruiting grounds. This would also be consistent with the rapid growth of 'targeting' in the

146 *Keith Dugdale*

Figure 8.1 Old and new* university graduate destinations, 1990–4

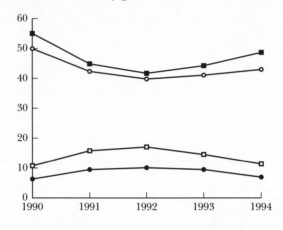

—○— Permanent UK employment, old universities
—■— Permanent UK employment, new universities
—●— Unemployment, old universities
—□— Unemployment, new universities

Notes: Data based on known destinations. *Including former polytechnics.
Source: Higher Education Careers Services Unit (1989–94).

Table 8.3 All male first degree graduate destinations, 1990–4

Category	1990	1991	1992	1993	1994
Permanent UK employment	52.6	43.6	40.6	42.1	45.8
Short-term UK employment	4.2	5.1	5.9	6.6	6.5
Further academic study	12.0	13.6	14.4	14.1	12.9
Teacher training	1.8	2.6	2.7	2.7	2.5
Other training	6.3	6.7	6.7	6.1	5.8
Employment overseas	2.3	2.5	2.3	2.1	2.1
Overseas students leaving UK	7.2	8.2	8.3	8.5	8.8
Unemployed	8.4	13.4	15.1	14.0	11.6
Not available	5.2	4.3	4.0	3.8	4.0

Note: Data based on total known destinations.
Source: Higher Education Careers Services Unit (1989–94).

early 1990s as large employers reduced their overall recruitment activities
to focus on a small number of preferred target institutions. On the whole,
these proved to be the old traditional universities.

Similar differences can be seen in Tables 8.3 and 8.4 which show the
varying success in the labour market of male and female graduates. Throughout the 1990s women graduates did consistently better in entering the

Table 8.4 All female first degree graduate destinations, 1990-4

Category	1990	1991	1992	1993	1994
Permanent UK employment	49.3	45.9	43.4	45.8	48.3
Short-term UK employment	5.9	6.4	6.9	7.5	7.6
Further academic study	8.3	8.8	9.8	9.8	9.1
Teacher training	5.4	6.6	7.1	6.8	6.4
Other training	9.7	9.1	8.9	8.0	7.3
Employment overseas	3.5	3.5	3.1	2.9	2.7
Overseas students leaving UK	4.4	5.2	5.3	5.4	5.8
Unemployed	6.9	9.4	10.6	9.3	7.9
Not available	6.6	5.2	5.0	4.6	4.9

Note: Data based on total known destinations.
Source: Higher Education Careers Services Unit (1989-94).

labour market than their male counterparts. In part, this may be accounted for by structural differences in their employment patterns in which the public and education sectors survived the recession better than manufacturing. In part, it may also reflect women's greater flexibility, and therefore employability, in a period when graduates were forced to seek employment at lower levels and in less traditional areas of the labour market.

Tables 8.3 and 8.4 also highlight the gender differences in the uptake of postgraduate study and training. A significantly higher percentage of men than women embark on further academic study, whereas the reverse is true for those entering more vocational postgraduate training.

Given the rapid rise in mature student entry, it is interesting to note from Figure 8.2 that changes in their immediate employment prospects mirrored those for graduates under 25. At the height of the recession, with larger employers reverting to more traditional recruitment targets, it could have been anticipated that older graduates might have fared worse in the market. However, it appears that their greater experience and better coping and survival strategies enabled them to seek out new openings and opportunities in a changing labour market.

Tables 8.5 and 8.6 reveal further detail of the changes in the graduate labour market in the early years of the decade. Table 8.5 confirms the impact of recession on opportunities in industry and commerce in contrast to the growth of graduate employment in the education sector. This decline in industrial and manufacturing employment is also reflected in changes in the type of work which adversely affected opportunities in research, design and development and environment, planning and construction.

Of longer term significance, the recession also led to fundamental restructuring within companies. Larger organizations emerged from the recession slimmer, with a commitment to flatter, less hierarchical management structures, more focused on their core business and more prepared to outsource other functions and services. At the same time, their contract with their

Figure 8.2 Comparison of all first degree graduate destinations by age, 1991-3

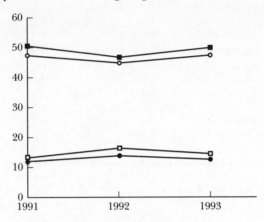

—○— Permanent UK employment under 25

—■— Permanent UK employment over 25

—●— Unemployment under 25

—□— Unemployment over 25

Note: Data from known destinations of UK university and college graduates excluding overseas students returning home.
Sources: Association of Careers Advisory Services (1995); *Universities Statistical Record* (1990-3); Committee of Directors of Polytechnics (various).

Table 8.5 All first degree graduate destinations, 1990-4 by type of employer

Employer category	1990	1991	1992	1993	1994
Public sector	21.5	23.4	23.1	21.2	19.1
Education	8.4	10.3	10.3	10.5	9.5
Industry and commerce	60.2	55.0	54.4	55.6	58.8
Miscellaneous	9.9	11.3	12.2	12.7	12.6

Note: Data based on total known destinations.
Sources: Association of Careers Advisory Services (1995); *Universities Statistical Record* (1990-3); Committee of Directors of Polytechnics (various).

employees changed. Flexibility became all important. The concept of a contract for life offering steady progression up a clear career ladder, was replaced by short-term contracts and more rapid career change; a world in which portfolio careers were increasingly becoming the norm and in which 'There is no such thing as a career path – it's crazy paving and you have to lay it yourself' (Association of Graduate Recruiters, 1996: 12).

The recession also reduced the dominance of the large traditional recruiter in the graduate labour market. In the boom of the late 1980s, the 400 companies in membership of the Association of Graduate Recruiters (AGR)

Table 8.6 All first degree graduate destinations, 1990–4 by type of work

Type of work	1990	1991	1992	1993	1994
Administration and operational management	8.9	9.8	9.9	10.5	10.7
Research, design and development	1.40	11.9	10.6	8.1	7.6
Scientific, engineering support	–	–	–	–	–
Environment, planning, construction	6.6	5.3	4.2	4.3	4.5
Sales, marketing and buying	7.5	7.4	8.2	8.5	9.5
Management services, computing	8.0	7.0	6.5	6.0	6.7
Financial	15.8	13.9	21.1	10.3	9.9
Legal	–	–	–	–	–
Literary, entertainment, creative	4.1	3.5	–	4.8	5.1
Personnel, health and social welfare	18.4	19.8	19.9	18.4	16.5
Teaching and lecturing	6.1	8.1	7.8	11.2	10.3
Others (including all above under 2 per cent)	10.6	13.3	20.8	17.9	19.2

Note: Data based on total known destinations.
Sources: Association of Careers Advisory Services (1995); Universities Statistical Record (1990–3); Committee of Directors of Polytechnics (various).

recruited 80 per cent of the total graduate output with single employers such as KPMG recruiting in excess of 1000 graduates. By 1995 AGR members' recruitment was down to 50 per cent of the total and falling.

From recession and restructuring it was the small firms sector which emerged as the main engine driving new job growth. The Labour Market and Skills Trends 1996–7 (Department for Education and Employment, 1996), shows that between 1989 and 1991 small firms created 330,000 net new jobs and at the end of 1993 there were 3.6 million businesses in Britain, an increase of 1.2 million since 1979. According to the Department of Trade and Industry (1996), 99 per cent of all British firms employ less than 50 people and account for the majority of people in the workforce (53.7 per cent).

Similarly, self-employment has also grown in importance as a major source of new job opportunities. Thus there are now 3.4 million self-employed people in Britain, 12 per cent of the work force compared to 6.6 per cent in 1979. Although the graduate destination statistics are not detailed enough to chart the movement of graduates into small businesses and self-employment, it is reasonable to assume that they are increasingly employed in growing numbers in both these sectors. This is confirmed by a study of 1000 graduates of the University of Sussex which showed that 40 per cent were working in firms of less than 200 employees and 15 per cent in firms of under 20 (Connor and Pollard, 1996).

The substantial increase in graduate output also helped to drive the expansion of the postgraduate sector. This rapid growth has led to a re-evaluation of the benefits of postgraduate education and the potential value of postgraduate qualifications in the labour market. The Harris review of Postgraduate Education concludes that the demand for a postgraduate education will continue to grow driven by the 'professionalization' of the work force, to deliver the requirements of individuals for lifelong learning, and to 'respond to the wish of individuals to differentiate themselves from the mass of graduates holding bachelors' degrees' (Harris, 1996: 27).

As regular career change becomes the norm, and as graduates are increasingly required to develop new skills and undertake additional training, so the need for lifelong learning will be reinforced. The fact that in 1994–5 60 per cent of taught postgraduate students were in the age range of 30–49 is an indicator of the growing inter-relationship between continuing study and mid-career development (Harris, 1996).

Similarly, the Harris Report concludes that, as in the US, 'The professions will need increasingly to draw upon postgraduate education for continuing professional development, as part of their requirement for lifelong learning' (Harris, 1996: 29).

Certainly the immediate value of a postgraduate qualification in the labour market is confirmed by a comparison of the first destination statistics for graduates and postgraduates. For example, a study of the labour market for postgraduates in 1991, a time of growing unemployment, showed a 4 per cent rate of unemployment for master's graduates and 3 per cent for PhDs compared to 10 per cent for first degree graduates (Connor and Jagger, 1993).

Changing patterns and changing skills

Given the speed and scale of change in both education and employment it is not surprising that it has been accompanied by a major debate about the purposes of higher education leading to an attempt by the Higher Education Quality Council to define graduate standards and the concept of 'graduateness' including the generic skills which might be expected of all graduates.

The Association of Graduate Employers (AGR) report *Skills for Graduates in the 21st Century* (1996) emphasized the need for graduates to develop 'self-reliance skills' in order to take responsibility for the management of their own careers. Thus, 'the self-reliant graduate is aware of the changing world of work, takes responsibility for his or her own career and personal development and is able to manage the relationship with work and with learning throughout all stages of life' (Association of Graduate Recruiters, 1996: 19).

During the early years of the 1990s and largely influenced by the Government's Enterprise in Higher Education Initiative, the debate about graduate skills focused on the need for students to develop personal transferable skills. The AGR report moved the debate forward by relating the skills graduates required to the new demands they would face in a mass graduate labour market. If employers required flexibility and offered short-term contracts rather than a career for life it was clear that graduates would

Table 8.7 Skills that are difficult to recruit

	All organizations
Interpersonal skills	36.2
Commercial acumen	29.3
Leadership	17.2
Technical skills	15.5
Enthusiasm	10.3
Innovation and imagination	8.6
Foreign languages	5.2
Programming	5.2

Note: No. of respondents specifying difficulties = 58.
Source: Association of Graduate Recruiters (1996).

need to learn how to manage their own careers, take responsibility for their own development and build their own networks to secure their future.

Similarly, the graduate penetration into the small and medium employer (SME) sector required new approaches and attitudes. The traditional two-year graduate training programme allowed graduates time and space to settle into employment, a luxury which the small firms sector could not offer or afford. Graduates were expected to 'hit the deck running'; they were required to 'make an immediate contribution to the bottom line'; and they had to bring with them up-to-date skills and knowledge. Not surprisingly, many of these potential employers, with little or no experience of graduate recruitment, have been resistant to the concept of recruiting a new graduate. Surveys of employers in the SME sector regularly underline the same barriers to the recruitment of new graduates, namely, that they are too expensive, lack experience and are difficult to accommodate in a small company (Rosa, 1994). As the pace of change has accelerated it is not just the SME sector that has required graduates to be more adaptable. As the 1997 'Graduates' Work' report concluded, 'In the delayered, downsized, information-technology driven innovation organisation there is likely to be less time for new recruits to "get up to speed"' (Harvey, Moon and Geall, 1997: 1).

Thus, larger recruiters have also often been critical of the new product emerging from our mass higher education system. Criticisms most frequently focus on graduates' ability, in particular their basic numeracy and literacy, together with their lack of well-developed personal skills. Table 8.7 identifies the skill areas where employers have the most difficulty in identifying good candidates. Despite the expansion of HE, and the greater emphasis on vocational subjects in the new university sector, it has remained the case that graduates from the traditional university sector appear to continue to be best placed in the job market. Indeed, the Performance Indicators Project (Pettifor, 1996) confirms that the traditional hierarchy of 'Oxbridge', red brick, plate glass and former polytechnics appears to have become more rather than less entrenched in the current graduate labour market.

This emphasis on quality is equally reflected in employer forecasts of their future demand for postgraduates. Thus the 'Harris' Report emphasizes the need to maintain quality while increasing output, and underlines the importance of generic skills training including project management, communication skills and problem solving (Harris, 1996).

The current employment scene

The major source of information on the immediate destinations of graduates is the annual First Destination Statistics survey (FDS) compiled by the Higher Education Statistics Agency (HESA). The annual graduate salary and vacancy survey conducted by AGR (1996) and the *Statistical Quarterly* produced by The Higher Education Careers Services Unit (CSU, 1996) provide a more detailed commentary on the graduate labour market. All these sources confirm that prospects for graduates have steadily improved since the low of 1992 and are better now than at any time in the 1990s. Table 8.2 illustrates this improvement in immediate employment prospects and gradual decline in unemployment levels. Figure 8.1 confirms the improved picture for both the traditional and new university sectors. The data used here relates to the graduating cohort of 1994. In 1996 responsibility for the publication of graduate destination data passed from the Universities Statistical Record (USR) and the Department of Education to HESA. HESA introduced a number of significant changes to the coding of destinations which makes overall comparisons with previous years impossible. However, the recording of those classified as unemployed six months after graduation has remained consistent and this confirms the improvement continuing into 1995 with unemployment levels down to 8 per cent (Higher Education Statistics Agency, 1996).

Given the expansion of higher education opportunities, it is important to monitor the performance of mature students, ethnic minorities and the disabled in the labour market. The 1995 HESA statistics show all three categories experienced higher levels of unemployment, suggesting that a more open education system had not yet led to a more equal employment market.

The 1996 AGR graduate vacancies and salary survey forecasts further improvements for 1997 graduates. AGR members predict a 9.9 per cent increase in vacancies with a significant variation between the industrial sector (+19.6 per cent) and non-industrial organizations (+5.6 per cent). This forecast increase in vacancies is mirrored by a rise in the proportion of AGR employers reporting recruiting difficulties: a rise from 39.4 per cent in 1995 to 44.5 per cent in 1996. Here again the industrial sector is experiencing greater difficulties than non-industrial employers.

According to the AGR survey (Table 8.8), these problems are particularly marked in computer science and IT, finance, accountancy and engineering. The Income Data Services survey of February 1996 highlighted similar

Table 8.8 Main areas of recruitment difficulties

	Industrial	Non-industrial	All organizations
Computer science and IT	25.4	15.8	21.0
Finance, accountancy and pensions	13.4	17.5	15.3
Engineering (unspecified)	19.4	1.8	11.3
Manufacturing/production	17.9	–	9.7
Electronics/electronic engineering	10.4	5.3	8.1
Lack of appropriate skills in applicants	6.0	8.8	7.3
Chemical engineering	9.0	3.5	6.5
Sales, marketing and purchasing	7.5	5.3	6.5

Note: No. of respondents specifying difficulties = 67 (industrial), 57 (non-industrial), 124 total.
Source: Association of Graduate Recruiters (1996).

problems and showed how significant the shortfall could be for individual companies. For example, Lloyds Bank was 23 per cent under its target, and HMV and Argos were both 50 per cent under. By contrast, only one public sector organization in their survey, the Inland Revenue, experienced a graduate shortage.

Subject differences

What this overall picture does not show is the significant variation in immediate career paths depending on the graduate's subject of study. Figure 8.3 reveals major differences which reflect a number of important trends, namely:

- *the importance of postgraduate study.* In the physical and biological sciences the percentage continuing on to postgraduate study has consistently been above 29 per cent throughout the 1990s. A postgraduate qualification has thus increasingly become a requirement for the pursuit of a career in scientific research. In contrast, the percentage of electrical and electronic engineers embarking on further academic study has been consistently below 12 per cent, an indication of both the greater availability of immediate job opportunities and lower employer interest in recruiting engineers at the postgraduate level.
- *vocational study and employment.* Press headlines often emphasize a link between studying vocational courses and enhanced job prospects, but the data reveals the superficiality of this comment. For example, law graduates have one of the lowest permanent employment records since the majority continue on to further studies for the Bar and solicitors' profession. In contrast, a far higher percentage of sociology graduates succeed in gaining permanent employment on graduation. This reflects the openness of the UK graduate labour market in which something

Figure 8.3 Subject comparisons of all first degree graduate destinations, 1994

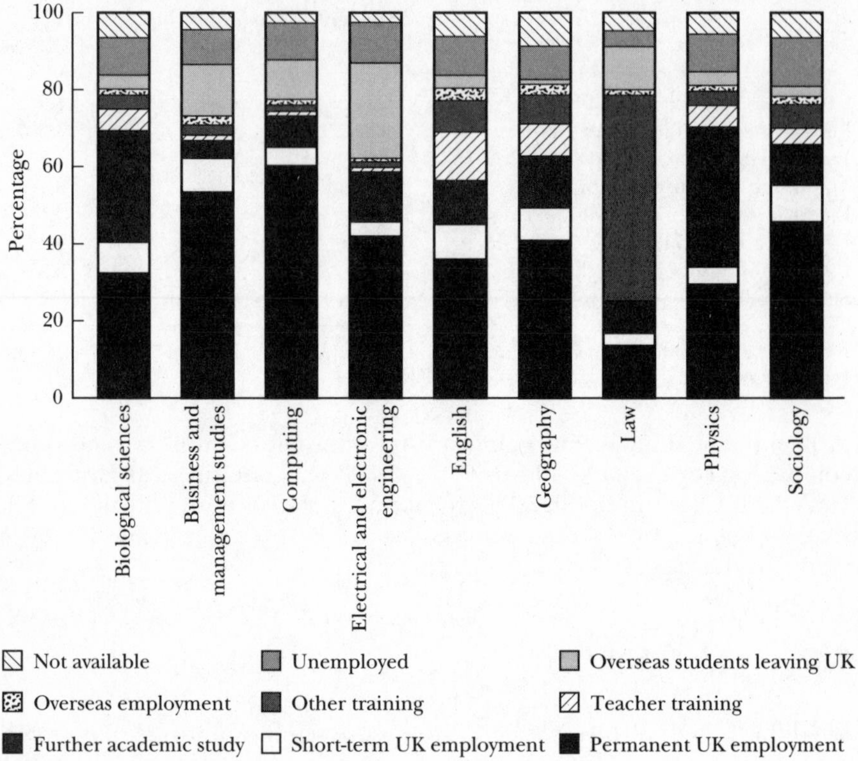

☒ Not available   ▨ Unemployed   ▨ Overseas students leaving UK

▨ Overseas employment   ■ Other training   ▨ Teacher training

■ Further academic study   ☐ Short-term UK employment   ■ Permanent UK employment

Note: Data based on known destinations.
Source: Association of Graduate Careers' Advisory Services (1995).

approaching 40 per cent of all vacancies are open to graduates of any discipline and the fact that large numbers of sociology graduates entered clerical and related occupations on graduation.

- *volatility in the market*. The severity of the recession in 1991 and 1992 revealed the greater vulnerability of graduates from more vocational subjects who had traditional expectations of a job related to their degree. Thus, the fall in employment for computing graduates, over 11 per cent between 1990 and 1991, was far greater than for English graduates where the fall was less than 4 per cent. Having embarked on a non-vocational course such as English, these students would be much more aware of the need for flexibility and have a more open-minded response to the opportunities available to them in all sectors of the labour market.
- *the value of temporary employment*. In career areas as diverse as social work, museum work and environmental conservation, temporary work is often a prerequisite for either further training or permanent employment. This short-term work cannot simply be equated with graduate

'under-employment' and higher than average levels of temporary work should not necessarily be interpreted as a poor performance in the labour market.

One important characteristic of the graduate labour market in the 1990s is the increased variation in routes into employment and a notable difference in the time it may take new graduates to move into their first established career position. Temporary employment is often an important means of gaining experience and paying off debts before embarking on a more formal career.

Immediate versus longer term prospects

Given that the First Destination Statistics graduate survey is a snapshot picture taken six months beyond graduation, it is not surprising to find significant variation in immediate job prospects. However, longitudinal studies tracing the movement of graduates within the labour market show that these differences quickly even out to leave no long-term significant variation in job prospects. The most recent longitudinal study into the destinations of Scottish graduates, provides a valuable insight into this process (Levey and McKenzie, 1996). Table 8.9 shows the substantial increase in employment (+34.1 per cent) and significant decrease in unemployment (−7.3 per cent) over the four-year period 1992–6. Table 8.9 confirms that this improvement in employment occurred across all subject groups, although there remained a difference in rates of unemployment by subject. Reference to the position of Mathematical Sciences shows how quickly the immediate destination picture becomes outdated. In 1992, they had the highest level of unemployment in the survey at 13.2 per cent but by 1996 this had fallen to a mere 0.5 per cent.

Postgraduate versus first degree prospects

The 1996 Higher Education Statistics Agency confirm the advantages of a postgraduate education for new entrants to the labour market. In 1994–5 only 2.8 per cent of UK PhDs and 5.7 per cent of other UK postgraduates were recorded as unemployed compared to 9.2 per cent for UK first degree graduates. Once again this snapshot reveals little about the quality or level of employment entered by postgraduates. In the mass labour market of the 1990s there is evidence both of increasing overlap and substitution between first and higher degree graduates. Qualification inflation has blurred the boundaries in the graduate job market, resulting in increasing competition between graduates and postgraduates. This is particularly true in areas such as personnel, marketing and computing where first degree graduates regularly compete on equal terms with students from one-year postgraduate vocational training courses.

Table 8.9 Changing Scottish graduate destinations, 1992–6 by subject group

Subject group	In employment		Further study		Not available		Unemployed	
	1992	1996	1992	1996	1992	1996	1992	1996
Allied to medicine	79.1	89.8	14.7	8.5	0.0	0.6	6.1	1.1
Biological sciences	43.4	68.8	43.4	26.3	4.5	1.6	8.7	3.2
Physical sciences	27.1	72.8	57.3	19.8	5.0	1.5	10.6	5.9
Mathematical sciences	58.0	93.8	27.3	5.7	1.5	0.0	13.2	0.5
Engineering and technology	64.7	92.8	19.8	4.4	3.0	0.8	12.6	1.9
Social studies	36.7	90.3	48.9	7.4	6.7	1.0	7.7	1.4
Business and administration studies	76.4	96.4	13.7	2.4	2.9	0.9	7.0	0.3
Language and related studies	34.2	80.5	46.8	14.0	8.9	1.8	10.1	3.7
Humanities	47.3	79.5	39.1	15.0	4.9	3.0	8.7	2.5
All groups	52.3	86.4	34.1	10.4	4.2	1.2	9.4	2.1

Source: Levey and McKenzie (1996).

In contrast, in the higher education sector and in scientific research and development, particularly in leading edge technologies in the pharmaceutical and biotechnology industries, a PhD is now established as the entry level qualification. As a result, graduates seeking entry to these fields and career development within them are increasingly required to continue their education beyond the first degree.

Graduate under-employment

It is often claimed that a mass higher education system has devalued the value of graduates in the labour market and led to significant 'under-employment of graduates' in career areas and at levels which would not traditionally be viewed as a graduate job. What is certainly true is that the definition of a graduate job has undergone a major change, so rendering meaningless any static definition of graduate employment. During the 1970s and 1980s this redefinition was a gradual process in which career areas such as retailing, purchasing and the police service emerged as new graduate jobs. The rapid expansion of higher education, radical restructuring within organizations and the reorganization of jobs has greatly accelerated this process of change. As the Graduates' Work survey concludes, 'Rather than graduate opportunities disappearing there is every indication that graduate opportunities are expanding, although outside the traditional ("high-flier") graduate career' (Harvey, Moon and Geall, 1997: 35). It is also important to note that this structural change may well have been accompanied by attitudinal change in which the new graduates of the 1990s might positively choose to enter lower-level non-traditional graduate-level jobs as their first entry point into the labour market.

Mason, in his study of the impact of mass higher education on graduate utilization in British industry, highlights the 'dangers of assuming that graduates are necessarily being "under-utilised" if they enter jobs for which university degrees have not "usually" or "traditionally" been required' (Mason, 1996: 95). He helpfully suggests that two conditions might be required to assess 'under-utilization': first, if the job has not been modified to take advantage of a graduate's skills, and second if no salary advantage is offered to graduates. By his criteria, his study of the steel industry showed minimal under-employment of graduates, whereas a comparison with the rapidly expanding financial services sector revealed up to '45 per cent of all graduates entering employment . . . in clerical, cashier and similar jobs rather than mainstream "graduate level jobs"' (Mason, 1996: 98). From his study, we might therefore conclude that there may be significant under-utilization of graduates in the newly emerging sectors of the graduate labour market.

However, this study once again focuses on immediate graduate employment and therefore what we may be witnessing is graduates starting at lower levels and in different non-graduate functions in order to gain experience before progressing in their careers. The longitudinal Scottish survey

Figure 8.4 Changes in the balance of employment, 1992 and 1996 – percentage of employed graduates entering non-professional and non-management occupations

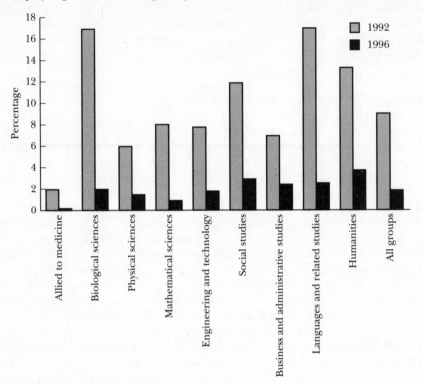

Source: Levey and McKenzie (1996).

lends weight to such an interpretation. Figure 8.4 demonstrates a significant move out of non-professional and non-managerial occupations in the period 1992–6.

This movement within the labour market is also underlined in the Scottish Survey by the fact that 25 per cent of the graduates had been in three or more jobs over the four-year period. Their salary progression over the same period is a further indication of upward career progression. However, what is clear is that for new graduates there is now a significant polarization in the job market. High flyers will continue to be in high demand, will attract high salaries and enter high level jobs commensurate with their skills and knowledge. For others, their immediate prospects will be far less attractive as they enter second-tier graduate programmes or more basic employment with less opportunity to use their skills and knowledge. In consequence, their immediate salaries will be less than those offered to their high-flying contemporaries.

International comparisons suggest that in a mass higher education system such a polarization may become institutionalized and persist longer term.

For example, the US Bureau of Labor Statistics show that the 'proportion of graduates classified as being under-utilized has increased from 11 per cent in 1969 to 20 per cent in 1990 and is projected to reach 30 per cent by 2005' (Connor *et al.*, 1996). Although not directly comparable, research in The Netherlands suggests that 20 per cent of graduates are under-employed, while in Belgium the figure is put at 25 per cent (European Commission, 1996).

Graduate salaries

According to the 1996 Incomes Data Services survey, in the first five years of their careers, graduates can expect to increase their salaries by around 10 per cent a year. Table 8.10 shows the variation in increase across the main employment sectors. Once again this longer term perspective points to the progression of graduates within the labour market. Table 8.11, derived from the August 1996 CSU *Statistical Quarterly*, indicates only a modest

Table 8.10 1995 salaries of 1990 graduate recruits by sector

	Sector (number)				
	Manufacturing (26) £p.a.	Finance (14) £p.a.	Service (13) £p.a.	Public (6) £p.a.	All (59) £p.a.
Minimum	16,000	16,400	15,300	19,260	15,300
Maximum	28,000	43,000	45,800	29,000	45,800
Median	22,010	18,960	25,000	21,709	22,000
Average	22,333	22,844	27,430	23,379	23,684
Average five-year lead (%)	60.8	43.3	72.4	88.5	60.8

Source: Income Data Services (1996).

Table 8.11 Salaries by subject of study, May 1994–May 1995

Subject area	Median salary
Life sciences	13,941
Physical sciences	13,100
Mathematical sciences and informatics	13,000
Engineering and technology	13,884
Social studies	13,144
Business and administration	13,000
Total all subjects	14,000

Source: Higher Education Careers Services Unit (1996).

Table 8.12   Forecast 1996 starting salaries by employer group

	Median starting salary (£)
Energy and water industries	15,000
Chemical and allied industries	16,000
Engineering	14,405
Electrical/electronic industries	14,750
Food, drink and tobacco	15,000
Other manufacturing	15,200
Construction	13,500
Hotels and catering	10,250
Retail industry	14,500
Transport and communications	15,500
Banking and finance	16,250
Insurance	14,575
Legal services	18,875
Accountancy	13,500
Other business services	14,875
Public services	14,000
All industries	14,750

Source: Association of Graduate Recruiters (1996).

Table 8.13   Forecast 1996 starting salaries by organization size

No. of employees	Lower quartile (£)	Median (£)	Upper quartile (£)
1–249	13,500	14,050	17,000
250–999	13,250	14,500	16,000
1000–2499	13,500	14,500	16,300
2500–4999	14,500	15,000	16,812
5000–19,999	14,000	14,750	15,500
20,000 +	14,475	15,000	16,119
All sizes	13,800	14,750	16,000

Source: Association of Graduate Recruiters (1996).

difference in graduate starting salaries by subject. The 1996 AGR Salary and
Vacancies Survey shows the major variations are by employment sector and
by size of organization (Tables 8.12 and 8.13).

Student debt

A review of career opportunities for graduates in the 1990s would be incom-
plete without reference to the growth of student debt. A number of recent
surveys have placed the average student debt on graduation between £2500
and £3000 (Barclays Bank, 1996; Purcell and Pitcher, 1996). The recent

study of 5000 undergraduates by Purcell and Pitcher shows high levels of debt are beginning to influence the ways in which graduates move into the labour market, so contributing to the greater variation in immediate career patterns. Two major trends of the 1990s can be seen to be influenced by student debt. They are:

- *short termism in the labour market.* This is reflected in the increasing number of graduates taking any job simply to pay off their debts before contemplating a longer term career commitment. According to the 1994/5 HESA statistics, of the 55 per cent of graduates who found permanent employment in the UK, only just over a half of these 'were paid, full-time and permanent' (Higher Education Statistics Agency, 1996: 97).
- *postponement of further study and training.* Both the Purcell and Pitcher study and anecdotal evidence from graduate careers advisers suggest that increasing debt levels are beginning to discourage graduates from immediately embarking on further study and training. Two quotes from undergraduates in the Purcell and Pitcher study illustrate this most graphically. 'Will have to go home to parents to live while I'm paying off my debt – also can't do MA as I wanted.' 'I have to find a job rather than do research, which I'd prefer' (Purcell and Pitcher, 1996: 22).

The influence of debt can also be seen to be a factor in the dramatic fall in applications for legal training at both the Common Professional Exam and Legal Practice Course level. Graduates already in debt are reluctant to incur a further £10,000 debt to train for a career in law at a time when the market is clearly over-subscribed and an immediate return on their investment cannot be guaranteed. In an improving labour market, with a greater number of jobs on offer, this may result in a fallback in the number of graduates proceeding immediately to full-time study and a subsequent increase in those opting for this two to three years beyond graduation.

Changing markets . . . changing expectations

That the graduate labour market has fundamentally changed in the 1990s is clear, what is less well understood is how far graduate expectations have also changed. The recent 'Great Expectations' study reveals helpful insights into current student expectations (Purcell and Pitcher, 1996). Figure 8.5 illustrates the types of jobs they expected to apply for and portrays a familiar picture which appears to have changed little in the 1990s. However, student comments made in focus group discussions did reveal an understanding of the changed market they were about to enter.

Take the quote from a woman student at a 'mid-century university' that 'There is no long term security; the days are gone when you had a job for life . . . I expect I will be confronted, in the main, with part-time, job share

Figure 8.5 Types of job that undergraduates expected to apply for, May 1996

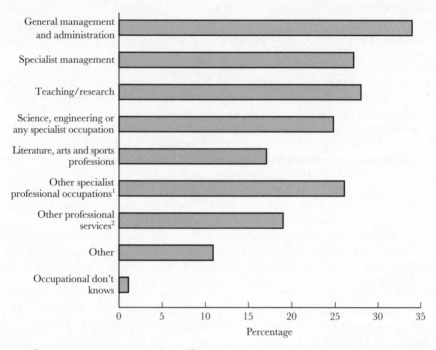

Notes: [1] For example, lawyer, accountant. [2] For example, systems analyst, advertising, copywriter.
Source: Purcell and Pitcher (1996).

and/or temporary work, or no work at all!' Similarly, the quote from a woman law student reflects the new reality where 'Few of my friends have found employment in the areas they hoped to pursue careers in and several of them who left last year are still working in mundane jobs' (Purcell and Pitcher, 1996: 38). That the graduate labour market is increasingly polarized is also reflected in the comments from these focus groups. Thus this pessimism was matched by more optimistic students who, recognized the changes but none the less 'basically hoped and expected to have the kind of career for which a degree has traditionally provided the entry' (Purcell and Pitcher, 1996: 40).

Interestingly, the undergraduates involved in the survey were fully aware of how important their degree classification would be to their future prospects. Thus, the students surveyed had 'a general perception that employers are increasingly regarding Upper Second Class Honours as a threshold, below which they do not short list candidates' (Purcell and Pitcher, 1996: 20). The 1994/5 HESA statistics show the reality of this perception, for unemployment amongst graduates with a First or 2.1 was less than 8 per cent but rose to 11.7 per cent for those with 2.2s and 16.6 per cent for those with Third Class Honours.

Figure 8.6 Characteristics important to undergraduates in applying for employment, May 1996

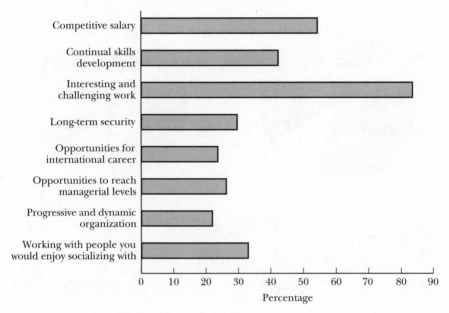

Source: Purcell and Pitcher (1996).

The survey further underlined how well their expectations matched the new realities of graduate employment with students, emphasizing the importance of interest and challenge at work and the relatively lower significance of long-term security (Figure 8.6).

Future graduate prospects

Without structural change in the labour market, the rapid rise in graduate output in the early 1990s would have inevitably resulted in a substantial increase in graduate unemployment. However, because of the demand for a more highly skilled workforce to enhance business competitiveness in an increasingly global market, graduate employment prospects appear set to continue to improve for the remainder of the century. Figure 8.7 provides an occupational comparison between 1981 and 1994 and shows that the employment mix has steadily favoured higher level occupations at the expense of lower skilled manual jobs. Thus, between 1981 and 1994 managers and administrators grew by 3.4 per cent a year, professionals 1.8 per cent and associate professionals by 2.7 per cent (Department for Education and Employment, 1996). The forecasts are that these trends will continue into the 21st century. The Institute of Employment Studies predicts that the

Figure 8.7   UK employment by occupation, 1981 and 1994

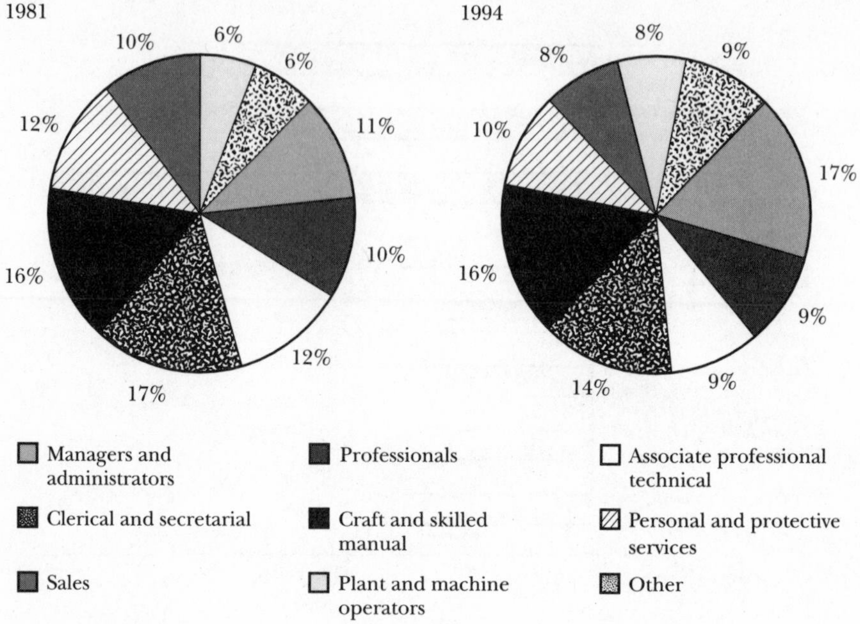

1981   1994

Managers and administrators	Professionals	Associate professional technical
Clerical and secretarial	Craft and skilled manual	Personal and protective services
Sales	Plant and machine operators	Other

Source: DfEE (1996).

employment of people with degrees is forecast to grow by 40 per cent between 1991 and 2001; a dramatic increase compared to their overall prediction of a 3 per cent growth (Connor *et al.*, 1996). If these forecasts are achieved, an additional 1 million graduates will be absorbed into the labour market in the decade 1991–2001. As these graduates seek to develop their careers they are increasingly likely to turn to postgraduate education both as a means to differentiate themselves in a mass market and as a route to career change and progression.

Although such forecast growth is substantial, it may not be able to keep pace with the supply of the highly qualified, particularly if age participation rates in HE rise from 30 per cent to 40 per cent as sought by organizations such as the Confederation of British Industry (1994). At other employment levels, this might be expected to result in substantial surpluses and a dramatic increase in unemployment. However, the experience of graduates in the early 1990s suggests this is unlikely to be the case. It is more likely that the surplus will be absorbed through a continuation of graduate substitution and displacement of the less well qualified and a continuing upskilling in jobs leading to 'qualification inflation'.

The graduates of the late 1990s and early 21st century will potentially be faced not with high unemployment levels but a major under-employment problem. As a result, the graduate labour market may become even more diversified, the differences in immediate employment patterns between subjects far more polarized and the salary and career options markedly different between the most and least successful in the mass market of the 21st century.

Conclusions

Although the rapid expansion of higher education, at both undergraduate and postgraduate levels, coincided with a severe economic recession, the data shows that, both in the short and long term, graduates have been successfully absorbed into the labour market. It also shows that the market has undergone fundamental structural change. Although large recruiters still set the standard by which a traditional graduate job is measured, the greatest growth in opportunities has occurred in the SME sector and in lower level employment. The nature of a graduate job has been redefined, the contract between employer and employee rewritten and the skills required by graduates to succeed in this new world reassessed.

The simultaneous expansion of postgraduate education has also blurred the traditional boundaries between first degree and higher degree jobs. Thus, first and higher degree graduates are increasingly in competition for entry level jobs particularly with traditional 'blue chip' recruiters or in the most competitive sectors of the labour market. The true value of a postgraduate education will increasingly be seen in longer term career development rather than immediate job or salary prospects.

Within less than a decade, the élite markets of graduate education and graduate employment have been successfully transformed into mass markets. Any mass market is inevitably more diversified and more complex and the new graduate labour market is no exception. Thus, the immediate destination patterns of graduates show greater variations in both the type and levels of employment/unemployment than in the more settled times of the 1970s and 1980s. The current debate about graduate under-employment reflects a labour market in transition. Attitudinally it harks back to a more static, more traditional concept of a graduate job rooted in an élite system. Structurally, it may reflect the reality of the new mass market in which under-employment becomes institutionalized. Longitudinal studies of the UK labour market suggest that under-employment is currently a short-term phenomenon, but US and other European experience indicate it may be part of the structural change accompanying the development of a mass HE system. Further longitudinal studies at both the first degree and postgraduate level are required to help understand this change in the UK market.

What is not in doubt is that employer expectations of graduates have changed for ever and the need for graduates as the core of the skilled labour force of the 21st century will continue to grow. Student expectations are also changing to match the new realities of the mass graduate labour market. The success of a mass HE system in the 21st century may be measured by its ability to produce the right graduates with the right skills and attitudes to match these new demands. Quality of output will be a critical factor in graduate employment and lifelong learning will be a key to long-term career progression.

References

Association of Graduate Careers Advisory Services (1995) *What do Graduates do?* Cambridge: Hobson.

Association of Graduate Recruiters (1995) *Skills for Graduates in the 21st Century.* Cambridge: AGR.

Association of Graduate Recruiters (1996) *Graduate Salaries and Vacancies,* summer update. Cambridge: AGR.

Barclays Bank (1996) *The National Graduate Survey, 1995.* London: Collective Enterprises Ltd.

Committee of Directors of Polytechnics (various) *First Destinations of Polytechnic Students.* London: CDP.

Confederation of British Industry (1994) *Thinking Ahead: Ensuring the Expansion of Higher Education into the 21st Century.* London: CBI.

Connor, H. and Jagger, N. (1993) *The Labour Market for Postgraduates,* Report 257. Brighton: Institute for Employment Studies.

Connor, H., Pearson, R., Court, G. and Jagger, N. (1996) *University Challenge: Student Choices in the 21st Century,* Report 306. Brighton: Institute for Employment Studies.

Connor, H. and Pollard, E. (1996) *What Do Graduates Really Do?,* Report 308. Brighton: Institute for Employment Studies.

Department for Education and Employment (1996) *Labour Market and Skill Trends 1996–97.* London: DfEE.

Department for Trade and Industry (1996) *Statistical Supplement.* London: DTI.

European Commission (1996) *Eures University Pilot Project 1993–96 Evaluation Report.* Brussels: Author.

Harris, M. (1996) *Review of Postgraduate Education.* Bristol: HEFCE.

Harvey, L., Moon, S. and Geall, V. (1997) *Graduates' Work.* Birmingham: University of Central England in Birmingham.

Higher Education Careers Services Unit (1989–94) *First Destination Statistics of Graduates.* Manchester: Higher Education CSU.

Higher Education Careers Services Unit (1996) *Statistical Quarterly.* Manchester: Higher Education CSU.

Higher Education Funding Council (1996) *Review of Postgraduate Education.* Bristol: HEFCE, CUCP, SCOP.

Higher Education Statistics Agency (1996) *First Destinations of Students Leaving Higher Education Institutions, 1994/5.* Cheltenham: HESA.

Income Data Services (1996) *IDS Pay and Progression for Graduates 1995–96,* Research File 37. London: IDS.

Levey, M. and McKenzie, K. (1996) *The Class of '92: Report on a Longitudinal Study of Graduate Destinations.* Glasgow: Scottish Graduate Careers Partnership.

Mason, G. (1996) Graduate utilisation in British industry: the initial impact of mass higher education, *National Institute Economic Review,* May, 93–103.

Pettifor, C. (1996) *Signposts to Employability, Performance Indicators Project*, Grantham: published by the author.

Purcell, K. and Pitcher, J. (1996) *Great Expectations: The New Diversity of Graduate Skills and Aspirations*. Manchester: Association of Graduate Careers Advisory Services (AGCAS)/Higher Education Careers Services Unit (CSU).

Rosa, P. C. (1994) *The Long Term Supply of Graduate Entrepreneurs*. Stirling: Scottish Enterprise Foundation.

Smithers, A. and Robinson, P. (1995) *Post-18 Education*. London: Council for Industry and Higher Education.

Smithers, A. and Robinson, P. (1996) *Trends in Higher Education*. London: Council for Industry and Higher Education.

Universities Statistical Record (1990–93) *First Destinations of Graduates*. Cheltenham: USR.

9

Graduate Employment Trends: Key Issues in the Labour Market of the Late 1990s and Beyond

Helen Connor

Introduction

Much has happened in both postgraduate education and the labour market during the last decade. Many of the traditional reasons for, and ways of, taking postgraduate study are changing. Postgraduates now enter a wider range of jobs and employing organizations and they face different kinds of career decisions and employment issues than their predecessors of even 10 years ago.

This chapter reviews some of the key issues, trends and developments relating to the employment of postgraduates in the UK. It draws off the available national statistics on the postgraduate labour market and recent research on employer demand for particular kinds of postgraduates.

It begins with a brief overview of the main trends and changes affecting the graduate labour market, highlighting specific issues of relevance to postgraduates. It then presents an aggregate picture of the current employment patterns of postgraduates, followed by a more detailed review of employer demand, in two fields of study, information technology (IT) and environmental sciences, which have been the subject of recent research studies.

Graduate labour market

Employment demand and opportunities for graduates in the UK have been subject to a period of rapid change over the last decade due to a combination of economic, social, technological and organizational factors. These are well documented (Goodman, 1993; Council for Industry and Higher Education, 1995; La Valle, Jagger and Connor, 1996). After a period during the mid- to late 1980s of booming graduate demand and widening opportunities for graduates when shortages were beginning to emerge, the situation changed swiftly with the onset of the recession in the UK economy to one of reduced demand and apparent surpluses of newly qualified graduates. The sudden downturn in graduate vacancies coincided with the start of a rapid expansion of higher education along with growing diversity of student intake (Connor *et al.*, 1996), and there were also longer term structural changes taking place in the labour market generally and in business reorganization and rationalization (Department for Education and Employment, 1996). As a consequence, graduate unemployment rose, the proportion of first degree graduates going into traditional types of graduate jobs and careers fell, and there were increases in entry to postgraduate study.

Since then, the graduate market has recovered somewhat. The situation today is one of improving demand for newly qualified graduates and there is a general upward trend in the UK economy for highly qualified people and increased educational requirements in many jobs (Institute of Employment Research, 1996). Market competition, however, remains high, especially for the most able graduates, and graduate unemployment levels are higher than an equivalent economic period in the 1980s.

The graduate market is no longer so dominated by a relatively small group of large employers and both small firms and self-employment play a more significant role (Connor and Pollard, 1996). Graduates are going into a wider range of work than before, sometimes displacing less well-qualified people or filling vacancies not previously associated with graduate entry. The definition of a 'graduate job' is changing. There is growing evidence of graduate 'underemployment' or 'under-utilization' by employers, more so in some sectors than others (Mason, 1995; Connor and Pollard, 1996), and a widening range of early graduate career patterns is evident. At the same time, there is increased attention being given in higher education to developing skills in students which are relevant to working life so that graduates are better prepared for successful entry to employment and career development (Council for Industry and Higher Education, 1996).

Postgraduates

What has been the impact of these changes on postgraduates? How has the postgraduate labour market been changing?

Before presenting some specific points of interest, it is worth noting that these structural changes in the graduate labour market and sudden swings in graduate demand will have affected postgraduates as well as undergraduates. This is because the recruitment needs of the private sector for postgraduates are linked to those for graduates in general and there is considerable overlap between the first degree and higher degree labour markets outside of academic and research work. A second related and important point to note is that the slow process of change in the function of postgraduate study began to quicken in the early 1990s. Previously, postgraduate study was seen primarily as very specialist, mainly providing teachers and researchers in universities, and also researchers for industry in the case of the natural sciences. It now has much wider relevance to industry and commerce. In many of the professions, a postgraduate qualification has now become a prerequisite for entry (e.g. law, education, social work) while demands for higher levels of knowledge and skills in many areas of private and public services have increased the demand for postgraduate education in general. There is also growth in demand for postgraduate education coming from individuals' increasing desire for lifelong learning in its various forms.

Growth in supply

Postgraduate student numbers have been growing at a faster rate than those at undergraduate level, up by 76 per cent between 1988/9 and 1993/4 compared with an increase of 66 per cent for first degree students. The growth rate for postgraduates, which accelerated in the early 1990s (Connor *et al.*, 1996), has continued to be higher than first degree student numbers, which have been subject to capping since 1994.

Growing emphasis on part-time study

The growth in the number of part-time postgraduate students has been particularly marked – up by 98 per cent during the period 1988/9 to 1993/4. Currently, almost 60 per cent of students on taught postgraduate courses, and over a third of research students, are studying part-time (Higher Education Statistics Agency, 1996a). Part of the reason for this shift in pattern of study has been an increase in employer-led demand for postgraduate training and education for employees, but it is also a response to demand from individuals for continuing professional development (CPD).

Staying on to do postgraduate study

There is an increasing tendency for students to continue on to postgraduate study after completing first degrees. In 1995, 21 per cent of those graduating with first degrees continued in further study or research, and in science subjects the figure was higher at over 30 per cent (Higher Education Statistics Agency, 1996b). (Unfortunately, the changes in the first destinations survey of graduates means that it is not possible to compare this figure with earlier years.)

Growing diversity in employment

A growing number of employers are recruiting postgraduates to a wider variety of jobs. This mirrors trends in the first degree market, but it also reflects the vocational emphasis of much of postgraduate study, especially in fast-growing areas such as IT and business management. However, the main focus of PhD employment is still higher education and research-based organizations.

Contract work

There is an increasing pattern of fixed-term contract employment for those seeking academic careers. Those in industrial R&D are employed increasingly, too, on a fixed-term contract basis. This means that career patterns of many young postgraduates are likely to be different than those of their predecessors. They also require skills which enable them to be pro-active in the more competitive and commercial funding environment.

Low unemployment

Unemployment of postgraduates has been low historically, and consistently lower than for first degree graduates. In 1991, in the depths of the recession, unemployment among newly qualified doctorates was just 3 per cent and slightly higher at 5 per cent for other higher degree graduates from universities (compared with over 10 per cent for first degree graduates at that time) (Connor and Jaggar, 1993). Currently, the unemployment level among all holders of postgraduate qualifications in the population is 3 per cent, compared with nearly 5 per cent among first degree holders and almost 9 per cent among the population as a whole (Office for National Statistics, 1996).

Overlap and under-employment

Increasingly, postgraduates are entering jobs where a postgraduate qualification is not an entry requirement and are recruited alongside first degree graduates, sometimes at similar rates of pay. Although people often take postgraduate study because they believe it to be essential or likely to promote their career development, this is often not true, especially where employers do not see the relevance of the postgraduate course or graduates cannot demonstrate any benefits gained. Because of the overlap between first degree and higher degree employment and the widening range of employment being taken up by postgraduates, it is likely that 'under-employment' is a growing trend among postgraduates as well as first degree graduates (see above), but there is little research to date which has examined this issue in sufficient depth, although research in progress on graduate under-utilization is concerned with this issue (at Social and Community Planning Research, London, sponsored by the DfEE).

Employer–education partnerships

An increasingly important dimension in postgraduate education is employer links. There has been a growing recognition that students need to develop more work-relevant skills and that postgraduate education has a role in meeting economic as well as individual needs. It is also seen as aiding technology transfer and providing a source of external revenue to universities. An array of schemes and initiatives to involve employers more in postgraduate education has been successfully developed (e.g. Teaching Company Scheme) as well as individual course or department level activities (e.g. tailor-made MBA programmes). These are often used by employers as recruitment tools.

Emphasis on skills

The significance of personal skills in employment has been highlighted by many research studies, for example: Soskice (1993) has drawn comparisons with the US in showing that new patterns of work require interpersonal skill to a much greater extent than in previous decades; the Association of Graduate Recruiters (AGR) in a major study on graduate skills (1995) identified self-reliance as being key for graduates in managing career progression and effective learning; and the recent Institute for Employment Studies (IES) study on the labour market for IT postgraduates (Rick *et al.*, 1996; discussed in more detail below) highlighted the importance of non-technical as well as technical skills. A major difficulty, however, comes when trying to distinguish what generic attributes or skills graduates rather than non-graduates should (or do) possess. Employers' views vary considerably by sector and discipline, by work context and type of company (e.g. small and large firms). In the Higher Education Quality Council's 1996 work on graduate standards, there was general agreement about the kinds of attributes graduates should possess, but it was difficult to develop a single set of attributes which should be found in all graduates, and virtually impossible to develop any differentiation by level of qualification. Further development work is felt to be needed to identify qualities expected of graduates within a series of specific domains, such as the aims of particular programmes of study, institutional missions and the culture of specific subject areas.

The international dimension

There is a growing international dimension to the postgraduate labour market. This is seen on the supply side both in the expanding number of international students in the UK – over 40,000 postgraduate students in 1994/5 were from abroad – and in the development of joint degree programmes/research projects with universities in other countries where UK students spend time abroad (Higher Education Statistics Agency, 1996a).

Of particular significance, is the growth of the global labour market for scientists and technologists seeking R&D careers. In a survey of 100 major R&D centres across Europe undertaken by the Institute for Employment Studies in 1994 (Court and Jaggar, 1995), on average 10 per cent of scientists were foreign nationals, but nearer 30 per cent in some of the smaller European countries. The main reasons employers gave for recruiting non-nationals were (a) their needs for specialist skills and expertise not available locally and (b) the desire to build an international culture. Recruitment had often flowed from international collaborative projects and visiting fellowships. While the USA remains the key international player, there is growing mobility across Europe, in particular between France, Germany and the UK, and eastern Europe, encouraged in part by EU programmes.

Current employment profile

There are three main sources of national data on the employment of postgraduates in the UK. The Census of Population and the Labour Force Survey provide data on the stock of people in the UK economy with postgraduate qualifications, while the Higher Education Statistics Agency (HESA) provides data on the employment destinations of newly qualified graduates. Their coverage, however, does not provide sufficient data to analyse postgraduate employment in detail, mainly because of small sample sizes. They are usually supplemented by *ad hoc* follow-up surveys of graduates from particular courses, institutions or disciplines. In this section an overview is given of the current employment profile of postgraduates using the nationally available data to illustrate some of the points made above on the greater spread of postgraduate employment across the economy; while the next section investigates some issues on employer demand and skill requirements in more depth using data from recent discipline-based studies of postgraduates.

Postgraduate population

Between 1981 and 1991 the number of employed people in the UK with postgraduate level qualifications doubled, to reach 345,000. However, this still represented only 1.4 per cent of all employed people or 13.3 per cent of all graduates in the UK. In 1981, these percentages were 0.7 per cent and 10.3 per cent respectively. By 2001, the employment of postgraduates is expected to reach over 500,000, a further rise of 45 per cent, a slower rate of growth than in the previous decade. By that time, postgraduates will comprise almost 2 per cent of the workforce but will remain at around 13 per cent of all graduates in the population (because of the rapid expansion in first degree study during the 1990s). These are based on medium-term demand forecasts produced by the Institute of Employment Research (1996) at the University of Warwick.

Table 9.1   Employment of postgraduates by sector

Sector	Proportion in each sector (%)	Penetration rate (as % of total employees)
Manufacturing	7.8	0.6
Other industries	6.7	0.7
Distribution/transport	5.4	0.3
Financial services	2.9	1.1
Business services	13.2	2.6
Public administration/defence	8.0	1.7
Education	34.8	4.9
R&D	4.9	16.5
Medical/health services	7.6	1.7
Other	8.6	1.3
All sectors	100.0	1.4

Note: Total number of postgraduates = 332,000.
Source: Office of Population Censuses and Surveys (1994).

These overall postgraduate employment trends reflect of course the substantial growth in supply of postgraduates over the period. There is also a tendency generally for people with better qualifications to find jobs more easily, and have less likelihood of being unemployed, and there are also long-term changes taking place in the occupational structure of the UK economy with the number of jobs in professional occupations rising faster than other occupations, especially those normally associated with lower qualifications (Institute of Employment Research, 1996). Another factor is the growing 'post-graduatization' of some professions, such as the growth of postgraduate teaching qualifications.

Sector

There is uneven distribution of postgraduates across employment sectors, as Table 9.1 shows. Over one-third of the total are in the education sector (schools, colleges and universities) while around one in eight are employed in business services. The remainder are spread across a number of sectors including public administration, medical/health/vet services, R&D (research and development) activities, manufacturing and other industries. Their penetration rate (i.e. postgraduates as a percentage of total employment in the sector) is considerably higher in the R&D sector where one in six employees is a postgraduate. The lowest penetration of postgraduates is in manufacturing and other industries, distribution and transport (each under 1 per cent). The sectoral distribution varies by gender: for example, half of female postgraduates are employed in education, health or medical services, compared with 40 per cent of male postgraduates.

Table 9.2 Employment of postgraduates by occupation

Occupation	Proportion in each occupation (%)	Penetration rate (as % of total employees)
Managers and administrators	19.6	1.7
Natural scientists	10.0	28.8
Engineers and technologists	8.0	6.0
Teaching professionals	31.7	12.2
Business and financial professionals	2.8	5.5
Health professionals	5.4	11.3
Other professionals	6.9	6.5
Associated professional/technical	11.4	1.8
Clerical/secretarial	2.1	0.2
Other	2.1	0.1
All occupations	100.0	1.4

Note: Total number of postgraduates = 325,000.
Source: Office of Population Censuses and Surveys (1994).

Occupation

The breakdown by occupation shows a less diffused picture (see Table 9.2).
Almost 85 per cent of people with postgraduate qualifications are employed
in managerial or professional occupations, the largest group being in the
teaching profession (32 per cent). They also tend to be concentrated in particular occupations, for example: one in four natural scientists is a postgraduate, one in eight teaching professionals and one in ten health professionals.

There is evidence that postgraduates are increasing their penetration
rates in most occupations and spreading more across the occupation spectrum (Institute of Employment Research, 1996). Those occupations showing greatest growth of postgraduate employment include teaching, health
and other professions. Growth in postgraduate penetration rates has also
been seen in some non-professional occupations (though from very low
bases), a possible indication of growing levels of 'under-utilization' as more
postgraduates take up jobs previously associated with less qualified people.

Graduate destinations

Turning now to the new supply of postgraduates to the labour market,
the HESA (1996b) statistics on first destinations of graduates also show a
fairly broad sectoral pattern of employment (see Table 9.3). Half of male
postgraduates entered the education sector, 12 per cent joined industry,
15 per cent business and R&D services and 7 per cent public administration/
defence. Female postgraduates were much more concentrated in education
(73 per cent).

Table 9.3   Postgraduates entering full-time paid employment in UK by gender and sector of employment, 1994/5

	Male	Female
Manufacturing	9.7	4.2
Other industrial/agricultural	2.6	0.7
Business and research activities	14.5	5.4
Public administration/defence	7.3.	4.5
Education	50.6	72.7
Health and social work	4.3	6.9
Financial activities	4.5	1.5
Other commerce/services	6.7	4.3

Source: Higher Education Statistics Agency (1996b).

Figure 9.1   Employment pattern of postgraduates*, 1994/5

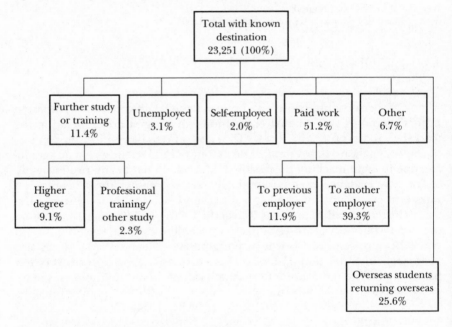

Note: *Doctorates and other higher degrees only.

Relatively small numbers of postgraduates did not enter employment but continued in further study or training (7 per cent) or were unemployed and seeking employment or training (6 per cent). The latter figure was made up of 3 per cent of doctorates, 6.5 per cent of other higher degree graduates and 8 per cent of graduates from postgraduate certificate in education.

Figure 9.1 further illustrates the breakdown of employment patterns of higher degree graduates. Of the 11 per cent going on to further study or

Table 9.4 First destinations of UK postgraduate students by subject, 1994/5

	Entered employment	Entered study or training	Seeking employment or training	Other	Base	Response rate
Medicine and dentistry	89.0	8.1	0.8	2.1	383	61.1
Studies allied to medicine	82.3	12.0	3.2	2.6	626	76.0
Biological sciences	82.9	11.0	4.4	1.8	904	75.5
Agriculture and related	75.9	16.0	2.8	5.2	212	78.5
Physical sciences	77.4	15.3	5.9	1.4	1386	77.4
Mathematical sciences	80.8	14.5	3.0	1.7	234	70.1
Computer science	81.8	10.7	5.7	1.9	807	70.0
Engineering and technology	79.5	11.3	7.5	1.6	1473	71.3
Architecture and related	83.6	5.6	6.1	4.7	342	62.2
Social, economic and political studies	77.3	15.0	3.5	4.2	1494	66.9
Business and administrative studies	88.9	3.7	5.9	1.5	1513	68.1
Librarianship and information science	88.1	4.9	6.0	1.1	268	74.9
Languages	63.7	27.1	5.5	3.8	584	65.0
Humanities	63.9	29.0	3.1	4.0	576	71.6
Creative arts and design	78.3	8.3	8.3	5.2	580	56.6
Education	89.7	1.0	6.8	2.5	14,312	84.4
Combined	75.3	15.4	5.3	3.9	636	83.4
All subjects	84.7	6.6	6.0	2.6	26,689	77.1

Source: Higher Education Statistics Agency (1996b).

training, the vast majority were taking higher degrees (mostly masters going on the PhDs). Self-employment was relatively rare at this stage. Interestingly, one in five graduates who entered paid work were returning to a previous employer.

There is considerable variation in postgraduate destination patterns by discipline, as Table 9.4 shows. A much lower proportion of postgraduates in languages and humanities entered employment (less than two-thirds) and a higher proportion continued in further study or training, compared to the average for all postgraduates.

PhD graduates have a narrower spread of employment sectors than master's graduates. Much more of the former remain in education (mainly in universities) and are concentrated in research-related activities. Unfortunately, the HESA data do not provide a sufficiently robust set of data to explore trends or pattern by level of postgraduate qualification.

Employer demand

These statistical sources provide a useful overview of how employment patterns are changing but say little about employer demand *per se*. The unemployment statistics are not a good measure of demand because of deficiencies in the data (mainly small sample sizes and low response rates for postgraduates in the first destinations surveys) and the tendency for postgraduates, particularly PhDs, to delay their job search activities until after their thesis writing has been completed. Also, as has been pointed out earlier, some postgraduates take up jobs not commensurate with their qualification.

Over the years, several studies have been undertaken, principally for the Research Councils, to help assess the size and nature of the labour market for postgraduate training. These have generally been discipline based and often commissioned to provide evidence of the demand for postgraduate training outside of the academic sector. For example, a large follow-up study of science PhD graduates was undertaken for the Science and Engineering Research Council (SERC) to find out about the success of students from different science disciplines in finding suitable work, and in particular the flows of PhDs from the academic to the non-academic sector (Connor and Varlaam, 1986). This was updated in 1993 by a more broadly based study of employer demand for PhD scientists (also for SERC and covering chemistry, physics, biology and materials) which included a survey of private and public sector employers and analysis of academic recruitment and employment trends (Connor *et al.*, 1994). The main findings were that employment of science PhDs in the private sector was concentrated in a very small number of organizations and that there was no evidence of a significant broadening of the PhD scientific labour market beyond its traditional research/ academic base, except possibly in mathematics. It also showed that demand and supply was roughly in balance, though there were concerns from employers about maintaining quality and standards in PhD output.

The employment of social science postgraduates was examined in several studies in the early 1990s (Pearson *et al.*, 1991; Pike, 1992) as part of a major review of postgraduate training in the social sciences at that time. These highlighted the greater breadth of the labour market for social science compared to science postgraduates but also that a distinct market for social science postgraduates, especially PhDs, was hard to discern. In follow-up surveys, undertaken as part of this research (Pearson *et al.*, 1991), a significant number of social science postgraduates who took up employment outside the academic sector were in jobs not related to their academic studies, and few employers reported a specific requirement for postgraduate qualifications (the main exceptions being some large consultancies, research organizations and parts of the Civil Service).

Other, more focused, studies have also been undertaken, for example of astronomy and particle physicists (Particle Physics and Astronomy Research Council, 1995) and of chemists (Science and Engineering Research Council, 1992), which have tried to measure the size of future employer demand, but these have not been wholly successful because of the uncertainty surrounding likely future graduate intakes in most organizations, the relatively small numbers involved, and the overlap between the first and higher degree markets.

More recently, two further research studies have been undertaken: one on the demand for graduates from advanced IT courses in 1996 and the other on employer priorities in the environmental sciences in 1995. Their findings are reviewed here in more detail as they bring out some particular issues of relevance to today's labour market.

Information technology

In the mid-1980s, new advanced courses in information technology (IT) were developed in the UK in order to meet a growing IT skills need. These included new conversion-type courses for first degree graduates from other subjects who wished to pursue careers in IT. Assessments of labour market demand at that time (Connor, 1986) showed them to be a satisfactory source of highly qualified recruits for employers and most graduates had little difficulties in obtaining suitable employment.

Since then, advanced IT courses have continued to attract funding and students; around 1000 studentships have been given each year by the SERC (now the EPSRC) on some 120 recognized (full-time) courses, though more students participate on a self-funding basis. However, the graduates from these courses face a different kind of labour market to that of the mid-1980s. The IT industry went into recession in the early 1990s and the fast-growing demand for IT skills slowed in pace; IT investment levels dropped, internal budgets were cut and IT graduate recruitment reduced. At the same time, the major expansion of first degree graduate output (see introductory section of this chapter) meant a growing number of graduates competing for the available jobs. Though there has since been some recovery in the IT labour market in the last few years, the key questions being asked were: Are the IT courses as relevant today? What is the nature and extent of IT graduate demand? Is there justification to continue to support IT conversion courses or should resources be better put elsewhere?

To address these questions, a major review of the IT graduate labour market was undertaken by IES for the Engineering and Physical Sciences Research Council (EPSRC) in 1996 (Rick et al., 1996). This research included a telephone survey of over 300 employers and a questionnaire follow-up to 1600 graduates who completed IT advanced courses in 1992/3 and 1994/5.

Overall, the research evidence showed that the IT courses *were* continuing to meet a labour market need. Despite the apparent slow-down in growth in the IT sector, most of the postgraduates from advanced IT courses in the two cohort years had succeeded in obtaining work or further study within 12 months of completing their courses. At the time of the survey, over 80 per cent were working in an IT-related job, and they were split roughly in a 40:60 ratio between the IT sector and non-IT sector (e.g. banks, public services, engineering industry). Almost two-thirds were working in small firms (of under 250 employees in size). This illustrates the breadth of the postgraduate labour market in this subject area. Unemployment was very low, and lower than for graduates as a whole in the relevant years.

But although most of the graduates had secured employment, few employers recruiting graduates for IT functions specified a need for a postgraduate IT qualification, and many of the IT postgraduates were recruited alongside first degree graduates to similar jobs. Similarly, a master's qualification was not a prerequisite for most of the jobs the IT postgraduates currently held but it was viewed as being helpful in getting them.

This lack of specificity on qualification reflects in part a reluctance by employers to be too prescriptive about qualification unless there was a clear identified need for very specialist and high level skills. However, there was general support from the small number of recruiters of IT postgraduates in the survey for a continuing need for postgraduate provision, and most were planning to continue recruiting postgraduates, but increasingly from particular courses only. These had been identified as being 'leaders in their field' and close links were being developed with them.

There were some interesting differences (and similarities) between conversion- and specialist-type courses. Employers' awareness of the conversion type courses was low in general. Most were unsure if they had recruited any graduates from them, but the small number who knew of conversion-type courses were negative towards them in general, though not of some individual courses. They were seen as an 'inferior product' or 'quick fix to an old demand problem'. In terms of graduate employment outcomes, initial unemployment among the most recent cohort (1994/5 graduates) was slightly higher for conversion than specialist courses (13 compared with 10 per cent), but a higher proportion of conversion course graduates were in jobs (75 compared with 65 per cent). Specialist course graduates were more likely to be in further study, taking PhDs. There was very little variation between the specialist and conversion courses in the sectoral and occupational patterns of the two groups of graduates. This was somewhat surprising given the different purposes of the two types of courses and the different backgrounds of participating students. However, as mentioned above, there were low levels of knowledge among most employers about the nature of IT postgraduate courses, which may be an explanatory factor. A recommendation of the research to the EPSRC was a review of the 'conversion' model and of the need for continuing with the policy of making a distinction between the two types of courses.

Recruitment difficulties were reported by a minority of employers in the survey. Only one in five experienced any difficulties relating to the supply of IT skills. Areas of fast-growing demand included object-oriented environments, fourth generation languages and rapid application development. Slightly more employers reported difficulties in finding suitable graduate recruits with 'complementary skills'. These included: poor communication skills, a lack of business awareness, and criticisms of teamworking skills.

These findings on graduate skill deficiencies reflect the greater emphasis employers in general now put on 'complementary' skills (see for example the regular AGR surveys, Association of Graduate Recruiters, various years). As IT permeates into all business areas, there is a greater need for computing staff with combinations of technical and non-technical skills, who can understand business issues and are able to communicate with non-IT staff and clients while at the same time keeping up their IT skills. Interestingly, the graduates themselves viewed the acquisition of non-technical skills on their IT course as being more important in their current job than the specific technical skills they had learned. Many universities have responded to these changing skill demands by adapting and broadening their postgraduate courses, but it seems clear that more need to be encouraged to do so.

Environmental sciences

A broader research study was undertaken by IES for the Natural Environment Research Council (NERC) in 1995 which examined the labour market for environmental scientists, and employer skill requirements and priorities in particular. It covered all scientists with postgraduate qualification within the NERC's remit, both PhD and master's/postgraduate diploma students, but focused on non-academic employment. It included a review of literature and data on employment, and interviews with a wide range of employers, professional bodies and industry organizations (Court *et al.*, 1995).

It, too, showed little problems relating to any numerical imbalance between supply of postgraduates and employer demand, except in some small specialist areas (e.g. hydrology, soil science) where recruitment was difficult, but it raised some now familiar issues, of a qualitative kind, on skills and especially combinations of skills. The main concern to employers was the availability of individuals with the 'right' combination of qualifications, skills and experience, though what exactly was meant by 'right' was often vaguely expressed and varied from employer to employer.

The greater need for a multidisciplinary approach to many environmental issues was highlighted in the research. This is a common theme of the Technology Foresight Panel reports on technological developments and future R&D investment (Office of Science and Technology, 1995). The priorities identified in the research as key areas for likely growing demand for postgraduates in environmental science in the future were: risk assessment, modelling, simulation and prediction, materials development, energy technology and life cycle analysis. A notable linking factor of these is that they are likely to involve 'hard science' skills in addition to advanced knowledge of an environmental science discipline (or disciplines). Some, such as risk assessment, require inputs from the social sciences.

Multidisciplinary needs were a consistent message from all sectors of industry (e.g. oil, public utilities, agro-chemicals) but they were expressed in different ways. Five types of multidisciplinary needs could be identified. These are the need to:

- be able to communicate with other scientific disciplines;
- understand information requirements and coordinate the gathering of information (e.g. within a team of geologists, petroleum engineers, soil scientists, etc.);
- integrate knowledge from a range of disciplines;
- be a multiple specialist or hybrid (e.g. chemist and hydrologist; forestry and agriculture);
- operate across the natural science–social science divide (e.g. cost benefit analysis, risk assessment).

A lack of technical skills was also a problem area for some where an increasing requirement for graduates with good scientific backgrounds was required (and emphasis was put on the importance of a good basic science first degree) and the mathematical or computing skills for modelling work. There was general dissatisfaction with the quality of technical skills and experience of many applicants.

The third set of skills highlighted by employers were the non-technical skills. Employers stressed a range of personal transferable skills including communication, team working, presentation, project and budget management, using initiative and motivation. Two areas given particular emphasis were the ability to communicate ideas to non-specialists and the ability to operate in different cultures and languages.

Outside of the research environment, employers tended not to differentiate on the grounds of qualification, and there was considerable overlap between first degree, masters and PhD level qualifications. As in other studies, little specific demand for PhD qualifications was identified, and no calls for increase in output. Attention focused more on maintaining the quality and standards of current postgraduate training in higher education, and providing more short courses for updating purposes, delivered in a flexible way to full-time employees. These were found to be increasingly attractive to employers.

Conclusions

The available evidence on employment trends shows that despite the rapid growth in postgraduate supply, supply–demand is not out of balance and unemployment levels have remained relatively low. The recent influx of postgraduates have generally found employment, but not always in traditional areas of postgraduate work and not always with financial advantages (at least initially) over less highly qualified recruits. There continues to be considerable overlap in the first and higher degree labour markets and difficulties discerning clear boundaries. There are some exceptions, where PhD or MSc recruits are specifically required; for example, in the case of PhDs, this is in organizations with substantial R&D activities, or where there are very high-level skills in specific technical areas. It is likely that postgraduates have displaced first degree graduates in some jobs, partly as a consequence of their increased availability but also because of changes to professional entry requirements and employer demand for higher education and skill levels. This is an area where further research would be useful to understand the factors influencing these trends and the benefits/drawbacks to employers and individuals.

There is considerable diversity in initial outcomes and career development for postgraduates from different disciplines, but deficiencies in the available trend data preclude detailed investigations at a discipline and qualification level. There is a widening labour market for master's graduates, but still concentrated mainly in professional jobs and in sectors such as public administration, health and medical services, and business consultancies. Employment of PhDs continues to be focused on the higher education sector. Although, there are a range of other career opportunities elsewhere, numbers required are very small.

Employers value postgraduate qualifications differently. Some seek graduates from particular courses (as in the case of some leading IT courses); others seek to recruit postgraduates with particular combinations of skills and expertise (as increasingly demonstrated in environmental science where a multidisciplinary approach and a good range of personal skills are increasingly required). A consistent message coming from employers is the importance of personal transferable skills, often talked about as work-relevant skills. Their availability among many postgraduates is a cause for concern, not just among private sector employers, but also in the public sector and academia. Universities need staff who can work with people in industry to secure research funds and other collaborative activities. Commercialization and contract work is a growing trend in public sector employment. Many universities are working to develop personal skills in graduates but often in a piecemeal way at a course or department level, and more needs to be done at a strategic level to embed skills development within higher education.

Future directions

It is likely that postgraduate education will continue to grow but its shape will alter dramatically in the years ahead, with much greater emphasis on lifelong learning, including professional development, delivered in flexible ways making more use of computer technology and electronic communications, and funded from various sources – the so called 'learning society'. The pattern of full-time postgraduate study following on from a first degree, so familiar today, will become less common. More individuals will seek out postgraduate education at different life stages, for a variety of reasons not all of which will be related directly to improving employment prospects or getting specific qualifications. Employers will be seeking more in the way of short courses and modules for updating purposes or for broadening the skills and expertise of graduate employees.

These changes will alter the labour market for postgraduates further, probably making the employment spectrum more diverse and the boundaries with the first degree market more blurred. The exception will be very specialist areas of PhD employment which will keep their academic focus. There are interesting times ahead, especially as the impact on the labour market, and on the demand for postgraduate education and training, of some of the current changes have not yet been fully assessed. These include, for example, the rapid rise in participation in higher education of young people in the early 1990s and the rapid expansion of part-time study.

In order to monitor the changes and, in particular, investigate student and employer demand for postgraduate study, improvements are needed to the quality of the current data on employment of postgraduates. In particular, significant gaps need to be filled relating to the growing number of part-time students and to the returns on taking postgraduate qualifications. More cohort-based studies would be useful so that the various pathways and progression in and out of periods of postgraduate education and employment can be properly investigated.

References

Association of Graduate Recruiters (various) *Graduate Salaries and Vacancies*. Cambridge: AGR.

Association of Graduate Recruiters (1995) *Skills for Graduates in the 21st century*. Cambridge: AGR.

Connor, H. (1986) *IT Advanced Courses 1984/95: the Labour Market for Postgraduates*. Brighton: Institute for Employment Studies.

Connor, H., Court, G., Seccombe, I. and Jaggar, N. (1994) *Science PhDs and the Labour Market*, Report 266. Brighton: Institute for Employment Studies.

Connor, H. and Jaggar, N. (1993) *The Labour Market for Postgraduates*, Report 257. Brighton: Institute for Employment Studies.

Connor, H., Pearson, R., Court, G. and Jaggar, N. (1996) *University Challenge: Student Choices in the 21st Century*, Report 306. Brighton: Institute for Employment Studies.

Connor, H. and Pollard, E. (1996) *What Do Graduates Really Do?* Report 308. Brighton: Institute for Employment Studies.

Connor, H. and Varlaam, C. (1986) 'Employment and Careers of Science Postgraduates'. Unpublished Institute for Employment Studies report to the Science and Engineering Research Council.

Council for Industry and Higher Education (1995) *A Wider Spectrum of Opportunities*. London: CIHE.

Council for Industry and Higher Education (1996) *Helping Students Towards Success at Work*. Paper produced for the Employer Study Overview Group (ESOG). London: CIHE.

Court, G. and Jaggar, N. (1995) Recruitment of non-national scientists and engineers in Europe, *Industry and Higher Education*, 9(3), 186–91.

Court, G., Jaggar, N. and Moralle, J. (1995) *Skill Requirements and Priorities in the Environmental Sciences*, Report 297. Brighton: Institute for Employment Studies.

Department for Education and Employment (1996) *Labour Market and Skill Trends 1996/97*. London: DfEE.

Goodman, C. (1993) *Roles for Graduates in the Twenty-first Century: Getting the Balance Right.* Cambridge: Association of Graduate Recruiters.

Higher Education Quality Council (1996) *Graduate Standards Programme (draft report and recommendations).* London: HEQC.

Higher Education Statistics Agency (1996a) *Students in Higher Education Institutions 1994/95.* Cheltenham: HESA.

Higher Education Statistics Agency (1996b) *First Destinations of Students Leaving Higher Education Institutions 1994/95.* Cheltenham: HESA.

Institute of Employment Research (1996) *Review of the Economy and Employment: Future Employment Prospects for the Highly Qualified.* Warwick: Institute of Employment Research, University of Warwick.

La Valle, I., Jaggar, N. and Connor, H. (1996) *The IES Annual Graduate Review 1996–97.* Brighton: Institute for Employment Studies.

Mason, G. (1995) *The New Graduate Supply Shock: Recruitment and Utilisation of Graduates by British Industry,* Report Series 9. London: National Institute for Economic and Social Research.

Office for National Statistics (1996) *The Labour Force Survey of Great Britain, March–May 1996 Quarter.* London: ONS.

Office of Science and Technology (1995) *Technology Foresight through Partnership* (in 14 volumes on different sectors; see for example Vol. 11: Agriculture, natural resources and environment). London: HMSO.

Office of Population Censuses and Surveys (1994) *1991 Census.* London: HMSO.

Particle Physics and Astronomy Research Council (1995) *Astronomy and Particle Physics Students Career Paths.* Report by PEIDA. Swindon: PPARC.

Pearson, R., Seccombe, I., Pike, G., Holly, S. and Connor, H. (1991) *Doctoral Social Scientists and the Labour Market,* Report 217. Brighton: Institute for Employment Studies.

Pike, G. (1992) 'Academic Staff in Higher Education: Modelling Future Recruitment', unpublished Institute for Employment Studies report to the ESRC.

Rick, J., Perryman, S., Jaggar, N., La Valle, I., Connor, H. and Frost, D. (1996). 'EPSRC IT advanced courses', unpublished report to the Engineering and Physical Sciences Research Council by the Institute for Employment Studies.

Science and Engineering Research Council (1992) *Survey of Requirements for Chemistry PhDs.* Unpublished report by PREST. Swindon: SERC.

Soskice, D. W. (1993) Social skills from mass higher education: rethinking the company based initial training paradigm, *Oxford Review of Economic Policy,* 9(3), 101–13.

10

A Note on Reshaping the Graduate Education of Scientists and Engineers

Mary J. Osborn

This chapter summarizes major findings and recommendations of a 1995 study on graduate education in the sciences and engineering carried out by the Committee on Science, Engineering and Public Policy (COSEPUP) of the US National Academies of Science and Engineering and the Institute of Medicine. The study originated in the common wisdom that we are in a period of explosive growth of knowledge and opportunity in many fields of science and engineering, and that this is occurring at a time of exceptional stress and economic uncertainty in academia, government and industry. The investigation focused broadly and generically on issues of doctoral education in engineering and the natural sciences, and, recognizing the large differences between and within disciplines, sought to address two major questions that broadly cross disciplinary boundaries: (a) what is the shape of career options and job markets for PhD scientists and engineers in the US in the foreseeable future? and (b) do current methods of graduate education optimally prepare students for the full spectrum of career options and opportunities that will be available? (The preface to the Report is reproduced in Appendix A.)

COSEPUP's considerations were guided by three fundamental convictions: First, the business of graduate education is *education*, not training. We often speak of graduate training and too often we think in terms of graduate training and in this we do a significant disservice to our students and to graduate education. The goal of training is development of specific skills, and training programmes are thereby encouraged to focus narrowly, to think technically and to produce graduates who are skilled in the technologies of the day. The goals of education by contrast are development of a broad base of fundamental knowledge and the ability to think independently and creatively about whatever new problem arises to be solved.

Second, the Committee strongly believes that the US will continue to require a vibrant base in fundamental research and technology, and that education of doctoral-level scientists and engineers will necessarily continue to be a national priority. The future health of the nation, both economic and in quality of life, will depend heavily on the ability of the nation to maintain leadership in science and technology. This necessarily, over the long run and despite local perturbations, means growth in the national need for PhD scientists and engineers who have sufficient breadth and flexibility to adapt to rapidly changing landscapes.

Third, the US system of advanced education offers a remarkably effective preparation for the traditional independent research career. Whatever changes might be appropriate to render the system more responsive to new situations must not compromise or dilute this quality.

In the course of the study, the Committee surveyed available data (which were not very adequate) on demography and labour patterns and heard witnesses from a broad group of constituencies, including students and recent PhDs, graduate faculties and deans, professional societies and a variety of academic and non-academic employers. As might be expected, these inquiries solicited a diverse collection of concerns and opinions, many of which were at odds with each other. However, several general themes and issues did emerge clearly. (The recommendations of the Report, taken from the Executive Summary, pp. 4–7, are given in Appendix B.)

Job markets and career options

Graduate education in science and engineering generally (and perhaps most notably in biomedical science) has developed over the past 50 years hand in hand with unprecedented growth in research universities, and there is considerable truth to the cliché that PhD programmes are principally geared toward entry into academic and related research careers. However, the academic job market in the US has never amounted to more than 60 per cent of PhD employment overall in science and engineering; in 1992, the most recent data available at the time of the study, academic employment accounted for slightly under half the total.

In addition, the landscape is changing for both universities and industry. Expansion of universities has slowed or halted in most classical fields of science and engineering. The end of the Cold War, coupled with concerns about global competitiveness, has led to abrupt reductions in industrial employment of doctoral scientists and engineers. Add the effect of federal deficit reduction, and the concerns of students and recent PhDs about their futures are compelling. On a positive note, there is also evidence that novel opportunities are emerging in newly important interdisciplinary fields, such as healthcare policy research, patent law, industrial ecology, informatics and in a variety of technology-related activities in government at all levels.

Access to information on career options

Whatever the shape and size of future job markets, it is self-evident that students contemplating entry into graduate schools need access to the best information possible to guide their choices of career. Students and recent graduates were uniformly emphatic, not to say caustic, about their frustration at the lack of realistic, current information on the totality of employment options that might be open to them and the qualifications deemed important by employers. The graduate experience too often leaves the new PhD poorly informed about the realities of the job market and ill prepared to cope with it.

Undergraduate advisers and graduate faculties need to increase their own awareness of the range of career options and sources of information in order to provide better mentorship. In addition, graduate programmes should encourage regular presentation of career seminars by professional societies and representatives of various types of employers as a means of disseminating first-hand expert information and also as a reality check on students' expectations. As a corollary, graduate faculties and graduate schools must understand and agree that a career choice outside the academic mainstream does not represent a failure of the system or of the student.

A major recommendation of the study was development of a national database, readily accessible on-line by students and their mentors, which would contain current information by field about career options and desirable qualifications, employment trends, profiles of available graduate programmes and so on. As a first step in this direction the National Academies have undertaken several actions: first, publication of a student guide to planning educational and professional careers in science and engineering (Committee on Science, Engineering and Public Policy, 1996); second, development of a career planning centre for the Academies' home page that includes a bulletin board for questions and advice, relevant databases, information on employment opportunities, etc., which is available on-line through the National Academy of Sciences home page; and third, development of a guide to effective mentorship which will be available on-line in 1997.

Changing shapes in graduate education

Given that only about half of new PhDs are currently entering an academic research career, and given a job market, both academic and non-academic, that is changing in unpredictable ways and is, for the immediately foreseeable future, very tight, how can graduate programmes best prepare their students for productive and satisfying careers?

Both academic and non-academic employers were essentially unanimous in their characterization of the ideal PhD job candidate, and this was independent of the specifics of the institution, business or industry. Individuals are prized who:

- are educated to think and to solve problems inventively;
- are broadly based, rather than narrowly oriented to a specific technology;

- can communicate effectively to non-experts as well as peers, both orally and in writing;
- understand technology transfer and can develop as well as initiate ideas;
- are able to work comfortably in a collaborative group environment and have respect for the employment milieu and their place within it.

Although traditional programmes and experiences do vary considerably, education toward the PhD is generally aimed largely at production of independent researchers in the academic mould. The sense is widely shared (though not universal) that the traditional path often lacks the kind of breadth and flexibility that will be increasingly necessary to prepare graduates for the more diverse spectrum of career paths that they may have to face. In addition, the time to degree has crept steadily upward in almost all fields over the past 20 years and this is perceived as a significant disincentive to entry into advanced education in science and engineering as compared with other career options, including law and medicine. Science and engineering, whether basic or applied, are becoming ever more multi- and interdisciplinary and new disciplinary entities are being forged between fields that used to be at opposite ends of the campus. Further, the kinds of knowledge and the ways of thinking that are most valued in scientists are increasingly being applied in non-research milieus in a broad range of governmental and business activities.

The report therefore recommends that universities and individual graduate programmes should, to a greater extent, differentiate their missions, depending on their individual strengths and regional needs, to provide educational opportunities that, in the aggregate, offer greater choice, flexibility and breadth. Many programmes would most certainly continue to emphasize the traditional research-intensive, academically oriented PhD education. Others, however, might choose to emphasize interdisciplinary or multidisciplinary options, including dual degrees such as molecular biology plus computing or engineering or law or teaching accreditation. Greater use of industrial and other placements can be encouraged where appropriate and industry should welcome and support such programmes. Predoctoral education should have the character of a branching pathway with multiple opportunities for choice, rather than the rigid pipeline it frequently appears to be. In addition, needs of students with respect to childbearing and child care must be recognized as legitimate, and suitably flexible programmes provided in supportive ways.

The predoctoral training grant programmes of the National Institutes of Health have an impressive history as a mechanism for catalysing creation of interdisciplinary programmes within the biomedical sciences, and the 1995 COSEPUP Report recommends broader use of this kind of mechanism to support development of new kinds of programmatic options.

Ever longer times to degree impose both psychological and added economic burdens on students, most especially under-represented minorities and women. Accordingly, the Report recommends that serious efforts be made by graduate schools and graduate programmes to decrease the average time to degree by better enforcing existing policies on time limits and by effective programmatic control of the undue prolongation of thesis research. The goal of reducing the normal time to PhD to something closer to five years is desirable and should be attainable. In combination with postdoctoral experience this can be accomplished without compromising breadth or educational rigour.

A final recommendation of the Report derives from the observation that, since the demise in 1972 of most federal training grants and fellowship programmes, PhD education in science and engineering in the US has relied primarily on grant-funded research assistantships for federal support of graduate students in their thesis years. As a consequence, graduate education towards the PhD is, in effect, a by-product of, and secondary to, federal support for academic research. COSEPUP is seriously concerned that this has significant negative implications for graduate students and the educational process. The primary goal of graduate education should be the best possible education for the student, not a ready supply of indentured labour for the professor's laboratory. The Report calls for initiation of a national dialogue to work towards defining a policy for human resources in science and engineering that will better serve the needs of the sciences and the nation. All parties to the enterprise – universities, professional organizations, industry and government – are urged to think seriously about the goals, policies, conditions and the many unresolved issues relating to graduate education in the sciences and to long-term national needs. To initiate this process, the National Academies complex held a Convocation on Graduate Education in the Sciences and Engineering in June 1996, the Proceedings of which are now available on-line through the National Academy of Sciences home page.

References

Committee on Science, Engineering and Public Policy (1995) *Reshaping the Graduate Education of Scientists and Engineers.* Washington, DC: National Academy Press.
Committee on Science, Engineering and Public Policy (1996) *Careers in Science and Engineering: A Student Planning Guide to Graduate School and Beyond.* Washington, DC: National Academy Press.
Griffiths, P. A. (1995) Preface, in COSEPUP, *Reshaping the Graduate Education of Scientists and Engineers* (pp. v–vii). Washington, DC: National Academy Press.

Appendix A
The focus of the report (Griffiths, 1995)

The Committee on Science, Engineering and Public Policy (COSEPUP) is a joint committee of the National Academy of Sciences (NAS), the National Academy of Engineering (NAE), and the Institute of Medicine (IOM) in the United States. In 1993 it issued the *Goals* Report entitled: *Science, Technology and the Federal Government: National Goals for a New Era*. In preparing that report, the Committee decided a further complementary volume was required that looked at the education of scientists and engineers. The result was the report entitled: *Reshaping the Graduate Education of Scientists and Engineers* that was guided by the following questions:

- What are the typical career paths for scientists and engineers, and how have they changed in recent years?
- Given present career paths, what are the most appropriate structures and functions for graduate education?
- How can science and engineering graduate students be prepared for a variety of careers in teaching, industry, government, and other employment sectors, in addition to research?
- Are we producing the right numbers of PhDs?[1]
- What should be the nation's goals for graduate science and engineering education?

Appendix B
Recommendations

General Recommendation 1: Offer a Broader Range of Academic Options

- To produce more versatile scientists and engineering, graduate programmes should provide options that allow students to gain a wider variety of skills.
- To foster versatility, government and other agents of financial assistance for graduate students should adjust their support mechanisms to include new education/training grants to institutions and departments.
- In implementing changes to promote versatility, care must be taken not to compromise other important objectives.

General Recommendation 2: Provide Better Information and Guidance

- Graduate scientists and engineers and their advisers should receive more up-to-date and accurate information to help them make informed decisions about professional careers; broad electronic access to such information should be provided through a concerted nationwide effort.

[1] Because of the concerns regarding PhD unemployment, the report focuses on the PhD.

• Academic departments should provide the information referred to above to prospective and current students in a timely manner and should also provide career advice to graduate students. Students should have access to information on the full range of employment possibilities.

• Students should be encouraged to consider three alternative pathways at the point when they have met their qualifying requirements.

• The National Science Foundation should continue to improve the coverage, timeliness, and clarity of analysis of the data on the education and employment of scientists and engineers in order to support better national decision-making about human resources in science and technology.

General Recommendation 3: Devise a National Human-Resource Policy for Advanced Scientists and Engineers

• A national discussion group – including representatives of governments, universities, industries, and professional organizations – should deliberately examine the goals, policies, conditions, and unresolved issues of graduate-level human resources.

Index

The Society for Research into Higher Education

The Society for Research into Higher Education exists to stimulate and coordinate research into all aspects of higher education. It aims to improve the quality of higher education through the encouragement of debate and publication on issues of policy, on the organization and management of higher education institutions, and on the curriculum and teaching methods.

The Society's income is derived from subscriptions, sales of its books and journals, conference fees and grants. It receives no subsidies, and is wholly independent. Its individual members include teachers, researchers, managers and students. Its corporate members are institutions of higher education, research institutes, professional, industrial and governmental bodies. Members are not only from the UK, but from elsewhere in Europe, from America, Canada and Australasia, and it regards its international work as among its most important activities.

Under the imprint *SRHE & Open University Press*, the Society is a specialist publisher of research, having over 70 titles in print. The Editorial Board of the Society's Imprint seeks authoritative research or study in the above fields. It offers competitive royalties, a highly recognizable format in both hardback and paperback and the worldwide reputation of the Open University Press.

The Society also publishes *Studies in Higher Education* (three times a year), which is mainly concerned with academic issues, *Higher Education Quarterly* (formerly *Universities Quarterly*), mainly concerned with policy issues, *Research into Higher Education Abstracts* (three times a year), and *SRHE News* (four times a year).

The society holds a major annual conference in December, jointly with an institution of higher education. In 1994 the topic was 'The Student Experience' at the University of York. In 1995 it was 'The Changing University' at Heriot-Watt University in Edinburgh and in 1996 'Working in Higher Education' at University of Wales, Cardiff. The 1997 Annual Conference is entitled 'Beyond the First Degree' at the University of Warwick.

The Society's committees, study groups and networks are run by the members. The networks at present include:

Access	Vocational Qualifications
Eastern European	Postgraduate
Funding	Quality
Mentoring	Student Development

Benefits to members

Individual

Individual members receive

- *SRHE News*, the Society's publications list, conference details and other material included in mailings.
- Greatly reduced rates for *Studies in Higher Education* and *Higher Education Quarterly*.
- A 35 per cent discount on all SRHE & Open University Press publications.
- Free copies of the Precedings – commissioned papers on the theme of the Annual Conference.
- Free copies of *Research into Higher Education Abstracts*.
- Reduced rates for the annual conference.
- Extensive contacts and scope for facilitating initiatives.
- Free copies of the *Register of Members' Research Interests*.
- Membership of the Society's networks.

Corporate

Corporate members receive:

- Benefits of individual members, plus.
- Free copies of *Studies in Higher Education*.
- Unlimited copies of the Society's publications at reduced rates.
- Special rates for its members, e.g. to the Annual Conference.
- The right to submit applications for the Society's research grants.
- The right to use the Society's facility for supplying statistical HESA data for purposes of research.

Membership details: SRHE, 3 Devonshire Street, London
W1N 2BA, UK. Tel: 0171 637 2766. Fax: 0171 637 2781.
email:srhe@MAILBOX.ulcc.ac.uk
World Wide Web:http://www.srhe.ac.uk./srhe/
Catalogue: SRHE & Open University Press, Celtic Court,
22 Ballmoor, Buckingham MK18 1XW. Tel: 01280 823388.
Fax: 01280 823233. email:enquiries@openup.co.uk

THE LEARNING UNIVERSITY
TOWARDS A NEW PARADIGM?

Chris Duke

Chris Duke addresses issues central to the evolution and future of higher education. He examines assumptions by and about universities, their changing environments, the new terminologies and their adaptation to new circumstances. He explores how far universities *are* learning, changing and adapting; and whether they are becoming different kinds of institutions or whether only the rhetoric is altering. He is particularly concerned with how far universities, as key teaching and learning organizations, are adopting the new paradigm of lifelong learning. He discusses how far the concepts and requirements for institution-wide continuing education have been identified and internalized in institutional planning; are they, for instance, reflected in programmes of staff development (in the continuing education of staff in higher education)? *Is* a new paradigm of university education and organization really emerging?

Contents

160pp   0 335 15653 3 (Paperback)